Reenvisioning Sexual Ethics

Selected Titles from the Moral Traditions Series

David Cloutier, Andrea Vicini, SJ, and Darlene Weaver, Editors

Reenvisioning Sexual Ethics

A Feminist Christian Account

KAREN PETERSON-IYER

GEORGETOWN UNIVERSITY PRESS / WASHINGTON, DC

The publisher is not responsible for third-party websites or their content. URL links were active at time of publication.

Library of Congress Cataloging-in-Publication Data

Names: Peterson-Iyer, Karen, author.
Title: Reenvisioning sexual ethics: a feminist Christian account / Karen Peterson-Iyer.
Other titles: Moral traditions series.
Description: Washington, DC: Georgetown University Press, 2022. | Series: Moral traditions series | Includes bibliographical references and index.
Identifiers: LCCN 2021020105 | ISBN 9781647122270 (hardcover) | ISBN 9781647122287 (paperback) | ISBN 9781647122294 (ebook)
Subjects: LCSH: Sex—Religious aspects—Christianity. | Sex—Religious aspects—Catholic Church. | Sexual ethics—United States. | Feminist ethics—United States. | Feminism—Religious aspects—Christianity. | Young adults—Sexual behavior—United States.
Classification: LCC BT708.P467 2022 | DDC 241/./664—dc23
LC record available at https://lccn.loc.gov/2021020105

∞ This paper meets the requirements of ANSI/NISO Z39.48–1992 (Permanence of Paper).

23 22   9 8 7 6 5 4 3 2   First printing

Printed in the United States of America

Cover design by Erin Kirk. Cover image courtesy of iStock.com/Galina Kamenskaya
Interior design by BookComp, Inc.

To my partner and spouse, Mohan S. Iyer,
whose love, encouragement, and commitment
to our shared life infuse each day
with hope and possibility.

Contents

Acknowledgments

Any book such as this one reflects much more than the work and ideas of the author. My insights are built upon the wisdom of so many thinkers who have inspired and shaped me, and to whom I owe an enormous debt of gratitude. I wish to offer special thanks to two extraordinary scholars from whom I have taken particular inspiration: Margaret A. Farley, RSM, and Karen Lebacqz. When it comes to Christian ethics, both of these remarkable women have "made the road by walking" and thereby struck a path for those of us who seek to follow, however imperfectly, in their footsteps. I feel fortunate to have been shaped by them in my scholarship, sensibilities, and posture toward the world.

I am immensely grateful to the many colleagues and friends who have inspired me (sometimes unwittingly) through their own work, engaged in robust conversation on these topics (at times over a tasty meal or an excellent bourbon), generously critiqued chapter drafts, or otherwise offered their steadfast encouragement through the weeds of the writing process. In particular, I offer my deep thanks to Kristin Heyer, Jim Keenan, SJ, Christopher Steck, SJ, David DeCosse, Cathleen Kaveny, Cristina Traina, David Clough, Jennifer Beste, Bridget Burke Ravizza, Donna Freitas, Emily Reimer-Barry, Jason King, Kari-Shane Davis Zimmerman, Sharan Dhanoa, Jeannie Crumly Cole, and my uplifting and supportive colleagues in Santa Clara University's Religious Studies Department, especially Pearl Maria Barros, Paul Schutz, Jim Bennett, Kitty Murphy, Teresia M. Hinga, Diana Gibson, Janet Giddings, Sally Vance-Trembath, and Margaret R. McLean. In addition, I am profoundly grateful to the late Paul Crowley, SJ, who died while I was writing this book; Paul's kindness, theological brilliance, courage, and faith have stood as a beacon for me, as for so many others. Also at Santa Clara University, my sexual ethics students over the years have bravely shared their stories and their struggles, their pain and their fears, and—most importantly—their hopes and their dreams. May their vision and imagination continue to elicit among us new ways of "doing ethics."

Enormous thanks are due to the editorial team at Georgetown University Press as well as others who have aided the editorial process. The steadfast encouragement, critique, warmth, and honesty of Andrea Vicini and Kristin Heyer have served for me as an exquisite model of both generous collegiality and kindhearted friendship. In similar fashion, I am indebted to Al Bertrand, who has struck the perfect balance of patience and encouragement throughout the process. GUP's anonymous reviewers provided careful readings and thoughtful suggestions. Erin Cole and Sarah C. Smith graciously helped with timely and meticulous copyediting, likely salvaging my equanimity at critical junctures. I of course take full responsibility myself for any errors in this book.

Finally, I offer my unending gratitude and love to the members of my family, the unsung heroes throughout the entire journey of writing this book. My now-adult children, Alex Iyer and Chris Iyer, have become superb ethical thinkers in their own right, bottoming out ideas, reading and critiquing chapter drafts, and generally providing both inspiration and cheerleading at every stage of the writing process. My mother, Nancy S. Peterson, has been a model of strength, perseverance, and support as we together have weathered several extremely challenging years marked by personal loss. Sarah Mather Peterson, one of the most incisive thinkers I know, was always ready to engage with me in deep, clarifying conversation about many of the knottiest questions addressed in this book. Last but far from least, I offer boundless thanks to my spouse, Mohan S. Iyer, to whom this book is dedicated. Without Mohan's steadfast support, enthusiastic encouragement, and buoyant energy, my relationships, my thinking, and indeed my entire life would be greatly impoverished. Insofar as I am able to see not only the struggles and challenges of this world but also its possibilities for hope and beauty, it is largely thanks to him.

Sexual Flourishing
in an Unjust World

Conversations about sex, particularly when approached in the light of Christian tradition, elicit a wide range of responses in the US context today: anger, fear, fascination, curiosity. Both within the academy and within ecclesial communities of different stripes, we are often at a loss to have meaningful and relevant interchanges. On the one hand, sex lies at the heart of multiple US cultural disagreements, ranging from marriage equality and trans* people's rights to abortion and even contraception policy. These debates derive much of their depth and vitriol from an inchoate awareness of the *power* of sex—that is, the power it exercises over individuals as well as the ways it shapes and influences our larger social expectations, practices, and institutions. On the other hand, academic circles have historically trivialized sexual subjects, often marginalizing them in the curriculum and arguing that they lack the intellectual import of other sorts of ethical concerns—such as climate change, war, and peace, or economic justice.

Recent awareness on this count has begun to shift dramatically, however. From the sexual abuse scandals in the Roman Catholic Church to the 2015 US Supreme Court decision outlawing state-level bans on marriage for same-sex couples, it has become painfully clear that Christians cannot afford to downplay sex or rely on outdated assumptions about sexual well-being or inadequate normative understandings of sexual activity. In fact, Christian ethics as a discipline has real work to do if it is to remain honest, relevant, and able to speak to a population increasingly disenchanted with organized religion, particularly in the sexual realm.

The work could not be more urgent. With the widespread growth in use of the internet over the past fifty years has also come the explosion of "porn culture"—the pervasive and sometimes violent pornographic representation of sexual conduct that has leaked into popular culture. Porn culture—especially in its freely available, more hard-core adaptations—has shifted popular sensibilities about what is considered desirable and fitting expression of human sexuality. At the same time, sexual ethics in the secular sphere has drifted further and further in the direction of espousing freedom of choice as the sole arbiter of what counts as morally acceptable. Popular feminist authors such as Jessica Valenti rightly criticize the ways in which traditional religious teachings have undermined women's sexual well-being, but they offer little beyond sexual education or free agency to describe what "good" sex might in fact look like in Western society today.[1] Thus, sex is increasingly understood as *purely* a matter of individual choice—that is, what people choose to do in the privacy of their own bedrooms is up to them, as long as it is consensual.

The result of these twin trends has been a strange mixture of hypersexualization on the one hand and an absence of meaningful ways to navigate it on the other. On the more conservative end of the Christian theological spectrum, Christian ethicists and moral theologians have sought to articulate vigorous norms that sustain the spirit of traditional church teachings but present them in a manner more acceptable to a twenty-first-century audience. Christopher West's wildly popular articulation of Pope John Paul II's Theology of the Body is but one example; West uses distinctly modern parlance and references from pop culture to fan out John Paul II's highly traditionalist understandings to a popular and presumably younger audience.[2] In a more centrist or reformist vein, Vincent Genovesi, Todd Salzman and Michael Lawler, and David Cloutier have all thoughtfully and carefully probed, and in some cases rethought, the deeper insights of Catholic interpretations of human sexuality—while generally remaining within, as well as speaking back into, the parameters of the tradition.[3] Although these approaches differ dramatically from one another, to some degree they share an emphasis on relatively "thick" sexual norms such as chastity or a lifelong marriage commitment as the means to set boundaries around human sexuality. In so doing, they indeed provide an authentic alternative to individual choice as the solitary sexual norm, but they also at times skirt important questions related to sexual injustice and women's well-being.

By contrast, feminist approaches to sex, particularly in the Catholic tradition, have indicated an alternate way forward. The work of Margaret A. Farley, Lisa Sowle Cahill, and Christine E. Gudorf have laid theoretical foundations upon which to build when examining the ethical challenges of human sexual life today.[4] These authors write with one eye firmly set upon human sexual well-being and the other keenly aware of the ways that well-being, especially women's well-being, has not been served by traditional theological and ethical paradigms. Additionally, virtue ethical appeals such as those elaborated by James Keenan or Lisa Fullam provide important points of connection to traditions wherein we are asked to consider not just what we should *do* in sexual spheres but rather what sort of sexual people we should aspire to *be*.[5]

All of the above approaches have in common an unwillingness to give up entirely on quasi-universal standards of justice and well-being, including especially women's well-being, but they maintain this alongside the knowledge that such standards must always be provisional, historically situated, and open to deepening and ongoing wisdom and interpretation. My own intellectual affinities lie in this direction. In addition, I draw vision in these pages from several Protestant authors—including Reinhold Niebuhr and Karen Lebacqz—who alert us to the power of social sin as an interpretative category, including the thoroughgoing impact it has upon our sexual understandings and actions. And here lies a crucial piece of the puzzle: sexual flourishing, as I understand it, has to do not simply with the individual but also with the society in which we live. Thus sexual ethics is not only about who we are or what we do, sexually speaking; it is about the sort of society we live in, and the ways our individual actions, choices, and practices bolster or challenge patterns of injustice and marginalization in that society.

These pillars of thought have laid a strong theoretical foundation necessary for sexual ethics in the twenty-first century. My aim here is to continue that work and extend it with particular attention to the world today. Certainly others have done this before me; for instance, an especially interesting mix of practical concern with a focus on justice may be found in the work of psychologist and pastoral theologian couple Evelyn and James Whitehead, as well as that of Protestant ethicist Marvin M. Ellison.[6] The questions addressed in these volumes push the Christian tradition forward, and here I seek to move it even further along, bridging the more robust theological and ethical analysis with the practical sexual issues particularly confronting a college-aged and younger adult audience today. I seek to do this while attending both to provisional normative understandings of human flourishing and to the nearly ubiquitous structures and patterns of injustice that haunt contemporary young adult sexual experience. Indeed it is this very group who, in my observation, generally drive the assumptions about sex and gender that have progressively become more egalitarian and fluid in the public conversation.

It is time, then, for Christian ethics as a field to reevaluate and reorient itself around its best, most thoughtful, and wisest instincts regarding human freedom and well-being with respect to sex. I seek to specify these instincts as they express themselves through a Christian feminist anthropological framework—that is, a framework that values and articulates genuine human flourishing, giving serious attention to women's well-being and the need for gender justice. Thus, after first critiquing elements of traditional Christian sexual ethics in chapter 1, I turn in chapter 2 toward this more constructive project. There I endeavor to elaborate certain norms that characterize the best insights of a Christian vision of the human person, as they pertain to sex: freedom and agency, physical health, emotional integrity, relational intimacy, and mutuality and equal regard. Further—and of critical importance —it is my contention that this vision of genuine human flourishing must be articulated not simply with respect to bodies but rather with respect to *historicized* bodies. More specifically, humans so understood exist not solely as individuals but rather in a broader communal context marked by economic and gender-based social injustices, injustices that profoundly compromise human flourishing, especially for women. Indeed, the approach articulated here is avowedly feminist, both in its affirmation that all people, regardless of gender, deserve equal respect and social power *and* in its recognition that our social structures, thought patterns, and cultural tropes in fact function to falsify, downplay, and sometimes outright deny women's well-being in the sexual spheres of life. If Christian ethicists are to make honest and incisive claims about sex, we must explicitly scrutinize and speak into this harmful social and cultural context.

Employing this Christian and feminist anthropological framework, in chapters 3 through 6 of this volume I critically examine four contemporary social practices and phenomena wherein sex plays a central role: the "hookup" culture that predominates on college campuses; "sexting," that is, the sending of nude photos or videos via text message; the sex trade; and sex trafficking. These topics have particular relevance today, especially to a younger audience. Together, the chapters form a succession of feminist and Christian case studies of sorts. Each topic serves to highlight various contours of the values and virtues I outline in chapter 2; taken as a whole, these chapters compose, illustrate, and flesh out a moral portrait of sexual flourishing. As an integral part of that process, each chapter also scrutinizes the social structures and forces that potentially inhibit a truly just experience and expression of human sexuality, from the point of view of the various agents and institutions involved.

I hasten to add, however, that the list of topics covered in this volume is woefully incomplete and in fact omits certain key concerns that are vital to a full consideration of sexual ethics. I do not, for example, address marriage for same-sex and same-gender couples. This is not because the topic is no longer pressing or controversial in US society. It is simply because, in my observation, that controversy is lessening as time goes on and, moreover, is increasingly confined to an older generation. Many (though of course not all) younger Christians simply do not understand marriage as properly restricted to heterosexual, cisgender couples, applying at different times frameworks of justice, hospitality, or even revised and more inclusive understandings of sexual "complementarity" to arrive at an updated, more wide-ranging understanding of marriage. Likewise, I do not undertake the validity of divorce as a Christian practice. There remain many circles where divorced persons enjoy at best second-class status and are systematically excluded from full ecclesial participation. Sensibilities about divorce differ in Protestant and traditionalist Roman Catholic contexts, although the practice itself is at this point common throughout both. I do not care to wade into doctrinal differences here, noting instead that the widespread acceptance of divorce in so much of Western society makes it less interesting to me (and, I think, to many) as a topic of discussion.

There are many additional topics ripe for thoughtful examination within Christian sexual ethics, topics which I also do not address here in any detail— polyamory, asexuality, and trans* identity and experience, for instance. In large part this is a matter of scope; I aim to keep this volume to a manageable length. The sustained, careful, experientially based sexual analysis merited by these topics deserves far more attention than I am able to offer here.[7] Instead, I begin with matters about which we as a society (and as a church) already have a great deal of information—and yet for which we still seem to lack persuasive ethical frameworks that equip us to reflect in thoughtful, clear headed, egalitarian, and liberatory fashion. Hence, while the topics addressed here by no means exhaust the many issues that Christian sexual ethics might address in order for the discipline to reenvision itself, they are particularly pressing and captivating in contemporary life.

A word about my own positionality: I maintain affinities and affiliations in both Protestant and Roman Catholic environments and draw upon both traditions in all of my own ethical work, including this one. This is not a book, however, designed primarily to engage the detailed technical conversation internal to Roman Catholic moral theology, nor is it aimed solely or even primarily at Protestants. Rather, I seek here to build bridges, drawing upon what I consider to be the best insights from various corners of Christianity. I am also a straight, cisgender woman. As such, and from one perspective, I have little authoritative voice with which to speak to audiences of significant sexual diversity. Yet simply the fact that it is *difficult* for me to speak in these ways does not mean that I have the luxury of not speaking at all; rather, it means that when I do speak, I have an obligation to do so mindfully and cautiously, taking care not to assert my own conclusions as overly narrow universals. Finally, I am a white person, in an intercultural marriage and with bi-ethnic children. I have been shaped and formed in a largely white middle-class culture, even as I have also chosen, in my personal life, to build bridges of understanding spanning culture, race, and ethnicity. While I necessarily speak from my own point of view, I hope to place my discernments about human freedom and well-being into honest and sustained conversation with a broader audience. I am mindful that I still have much to learn, even as I put forth my own provisional understanding of human flourishing in the context of sexual, racial, and economic injustice.

Notes

1. Valenti, *The Purity Myth*.
2. West, *Theology of the Body*; and West, *Fill These Hearts*.
3. Genovesi, *In Pursuit of Love*; Salzman and Lawler, *The Sexual Person*; Salzman and Lawler, *Sexual Ethics*; and Cloutier, *Love, Reason, and God's Story*.
4. Farley, *Just Love*; Cahill, *Sex, Gender, and Christian Ethics*; and Gudorf, *Body, Sex, and Pleasure*.
5. Keenan, "Virtue Ethics and Sexual Ethics"; Keenan, "Contemporary Contributions to Sexual Ethics"; Fullam, "Sex in 3-D"; and Lisa Fullam, "Thou Shalt: Sex beyond the List of Don'ts," *Commonweal*, April 20, 2009, https://www.commonwealmagazine.org/thou-shalt.
6. Whitehead and Whitehead, *Fruitful Embraces*; and Ellison, *Making Love Just*.
7. I note that excellent theological and ethical analysis has begun on these subjects, particularly on trans* identity and experience. See, for instance, Ford, "Transgender Bodies, Catholic Schools"; Bader-Saye, "The Transgender Body's Grace"; David Cloutier and Luke Timothy Johnson, "The Church and Transgender Identity: Some Cautions, Some Possibilities," *Commonweal*, February 27, 2017; and Howes, "Mother, Father, Brother, Sister," 43–53.

CHAPTER ONE

Looking Back and Looking Forward

Human touch is powerful. Anyone who has ever interacted with an infant immediately knows of the mysterious ability of touch to soothe, to comfort, or simply to connect two previously separated individuals at a more-than-rational level. This experience is perhaps even more acute in the case of sexual touch, whose power is largely inchoate. Sexual touch can open up hidden forms of sentience and recognition, drawing us together in a profoundly humanizing fashion and leading us into deeper awareness of ourselves, our partners, even our place in the universe; alternatively, it can limit and even damage us in ways that extend far beyond our physical bodies. An appreciation of this power of sex—to expand or to diminish, to open us up or to shut us down—points us in the direction of a basic assumption that underlies this project: sex *means* something beyond its simple physical significance. In other words, sex potentially ties into something profound within us and reveals something important about human persons' relationships: to themselves, to each other, and, from a Christian perspective, to God.

When it comes down to it, however, Christian ethics has often articulated that deeper meaning in rather narrow terms—terms that privilege heterosexual marriage as the only or at least the most humanizing environment for sexual activity. Not only does this approach bypass other contexts as potential locations for sexual flourishing; it also deflects the sociopolitical analysis necessary to understand what, exactly, is going on with sexual activity in the real world, thus undermining an authentic and robust account of what is necessary to thrive, sexually speaking. It is not that the Christian tradition has nothing to offer to this conversation; on the contrary, Christianity offers wisdom and insights that shed genuine light on some of the thorniest sexual questions facing twenty-first-century society. But in order to tease out the best insights from Christianity, we must also be willing bravely to name the ways that it has fallen short.

Hence, the present chapter and the one that follows form a pair that together aims to critique, to retrieve, and to propose. Here in chapter 1, I trace the contours of a more traditional Christian approach to sexual ethics, highlighting some of the problematic tendencies and indicating *why* they are problematic, particularly for women. In chapter 2, I begin by combing the biblical tradition for its most life-giving discernments related to human sexuality, insights that shed genuine light on what it means for persons, including women, to thrive. Drawing upon those themes and insights, and together with feminist theological and philosophical accounts of what it means for women to flourish, I then propose a normative feminist framework that includes but moves beyond simple freedom of choice as a way of understanding the qualities of "good" sex. Together, these discussions pave the way for the analysis that takes place in the topical chapters that follow.

Locating the Tradition

Historically and traditionally in Christian thought, the deeper meaning of sex has been described to encompass both a *procreative* and a *unitive* significance. The first of these held a certain pride of place in Christian tradition for centuries. Augustine of Hippo, perhaps the first Christian thinker to systemize Christian sexual ethics, placed great emphasis on procreation as the central justifying feature of sexual activity and the passion that often accompanies it. Augustine's strong focus on the corrupting influence of original sin led to his belief that the passion of sexual desire must be subordinated to the influence of reason and will. Procreation thus constitutes the necessary rational purposing for sex, in the face of what Augustine termed *concupiscence*. In fact, according to Augustine's view, sex without procreative intent involves at least "venial fault," even if that sex takes place within the confines of a faithful marriage.[1]

As the tradition developed, sex became more clearly integrated under a natural law style of reasoning, especially evident in the thought of Thomas Aquinas. Thomas organized his views on human sexuality using principles of reason reflecting upon the "natural order" of things—a natural law perspective with a clear emphasis upon the physiobiological character and procreative logic of sex.[2] In Thomas's writings, procreation retains its status as the primary purpose of sexual expression and thus the chief end of marriage. Like Augustine, Thomas expressed a suspicion of the "deformity" of "excessive concupiscence" and held that this would not have existed in a state of inno-cence.[3] Thomas did place a greater emphasis than his predecessor upon the love that binds spouses, particularly understanding marriage to be a form of friendship that confers grace.[4] Still, the procreative norm continues to stand tall in Thomas's thought, driven ultimately by his stress on the strong function that human reason plays in discerning the physical and biological ends of sex.

This prioritization of procreation did noticeably soften, over time. The Magisterial Reformation disrupted the procreative paradigm, notably taking shape in the thought of Martin Luther. Luther continued to value procreation as a "good" of marriage, but he contextualized it among many other goods, including both social stability and the mutual cherishing of the spouses.[5] Luther accepted sexual pleasure as a created good, disordered by sin, and to be channeled by way of marriage in a postlapsarian world. A stronger suspicion toward sexual desire can arguably be found in the writings of John Calvin, who, in characteristically severe fashion, admonished his followers against "uncontrolled and dissolute lust" within marriage and urged that "each man have his own wife soberly, and each wife her own husband."[6] After the Refor-mation, Protestantism continued to diverge from a strictly procreative ethic, with most Protestant traditions eventually affirming artificial contraception and, more recently, some actively affirming marriage for same-sex and same-gender couples, whether or not procreation is in the picture. However, the tradition has continued to approach sexual pleasure itself with some degree of ambiguity. While modern Protestant traditionalists tend to be less appre-hensive about physical pleasure than their predecessors, until recently, few have explicitly lifted it up as a positive sexual value.

As for the Roman Catholic moral tradition, a similar softening of a strictly procreative norm has taken place. By the time of the Second Vatican Council (1962–65), the procreative and unitive functions of sex—the latter expressed as conjugal love and intimacy within marriage—were officially elevated as coequal.[7] A landmark event, however, took place in 1968 with the publica-tion of *Humanae Vitae*, where Pope Paul VI, rejecting the majority opinion of the Pontifical Commission on Population, the Family, and Birth Rate, instead determined that each and every act of marital sex should be open to procreation, thus effectively muffling incipient stress on interpersonal union.[8] Several decades later, the loose corpus of John Paul II's teachings referred to as the Theology of the Body portrayed the meaning of sex as stemming organ-ically from the body itself as revelatory of God's will. Relying heavily on the Genesis creation stories, the Theology of the Body simultaneously lifts up both procreative and unitive functions of sex, realized as a personalist mat-ter characterized by male/female complementarity.[9] According to this logic, loving heterosexual marriage that is fully open to procreation is the only context that adheres to the true meaning of sex, since anything else belies the "truthful" language of the body itself.

Throughout this history, the virtue of chastity has played a key interpretive role in Christian sexual ethics, particularly in the Catholic tradition. Thomas Aquinas defined chastity under the rubric of temperance; he framed it as the subset of temperance with respect to "venereal pleasure" and the property that curbs concupiscence.[10] This rather negative and primarily regulatory framing of chastity predominated for centuries; in one representative twentieth-century illustration, for example, chastity is designated "the moral virtue that controls in the married and altogether excludes in the unmarried all voluntary expression of the sensitive appetite for venereal pleasure."[11] Recent usage of the term has reflected a more positive and holistic understanding, however. The current *Catechism of the Catholic Church*, for example, defines chastity as the "successful integration of sexuality within the person and thus the inner unity of man [sic] in his bodily and spiritual being."[12] In spite of the way this definition moves beyond the realm of the purely physical and helpfully points toward the inner unity of the person—a more holistic posture, to be sure—it nevertheless remains squarely situated in the context of reasserted natural law teachings that stress the absolute inseparability of the unitive and procreative dimensions of the sexual act, teachings that (among other things) limit sexual intercourse to heterosexual married couples. Hence, a more traditionalist and physicalist understanding of natural law sexuality is arguably operative behind the scenes, even in this more expansive definition of chastity.[13]

Problematizing the Traditional Approach

There is no doubt that the strictly procreative ethic that once prevailed in Christian sexual ethics has relaxed over time. Yet, in spite of the fact that even Christian traditionalists have expanded the deeper meaning of sex beyond procreation, enormous problems still surface when the tradition is considered from a feminist point of view. While *feminism* is a term often mischaracterized and even misconstrued, I use the term here simply to designate a "conviction and movement opposed to discrimination on the basis of gender."[14] Such negative discrimination typically takes place both in personal and public realms, and feminism thus opposes both interpersonal beliefs and behaviors that support such discrimination as well as patriarchal social structures that codify and express it. In reality, many different types of feminism exist, differentiated by such factors as political or economic worldview, racial or ethnic identity, and any number of further qualifiers. Feminist approaches to Christianity generally seek to reconcile the aims of feminism as a whole with a religious tradition that has at times proved fundamentally non-inclusive and even harmful toward women. I understand these approaches to be neither anti-male nor anti-egalitarian but rather to hold as a central commitment the respect and equal social power of all people, in a world where women are de facto discriminated against, both personally and institutionally.

Adopting a feminist ethical lens reveals that the concept of gender complementarity runs like a red thread throughout traditionalist Christian perspectives, fortifying a rigid, binary, and overly simplistic understanding of gender. In this tradition, what it means to be "male" or "female" is more or less hard-coded into human biological reality, failing to account for historical and contextual influences on sexual identity—including the developing awareness that gender is often experienced in less binary ways. Additionally, traditional notions of gender complementarity downplay or even erase the negative impact of societal roles, the gendered distribution of power, and the reality of LGBTQ+ sexual experiences. To use postmodern terminology, false universals are thus wrongly projected into ethical discourse. In the case of women, the resulting account of "womanhood" found in the tradition maps onto a real-world disempowerment of women in the socioeconomic sphere, thus effectively baptizing their subjugation. Motherhood, for instance, is traditionally depicted as fundamentally constitutive of women's sexual identity[15]—a damaging and reductionistic portrayal that accounts neither for the breadth of women's experience nor for the deep socioeconomic inequalities in which women, including and especially mothers, are mired.[16] A portrayal of women as somehow essentially connected to the role of "mother," then, functions in the real world to justify theologically a structural disadvantaging of women in the economic sphere and an exclusionary posture toward women who are *not* mothers, whether by choice, circumstance, or biological impossibility.

This same reliance on notions of complementarity—whether in service to the procreative or the unitive norm—also operates negatively vis-à-vis the experience of LGBTQ+ persons. That is, the bodies and experiences of LGBTQ+ persons—which may be lacking the idealized version of heterogenital complementarity that characterizes, for example, John Paul II's Theology of the Body—are thus treated as nonnormative or even fundamentally defective. In response, some revisionist theologians have sought to retain the idea of relational complementarity but dissociate it from its more exclusionary and heteronormative limitations; Todd Salzman and Michael Lawler, for instance, helpfully propose "holistic" complementarity as an alternative and more flexible relational norm. Holistic complementarity, as they describe it, requires that truly human sexual acts be well integrated with the participants' whole selves—bodily, affectively, spiritually, and personally.[17] This move effectively unlinks the notion of complementarity from its more limiting, physicalist, and ultimately heteronormative implications.

But complementarity thus interpreted is not the only problem with traditional sexual-ethical frameworks. The deductive nature of such approaches too easily leads to an idealized picture of human sexual experience, belying the far-messier sexual realities faced by real people. Even the complex lived sexual experience of married heterosexual couples is largely distinguished by the "messy, clumsy, awkward, charming, casual, and yes, silly aspects of love in the flesh"—truths effectively obscured by the abstract definition of the sexual person found in more traditionalist theologies.[18] In other words, real-world people and experiences rarely conform to the idealized anthropology embedded within such theologies. As James Keenan points out in his own, more realistic sexual anthropology, each person's life and relationships are characterized by a certain "chaos" that provides the occasion for the virtue of mercy toward oneself and others.[19] Or, to put the point into bluntly contemporary pop-cultural terms, each of us is a hot mess—both within ourselves and in our relational lives. Idealized understandings of the procreative and unitive aspects of human sexuality that ignore the *complicatedness* of human persons and human relational life offer little useful guidance to ordinary people struggling with ordinary problems. Similarly, an idealized sexual ethic—one that deduces right behavior from abstract understandings of sexual or gendered reality—is bound to fall short in the context of real-world social problems such as extreme economic inequality, widespread sexual violence, or the economic, ecclesiastical, and cultural marginalization of women and LGBTQ+ persons.

Finally, it should be emphasized that chastity—represented as *the* defining virtue of sexual ethics—is itself a highly problematic concept from a feminist perspective. Chastity can, of course, helpfully point toward the authentic integration of a person's sexuality into that person's broader relationships and commitments. In addition, it can highlight a sort of "interior" unity that encourages and characterizes holistic well-being. However, in traditional views, the virtue of chastity is often utilized to cover *all* sexual sins and thus eclipses other virtues, including those less individualistic and more centered on our lives in community with one another.[20] In this way, a focus on chastity can function to detract from a broader, more justice-oriented lens with which to examine particular sexual practices, including the social contexts in which they take place.

From the perspective of women's well-being, chastity as a practical norm often translates today to a cultural emphasis on sexual "purity." "Purity culture" —common within both Roman Catholic and evangelical and fundamentalist Protestant circles, though taking a different cultural shape in each—responds to the sexualization of American popular culture by retrenching: purity advocates urge girls and women to remain sexually chaste until they are married (to men). In the Catholic imagination, this emphasis frequently finds expression in the reverencing of the virginity and motherhood of Mary, the mother of Jesus—who is seen to be the paragon of women's sexual virtue. Mary, who most likely was a teenage girl, is generally portrayed in the tradition as someone who had never had sexual relations and whose agency is defined simultaneously by her status as a virgin on the one hand and, on the other, her passive and obedient *acceptance* of the angel Gabriel's announcement that she would be "overshadowed" by the "power of the Most High" and subsequently give birth to a son. The problems with this interpretation are manifold—ranging from the nonrecognition of the radical political nature of Mary's story to the sidelining of her active acceptance of Gabriel's greeting and her agential trust in a God who is faithful and who affirms her own dignity and worth. Instead, Mary too often is simply uplifted as both passive and sexually "pure," precisely in her capacity as a virgin.[21] Alternatively, Protestant purity culture more often is expressed culturally in the form of "purity balls" (prom-like events promoting virginity until marriage) and "promise rings" (with which teenage girls pledge—usually to their fathers—to guard their virginity until they are married to men). Both traditions tend to default to an "abstinence-only" model of sexual education. This popular framing of purity thus functions to restrict human sexual expression to married, heterosexual spheres, as well as to place strong limits around sexual choice-making for women and girls.

Feminist cultural critic Jessica Valenti has incisively named this valorization of chastity in contemporary Christian popular culture as a "purity myth" that equates women's sexual status with their moral worth.[22] In other words, the elevation of chastity—and resulting emphasis upon sexual purity in popular culture—arguably perpetuates rather than refutes the hypersexualization of girls; in both cases, the worth of girls and women is once again tied strongly to their sexuality. As ethicist Bridget Burke Ravizza puts it, "Within this ethical system, if girls are sexually active, particularly if they 'lose their virginity,' they experience a loss of goodness and value."[23] Hence, an emphasis on sexual passivity, modesty, and abstinence-only education practically functions to disempower rather than support women and girls. Not only does this actively contradict their well-being; it also eviscerates their genuine sexual agency, infantilizing them in both the public and private spheres.

The popular association of moral worth with purity has other insidious consequences, as womanist theologians have underscored. For instance, Kelly Brown Douglas highlights the ways that, in the development of Anglo-Saxon heritage in the American context, whiteness has come to signify purity and moral innocence, while blackness has been popularly linked with "lewd, dangerous, and immoral people."[24] Similarly, Catholic womanist theologian M. Shawn Copeland notes the cultural association of the color white with cleanliness, innocence and virginity, chastity and purity, virtue and beauty, light and intelligence; and the color black with filth, depravity and immorality, promiscuity and pollution, vice and ugliness, and dark and ignorance.[25] Even the most cursory examination of slavery in the United States reveals the loathsome way female Black bodies were objectified, raped, beaten, blamed, and otherwise violated for the benefit of white slaveholders. Thus, when Christianity elevates purity as a signifier of virtue or moral worth, it simultaneously papers over and exacerbates the racist undertones with which the concept is associated and the violence in which it has been complicit.

In related fashion, elevating sexual purity as a virtue may readily be used to justify, ignore, or conceal racist motivations for contemporary violence and even murder. For example, in March 2021 in suburban Georgia, eight people—including six women of Asian descent—were murdered by a white, Christian gunman who claimed he killed them in order to eliminate the "temptation" he was experiencing in conjunction with his "sexual addiction."[26] The racist propensity to understand women—including Black, Latinx, and, in this case, Asian and Asian American women—as exotic and hypersexualized objects of male desire is heinous in its own right. Yet when combined with a shame-based Christian elevation of purity and an associated call to resist sexual "temptation," it becomes dangerous and even deadly. Moreover, such a posture fortifies the victim-blaming mentality that characterizes rape culture more broadly—a topic that arises throughout this volume.

The above criticisms are searing. But even as they demand that we soundly reject an older normative framework—one characterized by procreative and unitive norms, and chastity as the central defining sexual virtue—they also invite us in a new and more constructive direction. That is, a more adequate, realistic, and holistic sexual ethic must refocus us: toward the power of pleasure itself; toward the critical importance of freedom—robustly understood—in sexual well-being; toward the value of relational intimacy, including outside the bounds of traditional marital structures; and toward the way sex can elicit deep and life-giving insight into one's personality. In addition, a more traditional reliance on concepts such as procreation, gender complementarity, and romanticized ideals of "spousal cherishing" has practically functioned to mute the impact of social structures on sexual well-being—including the massive injustices that shape human experiences of sex in the real world today. Thus, in promulgating its oversimplified normative frameworks, the Christian tradition has ended up in fact contradicting women's authentic freedom and well-being and at times effectively baptizing unjust and heteronormative social patterns. A more adequate sexual ethic—one that seeks to take genuine account of and work against these unjust social patterns—must squarely address them in its analysis and proposals.

All of the above Christian theorizing, however, takes place in the midst of a US cultural context increasingly characterized by the revering of privacy and individual choice, particularly within the realm of human sexuality. Partially in response to the perception that traditionalist frameworks are overly restrictive, gender reductive, and otherwise oppressive—a perception with which I sympathize—the calls for women's "liberation" in the popular sphere have often articulated that liberation solely in terms of sexual freedom of choice, broadly construed. But what, exactly, is the *aim* of that freedom of choice? What are we liberated *for*? Well-deserved critiques of Christian-based ethical norms such as chastity or virginity have sometimes done a better job at picking apart the problems with the concepts than they have of developing new, more humanizing and appropriate—and less individualistic—norms. In other words, too often, a simple and untextured call for freedom of choice and consent in sexual decision-making substitutes for a meaningful, robust ethic. While freedom and the resulting emphasis on personal consent is indeed indispensable to an adequate feminist sexual ethic, it is not enough; we need a more explicit and full-bodied account of human well-being and what it asks of us.

A Word about Method

Clearly, there exists no lack of feminist critique of more traditionalist Christian paradigms. Both from within and outside the Christian tradition, feminists have rightly identified the myriad ways that Christianity in general and Christian sexual ethics in particular have remained mired in outdated assumptions regarding human sexuality and failed paradigms of sexual flourishing—some of which I elaborate above. Further, *white* feminism has fallen short in its own critique and normative proposals. Intersectional feminism—including womanist, *mujerista*, Latina feminist, postcolonial, and decolonial feminism—has rightly taken white feminism to task for projecting white women's experience onto women as a whole, thereby failing to attend to the genuine breadth and diversity of women's experiences and contributions to theology and ethics.[27]

Along similar lines, feminist deconstructive philosophical analyses have challenged metanarratives about the body, sexuality, and gender. Finding roots in a Foucauldian critique of objectivity, a postmodern rhetoric of *difference* rejects ethical understandings that reify patriarchal patterns or falsely universalize white, middle-class, heterosexual, and cisgender women's experience as if it encompassed all women. Such analyses hold that "universalizing" arguments—even those promoting qualities such as human well-being or equity—in fact flatten moral truth and thereby replicate social power differentials. Influential feminist philosopher Judith Butler has taken this deconstructionist impulse a step further; she stresses that sexual identity is fundamentally performative and that bodies themselves are indistinguishable from cultural frameworks of meaning and signification—so that, as far as human sexuality is concerned, gendered categories such as "woman" cannot properly be given any fixed referent. Indeed, her view pushes toward a position wherein there finally exists no finished or stable access to moral truth.[28]

Yet many feminists—particularly those who seek to remain within the bounds of Christianity—have pointed out that this sort of approach, although valuable and necessary practically speaking, is also potentially problematic when taken too far. According to this stream of thought, an extreme form of deconstructionism paves the way for moral relativism or even nihilism (a charge Butler herself resists). The fear, from the point of view of practical ethics, is that relinquishing agency and identifiable bodily reality to an extreme degree ultimately risks also eviscerating a common cry for justice, one that stretches across boundaries of culture and history. Lisa Cahill, for instance, writes, "The rhetoric of difference, when elevated to the level of a philosophical principle, can devitalize the cause of justice on behalf of those whom it was initially aimed to serve. It threatens to place the 'different' beyond the scope of one's own moral comprehension, concern and responsibility."[29] Further, in the absence of some sort of articulated normative framework about human sexual well-being, Enlightenment values such as autonomy and freedom have a way of sneaking back into avowedly deconstructionist accounts of sexual ethics as "tacit universals."[30] Thus, while rejecting abstract universalism and timeless absolutes, these feminist thinkers nevertheless seek to articulate a more historicized and nuanced understanding of human well-being that retains room for difference without relinquishing normative claims altogether.

Like these Christian ethicists, I approach moral knowledge with a posture of cautious critical realism, believing that it is indeed possible to attain genuine knowledge about the world, even if that knowledge is provisional, situated, and imperfect. Put differently, a "good life" is a real thing, not *only* a matter of preference, and, within limits, it is possible to articulate its contours—ideally the project of a modified, historicized, or "low-flying" natural law style of reasoning. Yet that articulation must never be done in simple deductive fashion, divorced from the specifics of history and embodied relationality. Rather, we must begin by explicitly acknowledging that "the universal can never be fully articulated,"[31] and thus that reasoning about human flourishing should remain flexible, revisable, practical, and heavily inductive, even as it strives to articulate more general ethical aims or principles.

Simultaneously, a feminist approach that retains liberationist *theological* commitments requires the promotion of substantive norms of well-being— norms that seek to positively impact the welfare of women, LGBTQ+ people, and indeed all persons who are harmed or marginalized by unjust social structures and expectations. My claims here are thus relatively modest but nonetheless vital: even in a world of postmodern sensibilities and sensitivities, one can begin to specify the broad outlines of shared human values related to sex, values that support the authentic freedom and well-being of all persons, including and especially women. What is needed is a careful, provisional, but nevertheless unabashedly feminist account of what it can mean to thrive, sexually speaking, in the context of an unjust—indeed, "fallen"—world. This will involve an effort to articulate the place of freedom and autonomy, to be sure, but also to specify embodied relationality as it contributes to human flourishing.

Such an approach always must begin with a contextual, historically conscious reality of the human person. Importantly, this person exists simultaneously in realms both universal (thus conferring an obligation for basic respect) and particular (leading to specific treatments based upon historical and relational contextuality). Not only should Christians pay attention to the customary moral sources such as scripture and tradition; human experience and more "secular" disciplines play a key role in leading us to new and more honest (not to mention relevant) normative guidelines. In sexual ethics, we must pay attention to what science and experience tell us about the economic and social context of sex; the existence (or, rather, lack thereof) of a strong sexual binary; the expectations of gendered social life; or the level of human satisfaction that ensues from sexual practices such as hookup sex or paid sex work. Moreover, in a liberationist context, paying attention to human experience means paying *particular* attention to the experiences of those on the "underside" of history—that is, those who have been marginalized by dominant social expectations and practices, sexual or otherwise.

In order to avoid epistemic overreach, however, even values derived with feminist and liberationist commitments must be understood to be fundamentally inductive and revisable. As Reinhold Niebuhr described, *all*

historic norms are touched by finitude and sin, so ethical propositions necessarily retain a tentative and provisional quality.[32] Thus, even as the attempt
to articulate what counts as good, fulfilling, life-giving sex here possesses a
rather Catholic flair, the account is tempered by Protestant sensibilities about
the pervasiveness of human sin and its destructive power vis-à-vis our ability
to articulate accurately that sexual good. And since people exist in social
and historically concrete settings, human sinfulness not only takes place at
the level of the individual but also extends into social and structural realms.
Social injustice is pervasive, and its consequences can be deadly. Thus, while
our norms must be specified carefully and offered up tentatively, we simply
do not have the practical luxury of failing to offer them up at all.

Again, to be crystal clear: it will be impossible for real people with a diversity of perspectives to agree on what constitutes human flourishing, in every
time and place. Yet even as Niebuhr himself described love as an "impossible
possibility,"[33] sexual ethics must make the attempt to get *closer*, to condemn
commonly recognized forms of injustice, to lift up commonly (if perhaps not
universally) desired goals, and finally, to revise, revise, revise. A shared moral
vision—even a humble one—deriving from our shared humanity is a worth-
while goal, in a world where moral atrocities are far too common and exact far
too much suffering and anguish.

Sex is indeed a bodily reality, but one that is deeply shaped by history,
culture, and particular concrete location—all of which ground and enable
unique forms of connection among persons. Further, and to return to where
I began, sex is powerful: sexual well-being and joy can heal and transform
lives, instill a sense of personal and interpersonal power, and infuse a life with
creative potential.[34] For such a profound and complex aspect of human existence, the simple norm of consent—while of critical importance—is insufficient to guide a full account of sexual flourishing. What Christian ethics needs
is neither the rigid and limiting ethical norms of its past nor the uncritical
acceptance of the thin version of individual consent that we find in popular
Western culture today. Rather, what is needed is to draw upon the tradition's
own best insights, in conversation with and refined by feminist philosophical
and theological thought, to construct a more nuanced and flexible version of
human flourishing that affirms persons in all of their beauty, their messiness,
their freedom, and their possibilities. Only then will sexual ethics serve the
demands of justice.

Notes

1. Augustine, "The Good of Marriage." For a fuller elaboration of these positions, see Peterson-Iyer, "Sex and Sexuality."
2. For a more complete account of these early contributions to the tradition, see, for instance, Genovesi, *In Pursuit of Love*, 118–21.
3. Aquinas, *Summa Theologica*, I.98.2.
4. Rickaby, *Of God and His Creatures*; and Aquinas, *Summa Theologica*, II-II.26.11. See also Farley, *Just Love*, 44.
5. Luther, "The Large Catechism (1529)," 335.
6. Calvin, *Institutes of the Christian Religion*, 2.8.44.
7. Paul VI, *The Pastoral Constitution*.
8. Paul VI, *Humanae Vitae*. For the rejected majority report of the commission, see *Majority Report of the Papal Commission*. The majority report recommended that married couples be allowed to regulate conception, including the use of what is ordinarily termed "artificial" birth control. For an extended discussion of the unfolding of the controversy, and especially the role of minority report coauthor John C. Ford, see Genilo, *John Cuthbert Ford, S.J.*
9. Salzman and Lawler, *The Sexual Person*, 84–91. See also Salzman and Lawler, *Sexual Ethics*, 63–86.
10. Aquinas, *Summa Theologica*, II-II.141.4 and II-II.151.1 and 3.
11. Davis, *Moral and Pastoral Theology*, 2:172, cited in Catholic Theological Society of America Committee on the Study of Human Sexuality, *Human Sexuality*, 100.
12. *Catechism of the Catholic Church*, 2337.
13. Salzman and Lawler, *The Sexual Person*, 120.
14. Farley, "Feminist Ethics."
15. John Paul II, *General Audience*. See also John Paul II, *Familiaris Consortio*; and John Paul II, *Mulieris Dignitatem*. For more on this point, see Cahill, "Catholic Sexual Ethics," 145–46.
16. A full elaboration of the historical economic disadvantaging of women would be impossible in this short space, and indeed, I take the point as already sufficiently demonstrated that women do not enjoy anything close to full economic and social equality in modern society. What often comes as a greater surprise, however, is that motherhood itself functions as a primary agent of that socioeconomic disadvantage; see, for instance, Crittenden, *The Price of Motherhood*, esp. 6.
17. Salzman and Lawler, *Sexual Ethics*, 72–82; and Salzman and Lawler, *The Sexual Person*, 85–91.
18. Johnson, *The Revelatory Body*, 24–25. David Cloutier and William C. Mattison also highlight the ways that the focus on purity and idealized portrayals of human sexuality in the Theology of the Body belie a more positive, prophetic, grounded, and honest understanding of Christian love. See Cloutier and Mattison, "Bodies Poured Out in Christ."
19. Keenan, "Virtue Ethics and Sexual Ethics," 192–93.
20. Salzman and Lawler, *The Sexual Person*, 120.
21. For an incisive feminist critique of how the figure of Mary functions in Catholic thought, see Johnson, *Truly Our Sister*, esp. chapter 10.
22. Valenti, *The Purity Myth*, 48–51.
23. Burke Ravizza, "Feminism a Must," 151.

24. Douglas, "More than Skin Deep," 8–9. See also Williams, "Sin, Nature."
25. Copeland, "White Supremacy and Anti-Black Logics," 62.
26. Richard Fausset, Nicholas Bogel-Burroughs, and Marie Fazio, "8 Dead in Atlanta Spa Shootings, with Fears of Anti-Asian Bias," *New York Times*, March 26, 2021, https://www .nytimes.com/live/2021/03/17/us/shooting-atlanta-acworth.
27. See, for instance, Williams, *Sisters in the Wilderness*; Lorde, "An Open Letter," 90–93; Isasi-Díaz, *Mujerista Theology*; Aquino, "Latin American Feminist Theology"; Aquino, "Latina Feminist Theology"; and Kwok, "Unbinding Our Feet."
28. See esp. Butler, "Contingent Foundations," 50–54. See also Butler, *Bodies That Matter*, 3–27; and Butler, *Undoing Gender*, chapters 1 and 4, esp. p. 87. For a more sympathetic reading overall of Butler, see Grimes, "Butler Interprets Aquinas"; and Ford, "Transgender Bodies, Catholic Schools."
29. Cahill, *Sex, Gender, and Christian Ethics*, 28. See also Farley, "Feminism and Universal Morality"; and Traina, "Feminism and Natural Law." Finally, Lisa Fullam articulates a helpful position that acknowledges physiology without making anatomy destiny; Fullam assigns a "low predictive value for sex vis-à-vis gender, without discounting it entirely." See Lisa Fullam, "'Gender Theory,' Nuclear War, and the Nazis," *Commonweal*, February 23, 2015, https://www.commonwealmagazine.org/gender-theory-nuclear-war-and -nazis-0.
30. Cahill, *Sex, Gender, and Christian Ethics*, 2.
31. Grimes, "Butler Interprets Aquinas," 203. Grimes here makes a strong case for how this more flexible and inductive understanding of human flourishing is consonant with Thomas Aquinas's own natural law reasoning.
32. Niebuhr, *The Nature and Destiny of Man*, 284.
33. Niebuhr, *An Interpretation of Christian Ethics*, 19.
34. Parker, "Making Love," 9.

CHAPTER TWO

Moral Anthropology, Justice, and Sexual Ethics

Having traced the contours of traditional forms of Christian sexual ethics, including some of the key ways in which they fail to serve the agency and holistic well-being of women and other sexually marginalized communities, it is now time to take a more positive turn and seek to articulate the outlines of a normative feminist Christian framework for sexual ethics. To be sure, like most feminist approaches, that framework includes an important place for sexual freedom and agency. But it also enumerates and elaborates broader dimensions of well-being, including physical health, emotional integrity, relational intimacy, and mutuality and equal regard as they intersect with and bolster that agency—in a world marked by gender inequality and other forms of sexual and socioeconomic injustice. At its most basic level, the framework I offer here initiates a vision of human flourishing that takes women's sexual reality and experience seriously—including earnest consideration of both their personal and social well-being.

Seeds of a New Sexual Ethic: Insights from the Biblical Tradition

To arrive at such a vision—or, rather, a reenvisioning—of sexual ethics, it is vital first to identify the core, life-giving insights from Christianity that inform the *best* of Christian sexual ethics. It is true that Christian sexual ethics has often functioned more to tear down than to build up, demonizing pleasure, reifying chastity, overemphasizing procreation, ignoring sexual injustice, or otherwise relying on ethical frameworks that function to exclude or condemn. Yet that same tradition potentially offers seeds of insight, life-giving truths, and resources for transforming individuals and societies in a just and humanizing direction. Many of these discernments are rooted in the biblical tradition. It is not my project here to engage in a detailed scriptural exegesis in every case, nor am I particularly equipped to do so. My hope is not to glean extensive or concrete sexual guidance from scripture but rather to allow its paradigms to shape and inspire broad ethical awareness, "tutor[ing] the imagination" and fostering new ways for us to envision reality.[1]

Unity of Body and Soul

Some of the earliest roots of the Christian tradition affirm a unity of body and soul, but the theme has doubtless been compromised by the impact on Christianity from both Greek and Enlightenment directions of thought. Each of these influences contributed in unique ways to dualistic notions that functionally bifurcated the body from the rational or spiritual "soul." Yet the kernel of insight persists within Christianity: human sexuality rightly encompasses the deeply intertwined physical, emotional, rational, and spiritual realms. In truth, humans in their lived reality are unavoidably *embodied*. We exist both as "embodied spirits" and "inspirited bodies," so deeply composite that it is quite literally impossible to fully separate the two in freedom of choice and experienced lives.[2] Sex is but one example of this; the biological basis of sex is real, but from the start we deeply infuse sex with patterns of meaning and identity that extend far beyond the purely physical realm.

A close unity of body and soul, including its more rational and even intellectual components, is embedded throughout the Hebrew Bible. Even the language itself contains hints to this effect. For instance, as James Nelson has incisively pointed out, the ancient Hebrew verb for "to know" (*yādāh*) is used in places as a synonym for sexual intercourse, alluding to the close connection between *desiring* another and yearning for a deep *knowledge* of the other.[3] In fact, from the very start of the book of Genesis, there exists strong basis to acknowledge the body as more than incidental—that is, as good, beautiful, even sacred. This is perhaps clearest when God affirms the newly created humankind in God's own image, and as sexual beings, simultaneously giving them responsibility over the rest of creation and declaring them, along with that creation, to be "very good" (Genesis 1:31).[4] God instructs these humans to "be fruitful and multiply" (1:28), that is, to use their sexual capacities to continue the ongoing work of creation. In the second Genesis creation story, we are told that Adam and Eve were "naked, and were not ashamed" (2:25)—a clear affirmation of the sexual body, and one that stands in sharp contrast to the way the body later came to be associated in parts of the tradition with impurity, temptation, and fault.

The biblical affirmation of the human body as a *sexual* body is perhaps richest in the unapologetic celebration of desire within the sexual poetry of the Song of Solomon (also called the Song of Songs). It is difficult to avoid the raw sensuality, passion, and pleasure present within its pages:

> How graceful are your feet in sandals,
> O queenly maiden!
> Your rounded thighs are like jewels,
> the work of a master hand.
> Your navel is a rounded bowl
> that never lacks mixed wine.
> Your belly is a heap of wheat,
> encircled with lilies.
> Your two breasts are like two fawns,
> twins of a gazelle. (Song of Solomon 7:1–3)

Taken as a whole, the book elevates sexual intimacy as not simply a matter of bodily lust and admiration of beauty but also as expressing the deep connections—relational, physical, and spiritual—that exist between the lovers. Sexual desire and bodily pleasure are affirmed, and they comingle with the emotional connection shared by the lovers, a connection that impacts them profoundly and longitudinally:

> Set me as a seal upon your heart,
> as a seal upon your arm;
> for love is strong as death,
> passion fierce as the grave.
> Its flashes are flashes of fire,
> a raging flame. (Song of Solomon 8:6)

Here, sex is *more* than physical; erotic passion connects the lovers deeply to each other, "sealing" them one to the other on a relational and arguably even spiritual level.

While the backdrop of the poem is decidedly patriarchal, the author appears to reject or at least to disagree with the view that men can or should control women.[5] In the face of social structures that would constrain the female lover or deny her goal—for example, the "sentinels" of the city who beat and wound her as she ventures out into the city alone—the Song extols her resilience and celebrates her passion and sexual choice-making. Indeed, one might say that the woman's sexual agency emerges in and through the power of her erotic desire. Womanist scholar Keri Day extends this assessment further, arguing not only that the Song affirms women's sexual freedom and erotic flourishing outside of strictly heteronormative ideologies but also that it is precisely this empowered sexual agency that facilitates a deeper, sacramental understanding of sex. She writes, "The Shulammite woman embraces how sexual agency opens her up to life, thus connecting her to herself, her ability to love, and ultimately to a celebration of how her agency [therefore enables] divine encounters in and through her body."[6] In other words, it is specifically the agency of the woman expressed through her erotic power that adds gravity and significance to the poem, infusing her bodily encounters with theological magnitude.

The tradition has frequently interpreted the Song as an allegory for a more spiritual connection to the divine, likening the desire and love between the characters to God's love for Israel, for instance, or to Christ's love for the believer. Less common in churches or theological texts, however, is to lift up the passionate character of the poetry itself. Yet it is precisely this passion that is noteworthy from the point of view of a tighter unity of body and soul, for it is in the unity of passion and deeper meaning that we are reminded of the sacramental nature of human sexuality—the way embodied pleasure and sexual desire have something vital to communicate and signify about our relationships with each other, and indeed with the divine.

The biblical and theological motif of the body's goodness continues, of course, in the New Testament thematic of the Incarnation. Christians do not worship a God who is wholly or even largely separate, other, distant; rather, God shows Godself to have walked among us, in a human body subject to the vagaries, joys, and struggles entailed by real, embodied existence. God's radical presence in the person of Jesus affirms the sacred nature of our own human embodiment, originally indicated by the Genesis stories. Moreover, it offers strong theological justification for prioritizing human embodiment in Christian sexual ethics.

Human Dignity

A second bedrock of the Christian tradition central to a reenvisioned and revised sexual ethic is the dignity of the human person. Undergirding every aspect of Catholic social teaching, human dignity specifies the unearned, transcendent worth that stems from creation in God's image and likeness. Moreover, it implies a radical equality among persons; each life is sacred, and the social order itself must function to support and benefit the well-being of each person as well as to invite the *full* participation of both persons and groups. Thus, dignity acts as the starting point for a moral vision of society—that is, for constructive proposals of justice. Importantly, this includes a willingness to take responsibility for—and act to redress—social structures that effectively ignore, repress, or otherwise harm individuals or classes.[7]

Human dignity, and the deep value of life it affirms, stems not only from the sheer fact of creation in God's image described above but also from the tradition's fundamental affirmation that all persons are loved and redeemed by Jesus Christ. Surely this is the core wisdom of one of the most well-known verses of the Bible, John 3:16: "For God so loved the world, that [God] gave [God's] only Son, so that everyone who believes in him may not perish but may have eternal life." Even as Jesus himself was identified as "beloved" by God at his baptism in all three synoptic Gospels (Matthew 3:16–17; Mark 1:10–11; Luke 3:21–22), the concept reveals an intimate truth about how God wishes to relate to all human beings; in the words of Catholic theologian Henri Nouwen, "being the Beloved expresses the core truth of our existence" and contradicts the self-rejection that is so prevalent in modern times.[8]

Lutheran public theologian Nadia Bolz-Weber similarly hints at the power of this "belovedness" when she describes how God's voice and actions effectively declare humans to be clean, justified, forgiven, new—conveying a deep internal sense of worthiness and exiling shame as a primary driver of human behavior. In other words, God's grace is radical and inclusive, communicating profound worth and knitting together the fractured parts of ourselves back into wholeness. She writes, "God's voice . . . imparts to us a worthiness that has nothing to do with our efforts or our accomplishments or our becoming some imagined ideal," banishing the accusing voice from our heads and inviting us instead to love ourselves.[9] From this perspective, human dignity is not simply a straightforward pronouncement of human value and equality; it is also an invitation toward deeper self-affirmation and a healed self-esteem. In terms of sexual ethics, it asks that our actions and practices conform to and promote the profound worth of self and other, and a willingness to take ownership of and responsibility for the individual actions we choose and social practices in which we participate.

Liberation

A strong affirmation of dignity in the context of real-world cruelty and oppression leads us to an additional core biblical theme—that of liberation. It is impossible to overstate the importance of liberation in the Bible.

In particular, the story of the Exodus—which depicts the emancipation of the ancient Israelites from slavery in Egypt for their eventual deliverance to the land of Canaan—pervades Christian identity in a profound and ongoing way. The tradition continues in the Old Testament prophets, notably Isaiah, Micah, Jeremiah, and Amos. Isaiah in particular offers iconic words by which God's people, restored to Jerusalem, are called to organize their communal life:

> Is not this the fast that I choose:
> to loose the bonds of injustice,
> to undo the thongs of the yoke,
> to let the oppressed go free,
> and to break every yoke?
> Is it not to share your bread with the hungry,
> and bring the homeless poor into your house;
> when you see the naked, to cover them,
> and not to hide yourself from your own kin? (Isaiah 58:6–7)

A few chapters later, the prophet expands upon the liberationist mandate:

> The Spirit of the Lord God is upon me,
> because the Lord has anointed me
> He has sent me to bring good news to the oppressed,
> to bind up the brokenhearted,
> to proclaim liberty to the captives
> and release to the prisoners;
> to proclaim the year of the Lord's favor,
> and the day of vengeance of our God;
> to comfort all who mourn;
> to provide for those who mourn in Zion—
> to give them a garland instead of ashes,
> the oil of gladness instead of mourning,
> the mantle of praise instead of a faint spirit.
> They will be called oaks of righteousness,
> the planting of the Lord, to display of his glory. (Isaiah 61:1–3)

This theme of liberation—indeed Isaiah's very words—are echoed centuries later in Jesus's announcement of his own ministry, as told in the New Testament Gospel of Luke:

[Jesus] unrolled the scroll and found the place where it was written:
"The Spirit of the Lord is upon me,
because he has anointed me
to bring good news to the poor.
He has sent me to proclaim release to the captives
and recovery of sight to the blind,
to let the oppressed go free,
to proclaim the year of the Lord's favor."
And he rolled up the scroll, gave it back to the attendant, and sat down.
The eyes of all in the synagogue were fixed on him. Then he began to
say to them, "Today this scripture has been fulfilled in your hearing."
(Luke 4:17b–21)

Here, Jesus—drawing upon a long tradition of God's mandate to liberate the oppressed—articulates a vision of justice and freedom that includes within itself an explicit rejection of social patterns that bind, imprison, or otherwise afflict. And in the ministry that followed, Jesus indeed shattered religious and societal barriers by touching, speaking to, and even eating with those whom society considered unworthy or unclean—women, the poor, and other socially marginalized persons. In this respect, Jesus carried forward and extended the liberatory frameworks of ancient Israel to express a still more radical version of freedom.

It is worth here taking an even deeper look at how that freedom is interpreted later in the New Testament. The broader New Testament vision of human freedom is not primarily a negative freedom, a freedom *from*; rather, its pages also elaborate a more positive vision of freedom, a freedom *for*. This is particularly evident in the writings of the apostle Paul. In the book of Galatians, for example, Paul depicts freedom as closely connected to God's Spirit. Freedom here entails a choice: Christians must choose to pursue not "self-indulgence" but rather love and service to one another (Galatians 5:13b)—a positive ethic relevant to the real-life struggles faced by the Galatians, to whom he wrote. He warns them against the "works of the flesh" yet importantly does not mean by this only sexual or bodily sins but also evils that we might ordinarily think of as "spiritual"—such as hostility, jealous rivalry, and selfishness (5:19–21). Paul thus does not advocate in Galatians a retreat from corporeality but rather an embrace of the "fruits of the spirit"—love, joy, peace, patience, kindness, generosity, faithfulness, gentleness, self-control (5:22–23).[10] In sum, according to the apostle Paul's understanding, Christian freedom is not aimless or open-ended; rather, it liberates people *into* a life with a particular normative shape.

Relational Reciprocity

Alongside and embedded within these articulations of human dignity and liberation, the Christian tradition has also strongly emphasized the more *collective* dimension of human experience. Several biblical themes converge here: Israel's identity as a covenant people of God; Jesus's depiction of the "kingdom" of God and the relationships that characterize it; and Saint Paul's strong emphasis on the followers of Christ as his "body" in Romans (12:5), 1 Corinthians (12:12–27), and elsewhere. Additionally, and as already described, the intrinsic social dimension of sexual ethics is present in the work of Augustine, Aquinas, and Luther, as well as many other historical strands of Christianity.[11] Even an understanding of sin as a rift in the covenantal relationship with God frames the concept primarily in relational rather than individual terms. And the concepts of social and structural sin—that is, sin that resides within a group or becomes embodied and embedded into social structures—take a still stronger view of the central role that human relationships play in the core of human identity.

Of course, relationality by itself, though a central quality of human experience, is not always conducive to human flourishing. Traditional Christianity—characterized both theologically and ecclesiastically by hierarchical structures, kingship metaphors, and strongly gendered familial expectations—hardly provides a rich source for mining more egalitarian and reciprocal norms. Patriarchal kinship norms that understood women to be a form of property stand as a backdrop to much of the biblical story. Paul's very specific assertions of male "headship" in families (1 Corinthians 11:3 and Ephesians 5:23, for example) or denials that women should exercise leadership in churches (1 Timothy 2:11–12) have been used to justify women's second-class status in both private and public realms. These teachings have doubtlessly driven untold numbers of women away from Christianity altogether and have dogged Christian feminism from its inception.

Still, seeds of a more egalitarian framework also exist in the Bible, and they are arguably more central and normative than the above, more culturally specific, passages. Jesus occupies a place in the biblical tradition not only as the Christ or messiah but also as a powerful social prophet who criticizes the elites of his time and routinely transgresses religious and social boundaries. His relatively egalitarian treatment of women in his own society stands in marked contrast to less liberative biblical moments. In fact, Jesus rejects the prevailing purity codes that characterized his social world and instead advocates a wholly alternative social understanding, one marked by neighbor love and compassion. And Paul's theology of oneness in Christ, for instance in his letter to the

Galatians, expresses a strongly egalitarian understanding of persons: "There is no longer Jew or Greek, there is no longer slave or free, there is no longer male and female; for all of you are one in Christ Jesus" (Galatians 3:28).

A case for this more egalitarian and reciprocal understanding of human relationships may be supported by the theological concept of the Trinity. Womanist theologian Kelly Brown Douglas, for instance, points out that the Trinity reveals God as "internally and eternally relational. . . . God in God-self, the Godhead, is in a relationship of mutuality and reciprocity as creator, redeemer, and sustainer."[12] Feminist moral theologian Christine Gudorf carries this understanding of the Trinity specifically into the realm of marital love, arguing that trinitarian love functions as an analog: a "self-disclosing love between equals whose intimacy overflows onto the whole of creation."[13] Finally, Catholic ethicist Bryan N. Massingale, drawing in part upon the work of Elizabeth Johnson, elaborates an understanding of the Trinity as shorthand for an "erotic" God, characterized by constitutive relationality and a passion for mutual and noncoercive relationships. When combined with the Incarnation, this erotic Godhead provides theological basis for a similarly nondominative understanding of sex in the realm of human relationships.[14]

I consider the theme of mutuality more fully later in this chapter. Here my point is simply to highlight that it possesses roots in the Christian tradition—both biblically and theologically—that often go unrecognized or overlooked. When integrated with feminist social awareness and analysis, such roots provide rich material for a Christian sexual ethic concerned explicitly to promote women's well-being.

Reformulating a New Sexual Ethic: Visions of Freedom and Well-Being

The above themes—the unity of body and soul, human dignity, liberation, and relational reciprocity—represent what I consider to be the *best* of the Christian tradition. They point us in the direction of a refreshed framework for sexual ethics, one that reenvisions what it means for *all* people to flourish, attending to both freedom and well-being—especially (though not exclusively) women's well-being in the context of patriarchy. But what exactly are the normative contours of such framework? The remainder of this chapter is devoted to answering that question—that is, to shaping a rough vision that moves us beyond a narrow focus on free choice without, however, tossing us back into the procreationist, chastity-focused, and overly exclusionary sexual analyses of the past. What is needed is a nuanced and more sex-positive portrait of flourishing that develops various qualities—freedom, embodied physical well-being, emotional integrity, mutuality and equal regard, and relational intimacy—all in conjunction with an insistence on locating the human person in the milieu of real-world systemic and gender-based injustice.

But before beginning this revised account of human flourishing, what do broader, nonreligious understandings of sexuality have to say about sexual well-being? The World Health Organization (WHO) in 2002 put forth (and later revised) the following understanding of sexual health, intended not as an official definition but rather as a part of ongoing discussions related to the concept. They refer to sexual health as

> a state of physical, emotional, mental and social well-being in relation to sexuality; it is not merely the absence of disease, dysfunction or infirmity. Sexual health requires a positive and respectful approach to sexuality and sexual relationships, as well as the possibility of having pleasurable and safe sexual experiences, free of coercion, discrimination and violence. For sexual health to be attained and maintained, the sexual rights of all persons must be respected, protected and fulfilled.

Based upon this understanding of sexual health, the WHO derives certain rights due each person—rights to the "highest attainable" standard of health, including access to sexual and reproductive health care services; to seek, receive, and impart information related to sexuality; to sexuality education; to respect for bodily integrity; to choose one's partner; to decide to be sexually active or not; to consensual sexual relations; to consensual marriage; to decide whether, and when, to have children; and to pursue a satisfying, safe, and pleasurably sexual life.[15] On the one hand, the above description of sexual health itself is quite broad, promoting well-being in virtually all dimensions (physical, emotional, mental, and social) of human existence. On the other hand, the list of concrete associated rights is actually rather skeletal. The focus here clearly remains upon safety, pleasure, and well-being in addition to consent and freedom of choice and expression. But the definition invites us to fill out or enflesh the texture and nuance of sexual health according to more particular social, cultural, and religious visions.

A slightly more robust philosophical account of human flourishing that can shape an account of sexuality is found in the work of Martha Nussbaum. Nussbaum's "critical universalism" represents her attempt to assess human well-being—and especially women's well-being—across culture and history. Drawing on the work of economist Amartya Sen, Nussbaum describes both the broad "shape of the human form of life" as well as the capabilities necessary for functioning well in the world. These include:

1. to live to the end of a human life of "normal length";
2. to have good health and adequate nourishment, shelter, opportunities for sexual satisfaction and choice in reproductive matters, and mobility;
3. to avoid unnecessary and nonbeneficial pain and to have pleasurable experiences;
4. to use the senses, to imagine, think, and reason, informed by an adequate education and protected by freedom of expression and religious exercise;
5. to have attachments (including love attachments) of things and persons outside of oneself;
6. to form a conception of the good and engage in critical reflection about the planning of one's own life;
7. to show concern for others and demonstrate compassion, justice, and friendship;
8. to live with concern for animals, plants, and nature;
9. to laugh, play, recreate;
10. to live one's own life with a guarantee of some noninterference with certain personal choices especially definitive of selfhood—e.g., marriage, childbearing, sexual expression, speech, and employment;
11. to live one's own life in one's own surrounding and context; to enjoy freedom of association and (to some extent) the integrity of personal property.[16]

Among these, clearly germane to a discussion of *sexual* flourishing are the capability for sexual satisfaction as well as for choice (and relative noninterference) in reproductive and other highly personal matters, the opportunity to plan the contours of one's own life, the capability for pleasure (and the avoidance of pain), and the chance for interpersonal attachment, friendship, love, play, and recreation. These indicate the need to elaborate notions of freedom and well-being, both physical and emotional. However, also noticeable in Nussbaum's list is her emphasis on imagination and the meaning that humans create for themselves and within familial and friendly organizations. These qualities point not simply toward the emotional aspects of human existence but also toward the deeper significance people attach to sexual expression and the need to integrate that significance across one's identity and lifespan.

Nussbaum's list pushes a revisionist Christian sexual ethic to attend to genuine human well-being on multiple levels—physical, emotional, relational and interpersonal, and spiritual. It also reminds us that freedom itself is neither a *dispensable* aspect of human experience, nor is it *sufficient* to describe the breadth of human flourishing. Indeed, freedom and well-being represent two sides of the same coin of human flourishing. Nussbaum's account prompts us that, while Christian ethics can do more to articulate that flourishing than her philosophically generalist account is able to do, it also cannot afford to do less.

Another way of framing the job that lies before us is to articulate human flourishing in terms of the demands of justice. The classic rendition of justice—as rendering to each party his or her "due"—tells us little until we fill it out with an articulation of what each person is actually due. Here, of particular use to a Christian feminist account is the work of Margaret Farley. In her seminal volume *Just Love*, Farley elaborates upon the classic understanding by arguing that justice requires the affirmation of persons according to their "concrete reality, actual and potential"—that is, in their universally shared human qualities as well as in their untidy particularity. To fill out what this entails, Farley describes what she terms "obligating features of personhood," features possessed by every human being and that "constitute the basis of a requirement to respect persons . . . sexually or otherwise." She particularly focuses on *autonomy* and *relationality* as twin aspects of personhood that ground moral obligations and provide content for more specific moral norms for sexual ethics.[17]

Farley herself derives a list of "bottom-line requirements" from this conception of human personhood. The norms elaborated below are in some respects similar to Farley's but expand them in new and alternative directions—directions indicated above by my specific critique and retrieval of Christian sexual ethics, as well as by the contours of Nussbaum's portrait of specific human capabilities. Moreover, each of the norms depicted here intersects in critical ways with the concrete realities of socioeconomic, sexual, and gender injustice that profoundly shape embodied experience and even direct human life together. Thus, not only must our understanding of the human person remain deeply attentive to these social realities; our normative prescriptions must reflect a commitment to human flourishing that is both individually and socially articulated—a truly holistic account.

Freedom and Agency

Freedom of choice or consent has of course become a catchphrase for the modern West, particularly the United States. A post-Enlightenment individualism pervades most aspects of public discourse, manifesting as a strong, sometimes almost devout reverence for autonomy as the preeminent moral guidepost. This propensity is built into our legal system and civic expectations as well as popular culture's veneration of individual identity and personal preference. Indeed, individual choice on most legal or ethical matters has become the philosophical "default" position in the public sphere, such that contradicting it requires intense justification and concrete proof of harm to identifiable individuals.

Whereas freedom is also at times revered within Christianity, an under-nuanced and unqualified individualism runs counter to both Christianity as a whole and a feminist Christian approach in particular. In fact, the Christian tradition has exhibited a complicated relationship with the very existence of human free choice. Some parts of the tradition have adopted a highly suspicious assessment of human freedom, stressing the givenness of nature or (in the case of John Calvin and his later followers) attributing a near absence of genuine freedom to human activity. Yet perhaps more widely characteristic of Christianity is an approach that understands freedom as fundamental, a "gift flowing from human nature" (according to Roman Catholic thought) and closely connected to human beings' status as both dignified and morally responsible.[18] Some parts of the tradition have even elevated the term *co-creativity*, emphasizing the radical quality of humans' freedom and responsibility to shape and redirect the "givens" of nature as active participants in the ongoing process of creation.

Without fully resolving this tension, on balance it is safe to affirm that human freedom is of key importance within Christianity and indeed grounds particular moral obligations. Yet this does not mean that autonomy is somehow the archetypical human quality. Rather, autonomy constitutes an irreducible aspect of human capacity and experience, and one we should qualify and contextualize but not ignore. Along these lines, Farley describes an anthropology that includes both autonomy and relationality as fundamental (and interrelated) features of the human person. While humans indeed transcend ourselves in our relationships with others, we also, in crucially important ways, belong to ourselves. In other words, our *selves* and our *actions* are, elementally, our own; they belong to us and not to others, and they reflect something profound about who we are and about what and whom we love. Hence, we experience the power of free choice as self-determination, and, while not infinite, it is nevertheless sublime in relation to who we are as humans. It amounts to the capacity "to choose not only our own actions but also our ends and our loves. It is a capacity therefore to determine the meaning of our own lives and, within limits, our destiny."[19]

Such a capacity is of particular importance to women, who have in so many ways been denied that choice by patriarchal families, churches, and societies in myriad places and times. A feminist account must begin with the recognition that women have, in fact, been *denied* freedom of choice in important respects, particularly in sexual and reproductive matters. For instance, the existence of relatively safe and reliable forms of contraception is a fairly recent development, historically speaking, and artificial contraception remains inaccessible in many parts of the world and disallowed by the Catholic Church itself. And without wading too deeply into the waters of the abortion culture wars, it is important to recall that even partial access to legal abortion in restricted cases has only been constitutionally available to women since 1973, and such access remains uncertain even today.[20] In the medical world more generally, patriarchy's ignominious history includes a long chronicle of male control over women's reproductive capacities, depriving them of a measure of freedom over their own bodies.[21] Moreover, childrearing by and large remains the responsibility of women, often severely limiting their life choices and constraining their social power.[22] Indeed, Christian ethicist Beverly Wildung Harrison has identified procreative choice in reproductive matters as a worthy goal—and one not simply having to do with access to safe abortion but more broadly understood to include safer contraception, greater economic security, access to affordable childcare, and a reduction of racial brutality and violence against women as a social good foundational to women's well-being.[23] These realities indicate how challenging it is for many women to claim even partial "authorship" over their own lives and how, therefore, freedom of choice, particularly in sexual and reproductive matters, is essential to their flourishing.[24]

And yet part of the challenge of affirming human free choice in a postmodern and postcolonial context is that agency itself has come under attack. The humanist "universal" subject has been unmasked as not so universal after all, but rather as white, male, straight, cisgender, non-disabled, and middle to upper class. Moreover, we have rightly become attuned to the many cultural forces that constrain free choice in the real world, defining the parameters of what is possible or even fully comprehensible to a wider audience. Within these contexts, sociologist Sherry B. Ortner eloquently defines a new goal: to "restore agency without reproducing the bourgeois subject . . . to picture indissoluble formations of structurally embedded agency and intention-filled structures, to recognize the ways in which the subject is part of larger social and cultural webs."[25] As a way of doing this, Ortner proposes examining not the agent in and of herself but rather as a player alongside others in "serious games," projects, and webs of relationship that define the shape of life.[26]

For women in a patriarchal (as well as racist, classist, ableist, and hetero- and cisnormative) social context, we must conclude that human agency is inescapably impacted by power. We cannot afford to ignore this in any account of free choice, nor should we minimize its place within an understanding of human flourishing. Yet we also must not altogether abandon the quest to promote women's authentic freedom, however challenged it may be. To do so would be to relinquish women's possibilities prematurely, as well as to deny the very real and resilient (even if imperfect) ways that women express their agency and exercise their autonomy every day, under compromised circumstances. Along these lines, Kochurani Abraham has elaborated the virtue of *resistance* as a subversive expression of postcolonial Indian women's critical voice and agency under conditions that oppress and dehumanize. Through resistance, she argues, women can "reclaim their subjectivity and agency, and can cast away the robe of victimhood, refusing to remain 'inert and passive objects of defining discourses as people without any control over their lives.'"[27] In this way, women who resist oppressive realities—similar to the Shulammite woman in Song of Solomon—effectively choose "our ends and our loves," determining, within limits, the meaning of our own lives.

Hence, women's freedom must be understood to include the powers of deliberative moral choice and thus co-creative influence, even under circumstances of extreme constraint and limitation. This agency is more constitutive of human personality than the exercise of a simple negative freedom; rather, its genuine expression contributes to our identity and ideally connects us sacramentally with the divine. Thus, as we attend to the shape of freedom in the concrete contexts of women's lives under patriarchal and other forms of oppression, we must remain honest and attentive to the struggles to which women are subject—and also to the genuine agency that they are capable of expressing therein.

Embodied Physical Health: Pleasure and Pain

If freedom is important to but not exhaustively definitive of human well-being, what else is necessary to describe sexual flourishing? When we begin with the contextual particularity of persons, we must take account of their embodied health: the physical well-being of each person, in the fullness of their complicated historical and relational context. Right from the start, however, we run into trouble, for there exists no unmediated access to the physical, biological, material body; our encounter with it is always impacted by historicized and cultural expectation. As Judith Butler puts the matter, "Sex is made understandable through the signs that indicate how it should be read or understood. These bodily indicators are the cultural means by which the sexed body is read."[28] Thus, the body, always mediated by society and by the relationships in which a person is enmeshed, is only available to us in epistemically imprecise form. Moreover, the Christian affirmation of soul-body unity requires that we avoid "thing-ifying" the body, as if we could neatly separate it from the mind or the emotions, or describe it fully on its own terms apart from the relational human person in which it participates.

Yet a posture of cautious, flexible, and revisable realism does not allow us to stop there. Although bodies are malleable and subject to cultural interpretation (and reinterpretation), they are not infinitely so. There is, rather, something fundamentally recognizable about a healthy, well-functioning human organism, one that thrives according to some commonly held or at least broadly defensible understanding. Further, the Christian tradition holds, it is incumbent upon us actively to pursue the good represented by that healthy functioning. The tradition holds that bodies are, it must be repeated, fundamentally *good*. They reflect the goodness of created reality and they mediate that reality to us. Part of being human is to honor and protect that good.

Human sexual bodies are immensely powerful: to begin with, they often—though not always—have the astounding capacity to bring forth new life. While heterosexual intercourse does not inexorably lead to pregnancy, any account of its power cannot responsibly avoid an appreciation and respect for its potentially life-giving qualities. Incumbent upon a sexual ethic, then, is a clear-eyed responsibility toward that reality—including personal and social accountability for the birthed children to whom pregnancy ordinarily leads. Human freedom indeed may allow us to time and even to shape pregnancy, but it does not, finally, remove altogether the biological processes that enable childbearing—itself a fundamental (though not absolute) human good.

Yet as nearly all theologians would at this point agree, erotic encounter surely is about far more than procreation—which is, in fact, only even biologically possible for a small subset of the adult population at any given time. Returning for a moment to Nussbaum's list of human capabilities for functioning, it is apparent that well-being includes the enjoyment of pleasure and the avoidance (as much as possible) of pain. Sexual pleasure deserves particular attention, since Christianity has too often functioned to demonize pleasure; as elaborated, the tendency to associate sexual pleasure with evil runs like a red thread through the Christian tradition. An ethic concerned with women's well-being must resist this tendency straightforwardly and strongly. Erotic desire and sexual pleasure are among the central and elementary goods of human life, goods worth pursuing on their own terms. From the point of view of creation, human sexual expression has the power to participate in and reflect the goodness of bodies; insofar as it does so, sexual pleasure itself must also be recognized as good and genuinely reflective of the divine. Along these lines, Mark D. Jordan identifies bodily pleasure as a "touchpoint" of sex, a residual sign of approach to the original created order and an echo or trace of God's judgment of the world's goodness.[29]

The basis for valuing pleasure need not only derive from a theology of creation, however. For instance, Christine Gudorf identifies pleasure as a premoral good that is so not simply because God created it but rather for a more "commonsensical" reason: because it *feels good*. According to Gudorf, sexual pleasure is not unlike a cool drink on a warm day or a hot soak for aching muscles. Pleasure can surely be sacrificed for other goods, but it should be presumed to be good in and of itself. Moreover, pleasure communicates to human persons their *own* fundamental goodness—a quality particularly important to women, who have so often been socialized to ignore or even fear their own sexuality. Deliberately depriving persons of pleasure must therefore be done only if there exists vigorous justification.[30]

Beyond the impact on the self, pleasure also functions to move us toward other, deeper goods: love and trust of one another, and even communion with God. In other words, while pleasure may be understood as premorally *good* because of the way it benefits human persons in a more immediate sense, it also serves human well-being in a more holistic way. That is, pleasure potentially points us inward, toward trusting, honoring, and caring for our own deepest selves, and concurrently outward, toward our larger, relational context. Both, of course, happen simultaneously, since each of us is one whole person, existing both in our own interiority and also in the relationships that situate, form, and partially constitute us. In this way, sexual pleasure, when sought in a humanizing manner, in fact points far beyond itself. Along these lines, Lutheran theologian Dorothee Soelle speaks of sexuality more broadly as a sacrament: a sign of God's grace in bodily element.[31] Catholic feminist Cristina Traina echoes this sacramental attribute, holding that sexual pleasure can "outfit human beings for receptivity to or cooperation with the divine."[32] Pleasure on its own does not achieve this degree of communion; it must be channeled so that it builds persons up, individually and socially, and draws them close to God; thus it exists alongside other norms, yet to be discussed. But a sexual ethic concerned with genuine well-being can ill afford to ignore or downplay the positive impact of sexual pleasure on relations with the self, with others, and with the divine.

To be sure, embodied physical health is not only about fostering pleasure; it is also about preventing or at least minimizing pain. The human body can be a source of great gratification and fulfillment, but it also can be the locus of frustration, violation, and suffering. Even under the best of circumstances, sex itself, and in particular heterosexual intercourse, is simply not always pleasurable or healthy, especially for women. According to data analysis from the National Health and Social Life Survey, 43 percent of US women aged eighteen to fifty-nine experience sexual "dysfunction," far higher than the 31 percent of similarly aged men. More specifically, between 22 percent and 28 percent of women surveyed report that they are unable to achieve orgasm, most commonly during coitus itself.[33] And of the women surveyed, 33.5 percent—including 15 to 21 percent of women under age forty—report experiencing painful intercourse some of the time, while 25 percent of women report it virtually *all* of the time.[34] The mainstream privileging of vaginal-penile coitus as the norm for "real" sex likely exacerbates the problem, since, statistically speaking, men's enjoyment of this form of sex far exceeds women's. Similarly, heteronormative religious scripts that place sex primarily in the service of procreation, as well as binary social scripts that privilege men's sexual desire and orgasm, constitute a devaluation of women's as well as LGBTQ+ people's physical pleasure as a critical aspect of human sexuality.[35] A sexual ethic that seeks to take seriously *all* people's well-being must be alert to and actively resist these harmful tendencies.

Beyond frustration and physical pain, of course, sex can cause physical harm in other obvious ways. Notably, the incidence of sexually transmitted infection is increasing in the United States, particularly among adolescents and young adults; in 2018 combined cases of syphilis, gonorrhea, and chlamydia reached an all-time high, both in absolute and relative terms.[36] Religious and cultural programs that downplay or ignore the need for adequate education regarding these rates—including the ways access to contraception can help lower them—is inadequately attentive to concrete reality. Further, another crucial aspect of that concrete reality is the widespread incidence of domestic and relational violence. According to the National Coalition against Domestic Violence, one in four women and one in nine men have experienced severe intimate partner physical or sexual violence and/or intimate partner stalking with severe impact. Most commonly targeted are young adult women between the ages of eighteen and twenty-four, and LGBTQ+ individuals appear to experience domestic violence at equal or even higher rates than heterosexual people.[37] Further, it seems increasingly clear that shutdowns and job losses related to the COVID-19 pandemic beginning in early 2020 have only exacerbated this already scandalously high incidence of intimate partner violence.[38]

These numbers should haunt any account that does not acknowledge the potential for sex abuse. Not only can the body be a locus of suffering on a personal level; such suffering manifests socially and can be exacerbated by social, cultural, and religious practices and expectations. This is particularly true for women from BIPOC communities.[39] Legal scholar Dorothy Roberts elaborates at chilling length the various ways Black women's bodies, since at least the time of slavery and right up to the present day, have suffered ignorance, abuse, and direct attack at the hands of white America. Roberts thereby chronicles how individual and structural racism together have prevented Black women from maintaining control over their own reproductive labor—whether by way of brute sexual assault and other forms of violence, compulsory contraception and sterilization, racist welfare and drug policies, the forceable separation of Black mothers from their children, or racist application of reproductive medicine. Roberts's account lays bare a harsh truth: a narrowly conceived focus on individual autonomy is a necessary but insufficient norm to guide sexual ethics, for a great deal of the suffering that BIPOC communities have endured has taken place on a communal and structural level. Simply ensuring the presence of individual consent in all things sexual, or even attending to women's physical well-being in individual cases, will fail adequately to address women's well-being as a whole; much less will these steps tackle the particular struggles faced by women from BIPOC communities.

Emotional Integrity

I turn now beyond the more physical aspects of human sexual flourishing to investigate distinctly interior qualities. On Nussbaum's list, such qualities are reflected as the capability to think, imagine, and reason, including in ways that might be ordinarily termed "religious." I intend, however, for this category to extend beyond traditional religious concepts, to include the way sexual activity, choice-making, and even personal identity are deeply contiguous and well integrated with one's values (spiritual, religious, or otherwise) and life story. Emotional integrity necessarily points toward self-reflective matters, for instance the need to integrate one's sexual activities with one's deep hopes, fears, sensibilities, or sense of life purpose. It also simultaneously points to considerations beyond the self—that is, the sexual self in relation to the larger world and even universe. Catholic moral theologian Lisa Fullam engages in a related line of thinking when she names the sexual virtue of "insight"—a quality that "invites us to see the echoes of our relationships beyond the immediacy of partners to include family, society as a whole, and our relationship to God."[40] Here, sex is most decidedly not simply physical but rather potentially enables a deeper self-awareness as well as a more profound encounter with what lies beyond oneself. Without this kind of perception, sex is necessarily limited, walled off from one's larger personality, including one's social commitments and sense of meaning and identity.

Another way of getting at the concept of emotional integrity lies in what popular author Brené Brown has termed "wholeheartedness." In Brown's words, "wholehearted living is about engaging in our lives from a place of worthiness." It is about accepting ourselves, believing that we are fundamentally worthy of love, and rejecting the various ways our culture promotes shame in self-understanding that disconnects us from ourselves and others.[41] Brown's promotion of wholeheartedness as a key ingredient of human flourishing is echoed in the sexual ethic of Nadia Bolz-Weber, who endorses a version of emotional integrity that includes healing and freedom from shame—especially the sexual shame that too often has accompanied Christian approaches to human sexuality. She links this reintegration of the self with salvation itself, pointing out that the ancient Greek word for "salvation" (*sozo*) means to heal, bring wholeness, preserve. Part of the Christian promise, she maintains, is that God reconnects our fractured parts when we find ourselves emotionally disconnected from ourselves or others.[42] Finally, Catholic moral theologian Aline H. Kalbian links this insight back to the Catholic concept of *integrity*, that is, when one's "body and psyche" are in accord with one another. She highlights how historically the Catholic Church has understood integrity in the terms of gender complementarity—an approach proving highly problematic for trans* persons and for individuals who are only attracted to persons of the same sex. Kalbian's approach thus effectively urges a broader call to integrity—a "wholeness or completeness" that hints at a more flexible and inclusive understanding of the human person and sexual well-being.[43]

There can be no doubt that integrating one's sexual actions with a deeper sense of one's values and personal history contributes mightily to a sense of human well-being. Conversely, when one's sexual actions remain disconnected entirely from the fullness of self-understanding—for example, when one refuses to face particular sexual fears, struggles, or other sensibilities and vulnerabilities—it cannot *but* have a fragmenting impact on one's identity and welfare. As we examine concrete circumstances related to human sexuality in the chapters to come, then, a key normative lens will be how particular individual and social practices foster or inhibit emotional integrity. How much, for instance, do sexual practices allow or encourage persons to face and claim their own histories—to integrate their past, present, and future? How much (or little) do they invite persons to explore their deeper values, desires, and instincts related to the meaning of sex? Are these treated suspiciously, or with hope and encouragement? How readily do such practices make room for individual life stories and the joys, sorrows, and hopes that they proffer? These questions are difficult to evaluate in any precise way, but they nevertheless deeply contribute to sexual flourishing in any given concrete setting.

Relational Intimacy and Trust

Let us next return to the core idea of the human person as not simply autonomous but also relational—a key insight of both feminist and Christian thought. We humans cannot exist apart from our relationality; while it does not perhaps fully define us, it is impossible for us to thrive without attending to its patterns and moral demands. And sex is not simply about our personal choices, histories, or values, nor is it only about physical well-being. Sex, perhaps more than any other human activity, is about the nature of intimate relations with another person. In the context of modern society, relational intimacy as a norm resists the near-ubiquitous reverence for autonomy and ego that has come to characterize so much of Western thought. Indeed, many of the baseline human capabilities in Nussbaum's list—to show concern for others, to demonstrate compassion, justice, and friendship, and to laugh, play, and recreate—assume human relationality as fundamental to human experience. Her fifth capability explicitly centers human attachments to others "outside of oneself" as a basic good necessary for functioning well in the world.

In the same insightful depiction of sex through the lens of virtue ethics referenced above, Fullam characterizes intimacy as "the central goal of sex," recognizing that "sex expresses a personal reality, not a bodily one."[44] Intimacy describes not simply physical closeness but also emotional tenderness, an act of being present to the other in a way that transcends mere erotic affection. At least in the context of modern Western understanding, without intimacy, sex seems to lose its "heart," to be emptied of its sacred power and potential to touch the "inner being" of its participants. It is of course a valid question as to whether intimacy plays such a central role in human sexuality when examined with a cross-cultural lens. Yet while the association of sex with emotional intimacy is far from universal, even in the modern West, it seems that intimacy is a widely shared (if not widely practiced) value held by many in the United States today. Fullam cautions against the disregard of intimacy: "A person who is unable to achieve emotional intimacy may use promiscuity as a mask, substituting the physical for the deeper body-spirit-soul connection that is the aim of satisfying sexual relationships."[45] This sort of deep connection is indeed a hallmark of "good sex," inviting persons to transcend their own embodied realities and enter into a profound and mysterious connection with another.

Authentic intimacy, however, opens people up not simply to pleasure but also to suffering; that is, it makes persons deeply, and sometimes painfully, vulnerable. In fact vulnerability is perhaps the paradigmatic quality of being human—for as long as we are alive, and in particular for as long as we *love*, we are also profoundly exposed to pain and loss. This is part of what it means to live a fully human life: it is difficult to imagine a truly fulfilled life apart from the vulnerabilities that enable genuine relation. Such vulnerability is of course not limited to the intimacy of sexual interaction; we become vulnerable to each other when we disclose to another our doubts and fears, our weaknesses and foibles, and our hopes and dreams. When such vulnerability is received with respect, reverence, or even tenderness, it can strengthen both parties and usher in new and more life-giving forms of human relationship.

Theologian Elizabeth Gandolfo, in an examination of maternity and natality, probes how these human realities reveal an almost tragic quality to human existence—that is, goodness is both beautiful and fragile. The risk of harm in human life (vulnerability) indeed causes us great anxiety, but it also is the necessary condition for love, health, connection, and wholeness. Gandolfo urges an incarnational theological focus that both acknowledges the danger implicit in human vulnerability and encourages us to "inhabit our own fleshy, relational, ambiguous, vulnerable bodies with less fear, anxiety, and stasis and with more courage, peace, and adventurous compassion."[46] In this way, God summons humans to self- and other-respect and empowers them for healthy engagement in the world.

It seems that if relational intimacy—and the vulnerability it entails—is to serve human flourishing, it must be grounded by something more. And in the sphere of human sexuality, that will no doubt include a certain level of trust between partners. For many, if not most, sex has the capacity to tap into a level of such deep self-exposure that, without trust, easily results in disappointment, pain, or even emotional abuse. As Karen Lebacqz affirms in a short but powerful essay, "eros, the desire for another, the passion that accompanies the wish for sexual expression, makes one vulnerable. It creates possibilities for great joy but also for great suffering."[47] Trust gives sex room to grow and thrive, even as sexual partners find safe ways to reveal to each other their deepest vulnerabilities. Moreover, a high level of trust generally takes time to develop; while it may not require a lifelong commitment, it also does not often sail in on brief or businesslike encounters. Trust requires a significant degree of personal investment in the other, one that surpasses mere sexual attraction or even perhaps romantic love. To violate this sort of trust in the context of sex is a supreme violation, indeed; few who have experienced sexual betrayal would deny the profound emotional pain it engenders.

Mutuality and Equal Regard

Relational intimacy on its own is not enough, however. Intimacy, when separated from the constraints of mutual respect, easily and quickly degenerates into a pattern of controlling attachment on the one hand, or a codependent relinquishment of human agency on the other. Particularly from a feminist perspective, relational intimacy itself must be tempered by the norms of mutuality and equal regard. While the qualities on Nussbaum's list do not inexorably lead to these more egalitarian norms, they do push in that direction, since her list of human capabilities for flourishing apply to *all* human persons, not just some. And if feminist theory has taught us nothing else, it has taught us that the demands of mutuality and equal regard lie at the heart of human relational well-being.

Mutuality is a term often used in sexual ethics, though not often well explained. Farley perhaps describes it best as entailing both "active receptivity and receptive activity—each partner active, each one receptive . . . mutuality of desire, action, and response."[48] A mutual sexual relationship generally avoids the pitfall of one person always playing the role of giver and the other playing the role of recipient—whether of care, pleasure, or love itself. Rather, there is a certain fluidity to a genuinely mutual relationship, a back-and-forth style of participation that resists one-way power dynamics and patterns of domination. Mutuality rules out the overall instrumentalizing of one party to serve the other party's needs, for both parties must be sufficiently vulnerable to give and to receive, and to maintain a basic level of attentiveness and presence to one another and to the relationship.

Carrying this impulse a step further, equal regard is meant to ensure that neither sexual partner is fundamentally disrespected, inappropriately limited by, or excessively dependent upon the other. Equal regard implies a rough equality of power in the relationship. It denotes neither identical treatment nor a rigid tally sheet of benefits and burdens but rather an overall egalitarian posture of one toward the other. In a sexual relationship characterized by equal regard, both parties are understood to be valuable, both deserving of respect and authority, and neither exercising lopsided influence over the decisions and actions associated with the relationship itself. Hence, as is the case with mutuality, equal regard discourages patterns of domination and subjection—patterns that too often characterize sexual relations, even (or perhaps especially) Christian ones.

In the Christian tradition, obligations for mutuality and equal regard are grounded both in our shared human dignity and, as indicated above, in Christian doctrines of the Trinity. They also find purchase in an ethic promoting love as central to the divine will. Arguably, love for God and love for one's neighbor as oneself—the bedrocks of Christian discipleship—animate nothing if not mutual respect and care in relational patterns, a deeply reciprocal commitment to protect and promote our neighbor's dignity and well-being. This commitment entails not a form of top-down, paternalistic protection from one to another but rather a mutual recognition of and care for one another, where each party is active and each receptive, where each is seen and sees, where each is heard and hears. Together, mutuality and equal regard ask that we open ourselves to the genuine value and insights of the other as well as allow the other to impact our own deeper identities and sensibilities.

Practically speaking, in US popular culture, sex is more commonly associated with domination and subordination than it is with mutuality and equal regard. Christian ethicist Marvin M. Ellison has elaborated how Western society generally has eroticized a gendered inequality of power, promoting male control over a female partner as the primary model for erotic, pleasurable sex.[49] Popular media abounds with examples in support of Ellison's point, from the *Fifty Shades of Grey* book and film series to the heavily gendered violence that disproportionately dominates the landscape of mainstream heterosexual pornography. But one need not look to such extreme examples of inequality for evidence of mutuality's elusiveness. Farley, citing examples from both sociological studies and classic literature, has pointed out how difficult it is to achieve authentic and supportive mutual giving and receiving within intimate relationships, even well-intentioned and committed ones.[50] Our seeming inability to easily realize relational mutuality is surely complicated by gendered sexual expectations that discourage the fullness of sexual agency, especially in women. That is, historically speaking, traditional understandings of heterosexual sex have been replete with images of men as active and women as passive, belying the sort of genuine reciprocity that feminist ethics directs.

In spite of how difficult they may be to achieve, mutuality and equal regard together form a critical goal and an indispensable piece of an adequate sexual ethic. Partners grow and thrive when they not only articulate their own points of view but also hear and remain fundamentally vulnerable to the points of view of each other. This, more than anything, lies at the heart of genuinely respectful relationship. Put differently, the fullness of agency itself depends upon a "robustly intersubjective exchange, where the sexual agencies of both parties are dynamically interacting."[51] That is, the desire of each party must be taken as fundamentally *relevant* to any given interaction. This in turn demands some degree of mutual vulnerability—a recognition that one's actions, desires, and interests may be meaningfully impacted by the other.[52] Insofar as gendered social expectations cause us to discourage, disregard, demote, or even directly override the contributions and sexual choice-making of women, genuine mutuality and equal regard will remain impossibilities—particularly, though perhaps not exclusively, in heterosexual relationships.

From a Christian perspective, a key question surfaces at this point about the place of self-sacrifice within this vision of mutuality and equal regard. Indeed, self-love has at times been disparaged in the Christian tradition, even as self-sacrifice has in places come to represent the pinnacle of Christian love.[53] Yet this approach is particularly troubling from a feminist point of view, since, in a patriarchal society, too often it is *women* who are, practically speaking, expected to do the bulk of the sacrificing. In other words, the elevation of self-sacrifice to an ethical virtue generally fails to take adequate account of gender injustice and the imbalanced impact sacrifice exerts upon men and women. By contrast, more careful analyses of Christian love are distinctly circumspect about the role of self-sacrifice, revering it not for its own sake but rather placing it in the service of other-regarding love, or even of mutual love itself.[54] Certainly genuine neighbor love requires an openhearted willingness to suspend one's private agenda, at least periodically and temporarily, in service to the welfare of the other. But this sacrifice itself must generally be reciprocal in nature if it is to avoid degenerating into injustice masked as Christian love. Thus self-sacrifice retains a bona-fide place within an ethic of mutuality and equal regard, but only secondarily as it serves these larger goods.[55]

In fact, an ethic that promotes sexual pleasure or choice making in the absence of mutuality and power sharing amounts to a violent—even deadly—ethic. Taken to the extreme, the unilateral pursuit of pleasure can result in egregious violations of well-being along the lines of forceable domination, sexual coercion, intimate partner abuse, stalking, and rape. But even far less extreme violations of mutuality often entail the objectification of the sexual partner—turning that partner into a "thing," an object of sexual release for the sake of personal gratification. Further, while a requirement of consent may address the former, more vicious sorts of violation, it will do little to protect against the latter. Along these lines, Gudorf points out how mutuality in sexual pleasure is in fact prior to and more radical than mere mutual consent, for it requires of sexual participants a much higher commitment to respect, care, and responsibility for the results of their sexual activity.[56]

Human Persons in Social Context

Each one of these aspects of human flourishing—freedom, embodied health, emotional integrity, relational intimacy, and mutuality and equal regard—is aimed at persons who exist both within and beyond themselves, whose agency is both fundamental and yet, in important ways, restricted by historical and relational situatedness. *Good* sex—that is, sex that allows persons to thrive, grow, and flourish—takes place within the broader sociohistorical contexts in which persons and communities are embedded. Positively, this means that erotic attachment may itself stretch the participants beyond just themselves, building them up in such a way that their minds and hearts are opened to other people as well as to the struggles of the world. Theologian Dorothee Soelle describes love in this fashion, arguing that "the ecstasy we experience in love heightens our awareness of the violence that imprisons other people and denies them life's fullness."[57] Soelle's view here alerts us that sexual love, perhaps like all forms of love, necessarily draws persons out of themselves, not simply into the company of each other but also into the larger social world. To do otherwise would in effect render sexual love as solipsistic and closed in upon itself, existing as a "world apart" that more resembles the stuff of Hollywood fantasy than real-life human relationships.

The truth is that sexual love does *not* exist in a world apart but rather operates within and alongside the struggles, pain, and injustices of human social life. Traditionally, Christian ethics has done a better job incorporating broad social analysis into its consideration of *nonsexual* realms of the moral life, particularly in the fields of political and economic ethics. By contrast, sexual ethics has tended to remain fixated on discrete action and on the "right" and "wrong" choices made by individuals. Even in more popular thought, sex is too often relegated purely to the domain of the private and the personal, something that takes place behind closed doors and thus comes down to individual choice and especially consent.

Yet we know that the public and the private realms are not, finally, separable. The most ardent sexual attraction can prove destructive and even fatal on a collective level, and what at first glance appears to be domestic bliss can in fact turn out to be a smoke screen for the most heinous sorts of domestic and relational violence.[58] Moreover, human agency itself is limited by the imperfect and unjust aspects of the world in which humans live. In any given case, these could include the often damaging contours of neoliberal capitalism; the limited professional choices available to poor women under the constraints of patriarchy; the erasure of queer stories from Christian sexual education;[59] or, more generally, the rigid gender norms that shape our sexual expectations of self and other.

Disney-esque fantasies of popular culture aside, we do ourselves and our society a great disservice if we fail to begin an account of sex with a clear-eyed analysis of structural injustice in the world. The Christian concept of social sin provides an apt lens with which to do so. Kenneth Himes describes social sin as "the disvalue . . . embedded in a pattern of societal organization and cultural understanding," for example, systemic racism, sexism, or imperialism.[60] There exists no small amount of controversy regarding the level of personal, individual culpability for sin that manifests socially. In the past, the Catholic magisterium has sought to defend the rootedness of sinful structural realities in individual action, thus stressing personal responsibility even while acknowledging that "structures of sin" indeed exist.[61] In much of Latin American liberation theology, on the other hand, the language of social sin has tended more to emphasize the genuinely reciprocal nature of individual and structural sin, such that "when human beings sin, they create structures of sin, which, in their turn, make human beings sin."[62] This latter definition highlights the way social sin shapes us at a deep and ongoing level, such that individual actions and choices cannot be correctly interpreted apart from the social context in which they take place. While this does not deny the role of individual human agency and accountability, it can and should remind us that our accurate understanding of sexual practices, like any human practices, depends in part upon structural and social analysis.

The work of Protestant ethicist Reinhold Niebuhr is especially helpful in laying bare the radical impact of structural and social sin on human action. Of his many contributions to Christian theological ethics, particularly insightful is Niebuhr's recognition that group pride, while finding its roots in individual attitudes, nevertheless exercises a far stronger influence over persons—such that "the pretensions and claims of a collective or social self exceed those of the individual ego."[63] In this context, any given effort toward promoting individual right action or articulating the truth must be accompanied by a thoroughgoing recognition that group identity can both cloud our perspective and compromise our will. In other words, social sin does not only affect our desire or ability to *do* the good; it also negatively impacts our epistemic access to the truth itself.

Taken together, these understandings of social or structural sin point us toward the profound influence social arrangements have upon how we understand ourselves, each other, the world in which we live, and even the world we hope to build. Our social contexts form us, and they also impact the myriad ways that we respond to each other. The concept of social sin stands over our well-intentioned efforts as a constant reminder: solidarity itself—to use Niebuhr's language—stands as an "impossible possibility," a law and a judgment that motivates and compels us but whose fulfillment in concrete terms is always only approximately achieved.[64] Yet only a response that includes social and structural analysis alongside a corresponding posture of solidarity can adequately respond to the lived experience of actual persons and their material reality. Put differently, if the dignity of human persons is socially embedded, then our response to violations of that dignity must also be social and structural, not merely individual or personal.

Hence, recognizing and combating structures of sin that impact human sexual experience and activity is integral to an adequate twenty-first-century sexual ethic. Christianity in fact offers theological grounds for such a move in its concept of the Incarnation and the tradition of liberation that Jesus himself claimed. As Christine Firer Hinze writes, "In the incarnation we find solidarity's deepest theological ground and warrant. The redemptive economy of Christ's life, death, and resurrection . . . blazes the path that disciples are invited to follow by emulating Jesus's loving solidarity with God and neighbor."[65] Just as Jesus himself, following the prophets before him, unmasked the social patterns that afflicted and oppressed, a Christian ethic today must be alert to and actively seek to uncover the ways that contemporary society inflicts similarly harmful and marginalizing norms and expectations. Further, it must pay attention to the social dimensions of human flourishing and to the way that individual choices add to or detract from the common good. As Lebacqz has argued at length, we simply cannot create a world apart from the realities of injustice; therefore, any attempt to articulate what justice looks like must include a hermeneutic of suspicion regarding the social realities in which we are embedded. Deliberate acts of solidarity aimed at redressing past wrongs are essential to the doing of justice, and they must begin with such a recognition of injustice.[66] In the articulation of a sexual ethic, this will entail close attention to power dynamics and gendered expectations that dehumanize, marginalize, or otherwise harm.

Along these lines, the fierce promotion of personal freedom or autonomous choice—as is so often the case in contemporary society—*without* a simultaneous focus on social justice and equality is potentially disastrous. Prioritizing liberty ultimately works well only for those with the personal resources and social power necessary to act upon that liberty. By definition, therefore, such a narrow focus disproportionately harms women from economically or otherwise disadvantaged communities. In sexual ethics, this does not mean that autonomy itself is an unworthy goal but rather that it must be tempered by attention to social, economic, and racial justice. As Dorothy Roberts argues, speaking of the racial injustice and abuse historically perpetrated against Black women, "liberty protects all citizens' choices from the most direct and egregious abuses of government power, but it does nothing to dismantle social arrangements that make it impossible for some people to make a choice in the first place."[67] In this light, a focus on persons in their social context, and a promotion of social equality as a positive sexual norm, is imperative to the overall promotion of human flourishing.

Conclusion

This chapter has laid a normative foundation for what follows—that is, for the more specific ethical topics and questions that face contemporary persons and societies as they navigate sexual life, personally and socially. Here and in the preceding chapter, I have not only critiqued the historical Christian tradition of sexual ethics; I have also sought to integrate the *best* insights from that tradition with contemporary feminist theology and secular scholarship. These various sources of wisdom thus crystalize into a value-based framework for humans' sexual flourishing in today's world.

Ultimately, to affirm such a framework is not simply a matter of admonishing right-versus-wrong choices. It is, rather, a matter of urging persons to consider how they become their best selves and how they might live most fully and wholeheartedly in a broken world. Further, it is to ask how societies may shape themselves at the broadest levels to facilitate and sustain that wholehearted living for all their members. In the past, many if not most proposals for Christian sexual ethics have been truncated both by an individualistic, decision-oriented focus and by patterns of reasoning that reinforce harm and injustice toward women and queer people. Simultaneously, popular culture has come to affirm an "anything goes" model of sexual choice-making focused almost exclusively on consent; this model may work decently well for the socially powerful, but it can be disastrous for those who enjoy relatively less personal or social authority—including most women. For them, what is needed is a normative model that concurrently amplifies their own agency and also opens up new pathways and patterns of sexual well-being. All of this must take place within an open-eyed consideration of the very real injustices, sexual and otherwise, that characterize modern Western society.

In the chapters that follow, attention to particular social disparities and limiting expectations shapes the discussion of what it means to flourish, sexually speaking. Such social contours include, at a minimum, the disparity in economic and social power between men and women, particularly women from BIPOC communities; the violence against women that so often accompanies those power disparities, including within Christian environments; the exclusion of women and LGBTQ+ persons from positions of power and authority in both church and civic environments; the highly gendered and binary social expectations that straitjacket both men and women, compromising both agency and well-being; and the hetero- and cisnormative assumptions that broadly shape sexual and social opportunities, both publicly and privately, and often result in violence directed specifically against LGBTQ+ communities and persons. I take it as foundational that all of these forms of social injustice do in fact characterize our current society—and that all of them likewise should shape our quest to make that society a more welcoming and hospitable place for human persons to thrive, sexually or otherwise. Let us turn now to these more concrete contexts and to the social challenges that they pose for a reenvisioned sexual ethic.

Notes

1. Spohn, "Jesus and Christian Ethics," 105.
2. Farley, *Just Love*, 129.
3. Nelson, *Embodiment*, 32.
4. Here and throughout this volume, biblical references are taken from the New Revised Standard Version (NRSV) of the Bible.
5. Knust, *Unprotected Texts*, 29. See also De La Torre, *A Lily among the Thorns*, 62–63.
6. Day, "'I Am Dark and Lovely,'" 213.
7. For a fuller account of the role of *redress* in a Christian vision of justice, see Lebacqz, *Justice in an Unjust World*.
8. Nouwen, *Life of the Beloved*, 33.
9. Bolz-Weber, *Shameless*, 181.
10. Schweizer, "Σαρξ, Σαρκικος, Σαρκινος," 135.
11. Cahill, *Between the Sexes*, 139–40.
12. Douglas, *Sexuality and the Black Church*, 119.
13. Gudorf, *Body, Sex, and Pleasure*, 26. See also De La Torre, *A Lily among the Thorns*, 9–10.
14. Massingale, "The Erotic Life of Anti-Blackness," 193–94.
15. World Health Organization, "Sexual and Reproductive Health."
16. Nussbaum, "Human Capabilities, Female Human Beings," 83–85.
17. Farley, *Just Love*, 209, 212, and 209–32.
18. Boyle et al., *Catholic Sexual Ethics*, 113–52. Karl Rahner's work stands as a noteworthy celebration of the central importance of freedom in human identity. His discussion is both profound and nuanced; see, for example, Rahner, "The Experiment with Man."
19. Farley, *Just Love*, 211–14.
20. The debate regarding how Christians should understand and evaluate abortion is as long and convoluted as it is cantankerous. It is not my project to engage that debate here, since to do so would require an entire volume by itself. Excellent materials have been written on various sides of this debate, even from within an explicitly Christian framework. Indeed, in many ways Christian sensibilities have broadened the considerations and sensibilities found in secular spheres, such that Christian analyses engage not just questions of "choice" or "life" but also more nuanced considerations of personal and social well-being, and reproductive justice. For a feminist position that moves beyond a simplistic embrace of individual choice and supports free access to abortion as part of the larger project of

reproductive justice, see, for example, Peters, *Trust Women*; and Ellison, "Is Pro-Choice What We Mean to Say?," 99–114. A nuanced position that retains strong anti-abortionist commitments may be found in Camosy, *Beyond the Abortion Wars*. For a recent feminist reenvisioning of a Catholic pro-life position, see Reimer-Barry, "Another Pro-Life Movement Is Possible." Finally, for an older but still helpful navigation through seemingly intractable positions in the public domain regarding abortion, see Rudy, *Beyond Pro-Life and Pro-Choice*.

21. Ehrenreich and English, *For Her Own Good*.
22. Crittenden, *The Price of Motherhood*.
23. Harrison, *Our Right to Choose*, 38.
24. Here I rely on Cathleen Kaveny's description of Joseph Raz's definition of autonomy: the freedom for the opportunity to become the "part-author" of one's own life. See Kaveny, *Law's Virtues*, 7.
25. Ortner, "Making Gender," 8.
26. Ortner, 12.
27. Abraham, "Resistance," 104, in part citing Anindita Ghosh, ed., *Behind the Veil: Resistance, Women and the Everyday in Colonial South Asia* (Ranikhet, India: Permanent Black, 2007), 2.
28. Butler, *Undoing Gender*, 87.
29. Jordan, *The Ethics of Sex*, 162.
30. Gudorf, *Body, Sex, and Pleasure*, 90–94.
31. Soelle, *To Work and To Love*, 12.
32. Traina, "Maternal Experience," 395.
33. Laumann et al., "Sexual Dysfunction in the United States"; and Crooks and Baur, *Our Sexuality*, 432 and 436–37. Globally, these numbers hold true, even for premenopausal women; according to one meta-analysis, female sexual dysfunction (defined as persistent problems with sexual response or pleasure that cause clinically significant distress) was found to affect 41 percent of premenopausal women around the globe. See McCool et al., "Prevalence of Female Sexual Dysfunction."
34. Northrup, *Women's Bodies, Women's Wisdom*, 291. The statistic regarding women under forty may be found in Crooks and Baur, *Our Sexuality*, 439, citing Els Pazmany et al., "Body Image and Genital Self-Image."
35. Antus, "Was It Good for You?" For one particularly clear example of how male sexual satisfaction is prioritized in popular understandings of casual heterosexual sex, see Freitas, *Consent on Campus*, 76–77.
36. Centers for Disease Control and Prevention, "Sexually Transmitted Diseases"; and Keller, "Reducing STI Cases."
37. National Coalition Against Domestic Violence, "National Statistics"; National Coalition Against Domestic Violence, "Domestic Violence and the LGBTQ Community."
38. Evans et al., "A Pandemic within a Pandemic," 2302–4. See also Jagannathan, "'We've Seen an Alarming Spike.'"
39. In recent years, the term *BIPOC* has begun to supplant *people of color* to indicate Black, Indigenous, and (other) people of color, although consensus has not yet emerged as to which term is the more appropriate. *BIPOC* attempts both to avoid a merging of categories (and the related erasure of identity) and to center the unique experiences of Black and Indigenous people in US history. Whether or not the term endures in the public square remains an open question, and I use it throughout this book aware of some of the critiques that have been raised against it; for an example of the latter, see Andrea Plaid

and Christopher MacDonald-Dennis, "'BIPOC' Isn't Doing What You Think It's Doing," *Newsweek*, April 11, 2021, https://www.newsweek.com/bipoc-isnt-doing-what-you-think-its-doing-opinion-1582494.

40. Fullam, "Thou Shalt."
41. Brown, *Daring Greatly*, 10, 69, 83–101.
42. Bolz-Weber, *Shameless*, 18.
43. Kalbian, "Integrity in Catholic Sexual Ethics," 65.
44. Fullam, "Thou Shalt."
45. Fullam.
46. Gandolfo, *The Power and Vulnerability of Love*, 228.
47. Lebacqz, "Appropriate Vulnerability," 274.
48. Farley, *Just Love*, 221–22.
49. Ellison, "Reimagining Good Sex."
50. Farley, *Personal Commitments*, 61–62.
51. Cahill, "Unjust Sex," 756.
52. Cahill.
53. Nygren, *Agape and Eros*, 712–13; and Kierkegaard, *Works of Love*, 68 and 133–34.
54. See for instance, Outka, *Agape*, 278; and Gudorf, "Parenting, Mutual Love, and Sacrifice," 181–86. See also Farley, "New Patterns of Relationship"; and Andolsen, "Agape in Feminist Ethics."
55. I shall not elaborate further here the objections to a Christian theology of self-sacrifice that exist in feminist literature. For views similar to my own, see Farley, *Personal Commitments*, 103–8; and Gudorf, "Parenting, Mutual Love, and Sacrifice," 175–91. The pitfalls of a purely self-sacrificial understanding of love become particularly apparent in the discussion of sex trafficking in chapter 5 of this book.
56. Gudorf, *Body, Sex, and Pleasure*, 139–41.
57. Soelle, *To Work and To Love*, 151. Soelle's description of this outward dimension of love displays certain parallels with Margaret Farley's discussion of "fruitfulness" as a sexual-ethical norm. See Farley, *Just Love*, 226–28.
58. The 2014 Isla Vista shootings by Elliot Rodger serve as a particularly chilling reminder of how readily sexual obsession can transform into deadly violence. While the Isla Vista case involved more than simple sexual entitlement, the manifesto that Rodger made public shortly before these shootings clarified that his unfulfilled sexual desires played a central role. See Adam Nagourney, Michael Cieply, Alan Feuer, and Ian Lovett, "Before Brief, Deadly Spree, Trouble Since Age 8," *New York Times*, June 1, 2014, https://www.nytimes.com/2014/06/02/us/elliot-rodger-killings-in-california-followed-years-of-withdrawal.html. More broadly, relational violence often hides behind apparently loving behavior; see, for instance, the work of the National Domestic Violence Hotline, esp. "Playing their Part: How an Abusive Partner's 'Good' Behavior Is Part of the Act," accessed August 1, 2020, https://www.thehotline.org/2017/02/09/abusive-partner-good-behavior/.
59. I use the term *queer* somewhat guardedly. For many, and especially younger, LGBTQ+ persons, the term has a positive and empowering connotation. For others, it retains its formerly pejorative status. When I do use it, I intend the term as a broadly inclusive indicator for those whose sexuality and gender identity do not fall along exclusively heterosexual and/or cisgender lines.
60. Himes, "Social Sin and the Role of the Individual." For the outlines of the understanding of structural sin described here, I am indebted to the analysis of Kristin E. Heyer as

she employs the concepts in her discussion of immigration. See Heyer, "Social Sin and Immigration."

61. See, for example, John Paul II, *Sollicitudo Rei Socialis*.
62. González Faus, "Sin," 537.
63. Niebuhr, *Nature and Destiny of Man*, 208.
64. Hinze, "The Drama of Social Sin," 458.
65. Hinze, "Straining toward Solidarity," 171–72.
66. Lebacqz, *Justice in an Unjust World*.
67. Roberts, *Killing the Black Body*, 294.

CHAPTER THREE

Hookup Culture and Sexual Agency

For the past decade or so, a growing number of journalists and higher-ed professionals—from deans of student life to campus ministers to teaching and research faculty—have become captivated by the ever-more-casual tenor of campus sexual culture—that is, by what has come to be known as "hookup culture." It is not necessarily the case that young adults are significantly more sexually active or are engaging with more sexual partners than they once did. But while college students may not be having more sex, they surely expect to have it more casually. Anyone part of a campus community today knows that the casual sexual hookup is a social staple, an expectation that has gradually nudged to the side most other forms of sexual relating, including dating and incremental sexual activity in the context of a committed relationship. In other words, where once dating or committed relationships prevailed, now brief and utterly uncommitted sexual encounters are solidly embedded in mainstream campus life across the United States.

The expectations and informal norms that characterize hookups have provoked no small amount of reflection, including both celebration and hand-wringing. Journalist Hanna Rosin trumpeted in 2012 that "the hookup culture is . . . bound up with everything that's fabulous about being a young woman . . . the freedom, the independence, the knowledge that you can always depend on yourself."[1] Indeed, the assumption (and assertion) of free choice and individual agency operates as the backbone of hookup culture, which roots itself in a broader ethos of individualism and personal preference. This ethos, coupled with the media-fueled social script that college is a time for unbridled fun, experimentation, and unequivocal self-focus, results in widely held student reluctance to openly criticize hookup practices, individually or systemically.

In the Christian world, appraisal has naturally been more suspicious. Donna Freitas's 2008 publication of *Sex and the Soul* received widespread

attention and sounded alarm bells across the country, particularly on religiously affiliated campuses. Freitas here describes, in story after story, the
ambivalence, disappointment, objectification, mistreatment, double standards, and outright harms that too often accompany hookup culture among
college students.[2] Normatively speaking, some Christian thinkers (though
not Freitas herself) have lamented the cultural marginalization of individual
chastity as a regulatory sexual norm. Others have called for the promotion
of love and commitment as antidotes to the impersonal and uncaring social
script so commonly associated with hookup culture. Still others endorse justice as the most valuable and appropriate lens with which to dissect the culture's contours.[3]

    This last category of approach is the most promising. Indeed, a thorough-
going analysis of casual sex must focus not primarily on hookups themselves
but rather on the sociocultural assumptions that underlie the practice. This
underlying sociocultural context—characterized by hyperindividualism,
casual or even careless attitudes toward sexual partners, damaging objectification of women's bodies and discounting of women's sexual desire, and the
straitjacketing ideals of hypermasculinity—structures and restricts sexual
expectations for real people as they navigate sexual possibilities. A Christian
ethic that seeks to promote genuine sexual flourishing must critique these
social patterns even as it rejects the simplistic version of consent that prevails on today's campuses. Based in the more robust portrait of human flourishing developed in this volume, I thus propose that hookup culture best be
approached using an anthropology emphasizing authentic human agency—
that is, a more complex version of agency that challenges the multiple social
injustices structuring hookup culture and simultaneously prioritizes freedom
of choice *and* desire, mutuality, equal regard, and emotional integrity. Seen
in this light, hookup culture should be interrogated not on the basis of an
individualist, chastity-oriented sexual ethic on the one hand or a simplistic
assertion of sexual autonomy and consent on the other. Rather, what we need
is a holistic understanding of human flourishing animated by the demands
of justice. I conclude the chapter with concrete suggestions for fostering an
alternative, and more just, campus sexual culture.

Hookup Culture: A Primer

For all of the cultural hoopla that the practice of hooking up has generated,
it is notoriously difficult to define. Perhaps its vagueness is part of its allure;
as Rachel Kalish and Michael Kimmel have argued regarding heterosexual

hookups, the vague definitions utilized by college students serve both men and women who seek to appear publicly as if they are conforming more fully to gendered sexual expectations.[4] If there are in fact specifiable criteria that characterize a "classic" hookup, Donna Freitas provides as good a list as any: 1) a hookup includes some form of sexual intimacy, from kissing to oral, vaginal, or anal sex (and everything in between); 2) a hookup is brief, lasting anywhere from a few minutes to several hours; and 3) no one should get emotionally "attached" from a hookup, since it is intended as purely physical in nature and deprivileges forms of communication that might lead to deeper connection. It should be emphasized that these criteria represent a widely accepted social *script* regarding hookups; they are not necessarily internally embraced by all or even most people who actually engage in hookups. Along these lines, Jason King has helpfully distinguished "stereotypical hookup culture" from "relationship hookup culture," wherein participants actually hope for a relationship to result. While this latter hope may be the more common posture for all people, King describes how it nevertheless does not describe the dominant on-campus sexual culture.[5] For her part, Freitas argues that the third criteria (no attachment) is the most problematic for participants, for it requires them to ward off any trace of emotional intimacy that might lead to a meaningful connection with their partners—not an easy thing to accomplish, when people are sexually intimate.[6] In fact, in the days following a hookup, hookup partners frequently engage in a labored effort to pretend that the hookup never happened at all.

A hookup is often, though not always, accompanied by alcohol use. According to one study among sexually active college students, heavy alcohol consumption was more than twice as likely to be present in encounters involving "non-steady" partners relative to encounters involving steady partners.[7] More anecdotally, Jennifer Beste, in her lengthy ethnographic study of hookup culture, found that attending a party and becoming drunk were considered a "nearly mandatory" part of the college social scene, helping students to feel personally freed from full responsibility for their sexual choices.[8] Moreover, because college drinking culture is so often linked to fraternity life, hookups frequently take place within the heavily gendered and heteronormative social environment that characterizes most fraternity parties.

How ubiquitous is hooking up? The answer is complicated, and here I provide only the barest overall account. Certainly, sex on campus is all over the news—but not necessarily because it is any more common than it used to be. Indeed, some have claimed that we in the United States are in the middle of a "sex recession" among young people.[9] According to the Centers for Disease Control and Prevention, between 1991 and 2017, the percentage of high school students having had sexual intercourse dropped from 54 to 40 percent—so that now, well less than half of all high school teenagers are engaging in sexual intercourse.[10] Of course, this figure includes very young teens, and there exists dispute about whether a similar decline prevails among college students.[11] Still, at a minimum, it is unclear that college students are having significantly *more* sex, or more sexual partners, than their counterparts from bygone decades. According to the Online College Social Life Survey—a survey of more than twenty thousand students conducted nationally at twenty-one four-year colleges and universities—students average approximately seven hookups over the course of a four-year college career—that is, less than two per year. Between 24 and 42 percent of college students say that they have never hooked up, while approximately 28 percent have hooked up ten times or more. In general, men appear more likely than women to prefer hookups over dates.[12]

Yet, importantly, college students themselves seem to have a distorted view of the frequency of hooking up, commonly *perceiving* that their peers hook up far more often than they do—and that a hookup is far more likely to involve sexual intercourse than it is. This misperception fuels many students' insecurities about campus sexual norms, as well as their sense that genuinely few alternatives for sexual interaction exist. In other words, as far as sexual relating is concerned, hookup culture often seems as if it is the "only game in town."[13] Moreover, sociologist Lisa Wade has noted that hookup culture is apparently embraced most enthusiastically by students who are male, white, wealthy, heterosexual, non-disabled, and conventionally attractive. From one perspective, this indicates a certain "sexual privilege" prevalent among some groups on campus—that is, an unearned status that places particular categories of persons at the top of the campus sexual hierarchy. Those who occupy these positions are therefore able, intentionally or unintentionally, to dictate the conditions of mainstream sexual culture.

The existence of such privilege in turn means that other students may find themselves trapped within the parameters of a sexual environment—including its attendant social, economic, racial, and heteronormative assumptions—that does not suit them. As Wade herself puts the matter, "What we are seeing on college campuses is the same dynamic we see outside of colleges. People with privilege—based on race, class, ability, attractiveness, sexual orientation, and, yes, gender—get to set the terms for everyone else."[14] Indeed, a full 91 percent of college students agree that their lives are dominated by hookup culture, *even if they are not avid participants.*[15] Thus, while not everyone joins in, the widespread practice of hooking up engenders a *culture* that exercises disproportionate influence over college social life.

To drill down on but one aspect of this, campus hookup culture has a distinctly heterosexist bias, and in fact much of the research done about hookup culture reflects that bias. It is not that LGBTQ+ hookups do not exist; they most certainly do. Yet it is important to avoid assumptions that queer hookups take exactly the same shape or adhere to the same (largely unarticulated) rules as heterosexual hookups[16]—particularly since queer hookups are more likely to enjoy a certain transgressive posture within the broader heteronormative social landscape. Many sociologists agree that LGBTQ+ hookups take place less frequently via the campus party scene, since those parties—especially fraternity parties—tend to favor students with heterosexual social capital and thus are not always perceived as safe sexual environments for LGBTQ+ students.[17] Even when same-sex or same-gender coupling does find a place within the mainstream party scene—as is sometimes true of sexual encounters between women—such actions may reflect not only the authentic sexual desire of the participants but also at times a certain level of performativity, engaged in primarily for the benefit of a heterosexual male gaze.[18] When men do hook up with other men, they are significantly more likely to have sex than are men hooking up with women, though this is not true for the same activities in the context of a date (versus a hookup), nor is it clear that it is similarly true for women hooking up with other women.[19]

Further, hookup culture itself is squarely built upon and fortified by highly gendered social expectations about what it means to incarnate masculine or feminine sexual identity in a predominantly young adult environment. Indeed, the dominant sexual culture and scripts on college campuses today largely center on and feed off of heteronormative assumptions, fueled by these gendered expectations. For this reason, the power dynamics and vulnerability entailed in queer hookups may vary significantly when compared with straight hookups. In fact, some of the norms I associate with sexual flourishing (mutuality and equal regard, for instance) may be easier to achieve in a queer sexual relationship, where such heavily gendered scripts are at times tempered by a readier willingness to transgress social expectations.

Queer hookups often initiate in slightly different fashion than straight hookups. In fact, many queer students, and especially cisgender gay men, are more likely to use the internet rather than mainstream campus party culture to find sexual partners. While a large majority of college students of all sexualities use dating apps, LGBTQ+ students appear to rely on them more heavily. In fact, one recent Pew Research study found that LGBTQ+ persons generally use dating apps at twice the rate of straight people.[20] Heterosexual and queer students alike use Tinder, Bumble, OkCupid, and other apps for both dates and hookups. Another popular dating app, Grindr, is specifically aimed at queer people and enjoys particularly widespread usage among cisgender gay men—although gay Black men may find it less appealing than more general dating apps, in comparison with gay white men.[21]

In general, the use of dating apps has surged, particularly with the onset of COVID-19. In March 2020 Tinder (the most widely used dating app among college students) recorded its highest number of swipes on a single day, amounting to three billion; while the next most popular app, Bumble, recorded a 70 percent rise in video calls from March to May 2020.[22] Moreover, while dating apps are sometimes used for simple virtual connection or to facilitate in-person dating, some—including Tinder—are widely associated with more anonymous forms of hooking up. Tinder in particular facilitates a distinctly superficial, appearance-based reaction to potential partners, manifested in part by the low-risk, left-or-right swipes on profile photos for which it is known. This disproportionate emphasis on physical appearance dovetails with the depersonalizing quality of hookup culture more generally, effectively training users to believe that sexual connection need not be demanding, and that there is always someone more desirable just around the corner.[23]

It should be noted, however, that the use of dating apps need not always reflect this more depersonalized form of connection; some apps are in fact designed to encourage less superficial means of choosing a partner, often by prioritizing various nonphysical metrics (using personality-related questions, for instance) in the matching process. In addition, dating apps may at times provide a welcome means for people to bypass entirely the exclusive and heteronormative mainstream hookup culture of college campuses. In this way, dating apps can function to give some people (particularly women and marginalized persons) more up-front control about what exactly they seek in a connection, empowering them to set the agenda and to establish their sexual boundaries in advance.[24] Still, in spite of these more optimistic possibilities, it can hardly be said that dating apps are problem-free. Perhaps most troubling, women and LGBTQ+ persons experience harassment on dating apps with an alarming degree of frequency; for instance, a full one-fifth of women who use dating apps have experienced threats of sexual violence in the course of such use.[25]

Why, exactly, do college students hook up, generally speaking? There are various reasons: having fun, achieving social popularity, finding a pathway (perhaps the only pathway available to them) to a relationship, conforming to peer pressure, and so on. Pleasure is a significant motive for both men and women in hookups. However, when pleasure is narrowed only to the metric of orgasm, there exists a so-called pleasure gap in heterosexual hookups that falls roughly along the lines of gender; men and women claim equal amounts of pleasure, but men orgasm approximately twice as often as women, who are far more likely to reach orgasm in the context of a longer-term relationship.[26] Additionally, most heterosexual hookups are said to be "over" once the male orgasms; within hookup culture, female orgasm is generally understood to be far less socially important.[27]

Gendered differences in students' hookup experiences extend further. Beste in fact names gendered social expectations as a dominant reason that students engage in hookup culture in the first place. According to her analysis, popular culture depicts college as a time to enjoy frequent, no-strings-attached sex and to experiment sexually with as many people as possible. This popular portrayal trades on common expectations of what "fun" looks like in a college setting: boozy, breezy, and noncommittal. Drilling down by gender, college men within hookup culture are ushered into a hypermasculine peer culture and "player mentality" characterized by aggressive heterosexuality, competitiveness with other men, and the shunning of vulnerability and emotional ties in sex. By contrast, women in Beste's study appear motivated by the desire to be affirmed as sexually attractive and socially popular, and by the (often-unarticulated) hope that a hookup might ultimately morph into a longer-term relationship.[28] And while there has been less research done about hookup motivation among queer students, there is some evidence that gay men engage in hookups with the hope for relationship opportunities more frequently than straight men, and that lesbians are even more likely to pursue emotional attachment.[29]

Too often, however, hookups in fact end up compromising rather than fortifying student well-being. Beste relays that a full 90 percent of her student ethnographers concluded that some or most of their peers were privately unhappy with college party culture, as evidenced by blank stares, anxiety, and insecure behaviors at parties, as well as the disappointment and feelings of emptiness or loneliness so prevalent in the wake of many hookups. In fact, not a single one of Beste's ethnographers expressed being "happy" with a typical hookup.[30] Similarly, Lisa Wade and Caroline Heldman, in their study of first-year students at a private college, document that most students—both men and women—expressed dissatisfaction with hookup culture because it failed to deliver a sense of meaningfulness, empowerment, or pleasure. In fact, they write, "Even when sex was both consensual and wanted, students often reported highly unsatisfying sexual encounters. This was especially true for women, who discussed their sexuality as something they served up to men."[31] Other studies authenticate the feelings of regret, frustration, distress, and disappointment that often follow hookups, as well as the lowered levels of self-esteem, life satisfaction, and happiness that accompany more frequent hooking up over time. Such negative mental health outcomes seem particularly true for young women, although young men, too, may experience psychological distress in less obvious ways.[32] There is also growing evidence that hookup behavior correlates with increasing rates of sexually transmitted infection—belying the persistent ideological conceptualization found among many students that sex is fundamentally a private affair.[33]

Perhaps most troubling of all are the respects in which stereotypical hookup culture supports and sometimes even legitimates sexual assault. Reliable figures about the frequency of sexual assault on campus are notoriously elusive, but various studies place the rate of sexual assault of college women as one in five or even one in four, and the National Institute of Justice in 2000 accepted a figure somewhere in between.[34] Whatever the actual numbers, few would dispute that sexual assault is an enormous problem. LGBTQ+ students are at even greater risk than their heterosexual and cisgender peers.[35] Equally disturbing are the results of a (now admittedly dated) 1981 UCLA study concluding that 36 to 44 percent of male respondents said that they would "force a woman to have sex" if they could do so without getting caught.[36] Even naming unwanted forms of sex can at times be challenging; for instance, in Wade and Heldman's study of first-year college students, the authors report that many women surveyed "felt uncertain" about whether sexual coercion from men within hookups was acceptable, with some women identifying it as highly problematic but others actually normalizing it in their own assessment.[37]

Needless to say, it is imperative that we account for this dysfunctional context if we are to evaluate accurately the impact hookup culture has on the college experience. The most common type of sexual assault—as well as the least likely to result in criminal conviction—is acquaintance rape. Many of these assaults happen against the backdrop of campus party culture, including its attendant alcohol-fueled hookups. Of course, the connections between binge drinking and rape culture—understood as the qualities of broader culture that subtly normalize sexual violence—are complicated and hotly disputed, and certainly participating in the former does not predispose one to perpetrating sexual assault. Yet the likelihood of sexual assault occurring within a hookup does increase significantly with alcohol use.[38] And while the binge drinking that is so deeply associated with hookup culture does not *cause* sexual assault, it does set up *conditions* conducive to sexual assault and provides an impetus for perpetrators as well as a context that enables those perpetrators to hide.[39] By compromising clear communication, exacerbating gendered sexual scripts, and allowing or even encouraging students to cede their sexual agency ("the alcohol made me do it"), excessive drinking can smooth the pathway for sexual assault and allow perpetrators an environment in which their actions easily blend in with more broadly accepted sexual behaviors.

The Cultural Backdrop of Hookups

While individual hookups can be uncomfortable to consider for parents, administrators, and faculty, especially those with a Christian or otherwise religious focus, it is the *culture* of hooking up—and the way it clearly compromises human flourishing—that should disquiet us and command our attention. Here I distill three general categories of norms and assumptions associated with hookup culture that my own approach challenges, implicitly or explicitly: hyperindividualism, a casual or even careless attitude toward sexual partners, and gendered sexual scripts that ultimately deprioritize authentic mutuality and an egalitarian commitment to the well-being of women.

Hyperindividualism

The cultural nexus of privacy, tolerance, and sexual diversity found on most US college campuses naturally prioritizes individual choice in the sexual-ethical landscape. As so many college students are apt to put the matter, "You do you!" Sex is assumed to be a wholly individual and private affair, not subject to evaluation by anyone apart from the individuals directly involved. Further, students who reject or disapprove of hookup culture must do so silently, since open criticism is generally framed as inordinately judgmental.[40] In the face of a cultural unwillingness to posit a broader normative umbrella, individual preference assumes (rightly, at times) enormous moral importance.

The concrete ethical shape that this cultural backdrop assumes within hookup culture is the widely recognized requirement for individual consent; sexual activity is seen as justified if and only if it is consensual. Yet how much genuine sexual consent *is* there on campuses today? Donna Freitas notes that consent within hookup culture often lacks robustness; students frequently relay that hookup sex "just happens," without anyone seeming to know exactly how.[41] Culturally speaking, for many middle- and upper-class students, college is "supposed" to be a time of fun, sexual experimentation, and irresponsibility.[42] Sex, which plays a central role in this cultural trope, is often assumed to be consensual, absent clear indicators of sexual assault.[43] Yet consent may be compromised by any number of things, including poor communication, intoxication, direct peer pressure, or more subtle gendered cultural expectations—expectations that in fact animate hookup culture and discourage participants (especially women participants who partner with men) from expressing authentic sexual agency. Even among queer students—who, according to some studies, prioritize the importance of active, verbal consent more than straight students do—consent is sometimes still compromised by the persistence of a "dominant" male gender stereotype, especially in sexual encounters between men.[44]

The fiction of robust individual consent within hookup culture—and, coupled with it, a quasi-market approach to sexual interaction—nevertheless persists. According to this narrative, hookup sex takes place between two highly self-actualized individuals engaging in an independent form of sexual exchange, each asserting what they want and fairly bartering it with the other. All of this is supposed to take place absent any onerous, value-laden expectations such as fidelity, commitment, or care. As Beste rightly points out, hookups themselves actually appear highly *reasonable* if one's sexual goals center on this sort of individualistic marketplace exchange, characterized by a materialist understanding of sex, a high degree of self-awareness, and a complete lack of emotional entanglement.[45] Even some forms of popular feminist appeals are framed in this strongly individualistic way. Indeed feminist author Jaclyn Friedman wryly criticizes this trend as promoting the "fauxpowerment" of women. *Fauxpowerment*, as Friedman describes it, represents a quintessentially American individualistic solution to women's societal disempowerment. Rather than calling women to challenge systems or social structures that hold them back, fauxpowerment urges women in the direction of a purely individualistic solution: "just claim your sexuality, ladies!"[46] Here, women's collective sexual empowerment is treated not as a structural, systemic, or even communal matter but rather as little more than an assemblage of individual choices.

In the face of this hyperindividualistic environment—indeed, one that so heavily structures mainstream hookup culture—a holistic analysis will necessarily seek to broaden the conversation. That is, a myopic focus on self-contained decision-making and individual sexual desire stands in clear tension with broader public health concerns and the common good. In fact, the COVID-19 pandemic has laid bare this tension, as so-called private choices have had sharp and often devastating public health consequences. To wit: while clear causal analysis still needs to be done, it does seem clear that an alarming mid-2020 spike in COVID-19 cases was heavily concentrated in college towns.[47] It is no stretch to draw the connection between this spike and the way some students feel entitled to enjoy the social aspects of campus party culture, even in the midst of a pandemic, as an integral part of what it "means" to be in college.

Even on a more personal level, it is imperative to highlight the reality that individual subjectivity itself always stands in dynamic tension with the broader cultural discourses that shape and form us. Humans are never free-floating choice-makers. Rather, as author Lynn M. Phillips has maintained, examining the sexual lives of young women: our cultures live inside of us, even as we live inside our cultures. In this context, agency itself is murky and intertwined with complexities of power, desire, and individual choice.[48] Hence, if individual behavior and decision-making is the only level at which we understand sexual agency, we have failed to understand it at all.

Casual (Even Careless) Attitudes about Sex

Another central assumption animating hookup culture is the idea that genuine caring for one's sexual partners is an unnecessary or, worse, problematic expectation. Hookup culture is characterized by a pervasive casual attitude toward sexual interactions; some have even called this attitude "aggressively slapdash."[49] In fact, such nonchalance may be imperative if a participant is successfully to resist any attachment that entails emotional vulnerability toward sexual partners. In hookup culture, "catching feelings" is understood as weakness, with aloofness serving as the goal—at least in the initial stages of sexual relating. Someone who cares too much about a sexual partner ends up on the losing end (or at least the less powerful end) of the hookup equation. In other words, it is distinctly disempowering to be seen as wanting something too much. In brief, in hookup culture, "caring is creepy."[50] The culture instead demands from its participants, as Donna Freitas has put it, the "performance of the ambivalent shrug."[51] One might even say that today's college students who participate zealously in hookup culture knowingly or unknowingly cultivate a *competitive* form of ambivalence, where *non-caring* functions as a perverse sort of virtue developed over time. In a widely circulated essay, cultural commentator Alana Massey in fact has masterfully dubbed this quality of "chill" a "garbage virtue," one that is both sinister and pathological.[52] In this culture of chill, the one who cares less wins.

Ethicist Kari-Shane Davis Zimmerman, in a virtue analysis of the practice of hooking up, has accurately sounded a note of moral alarm about this process. Zimmerman maintains, "Men and women who hookup are learning skills that deter them from knowing what it means to be truly present and mindful of another person's desires because they themselves remain shut down emotionally and psychologically during a hookup."[53] In other words, the act of hooking up isn't best understood as a simple *act*. Rather, like most acts, it represents one brick in the walkway of character cultivation—in this case a character potentially marked by psychic disconnectedness and mistrust. The code of hookup culture asks its participants to "turn off" their emotional vulnerability to prevent them from getting hurt in the process.

Yet a posture of casual ambivalence toward sex not only prevents trust, vulnerability, and true interactivity; it also privileges noncommunication and thus quite naturally conduces toward sexual assault. Indeed, taken to an extreme, the logical conclusion of a thoroughly non-caring attitude toward a sexual partner is an unwillingness to hear or honor that person's agential choices. The expectation that one should not emotionally invest oneself in sexual activity reduces the likelihood of paying close attention to the other person's desires, feelings, and wishes—thus also making it far less likely that one will care or even *notice* when that partner participates in a less-than-enthusiastic fashion. Further, from an assault survivor's point of view, if one is not "supposed to" care much about *any* casual sexual interaction, one will remain that much more reluctant to name an actual sexual assault as such—since raising a charge of sexual assault means that one *has*, in fact, cared about what actually happened in the sexual interaction itself. In this way, a culture of ambivalent non-caring both disempowers victims and survivors and simultaneously empowers would-be perpetrators.[54]

From a perspective that values human wholeness, relational intimacy, and interpersonal trust, a careless attitude toward sex is problematic at best and intensely destructive at worst. More broadly, a culture that promotes such an attitude directly contradicts human flourishing and belies all but the thinnest understanding of sexual justice between participants.

Gendered Sexual Scripts

Finally, in spite of the cultural trope of hyperindividualized personal choice, there exist on US campuses robust and highly gendered social scripts associated with hookup culture. In fact, for participants who engage in heterosexual hookups, the culture itself hinges upon a stereotypical understanding of what it means to be a sexual woman or man. Even queer students may experience and internalize such gendered scripts and expectations, sometimes reproducing them within LGBTQ+ hookups.[55] Judith Butler has elaborated that gender itself is performative; that is, we act in ways that constitute and shore up culturally formed ideas about what it means to be a man or woman today.[56] And this performativity is visible everywhere in hookup culture, as students live into specific sexual expectations shaped within postmodern culture.

Among other qualities, sex in the twenty-first century increasingly is seen not only as biologically natural but also as an entirely normal and expected part of young adulthood. People of all genders are understood to want desperately or even *need* sexual fulfillment in order to qualify as healthy social participants.[57] This backdrop structures the broad acceptance of hookup culture as well as the performative expectations within it. The ubiquity of social media entrenches the tendency further; that is, social media has created an undeniable cultural pressure for young people to craft their public images in explicitly sexual terms. As *New York Times* journalist Vanessa Grigoriadis has put the matter, "Our digital age's instant, immersive space flattens us into avatars and demands constant attention to one's attractiveness and sex appeal."[58]

Against this background hypersexualized cultural drumbeat, clear and distinct differences nevertheless exist between feminine and masculine sexual expectations. For their part, women have been both over-identified with sex and simultaneously shamed for expressing their sexuality in an open or active way. In general today, women's self-esteem is socialized to be disproportionately tied to their sexual desirability. They are required to project "effortless perfection," a pedestal ruled by those who are conventionally pretty, cute, and thin and who conform to heterosexual men's expectations.[59] They are generally obliged to be both sexy and sexually available—without, however, coming across as *so* sexual that they risk being publicly slut-shamed, a label that may be applied to too-sexy clothing, too-frequent sexual activity, or too-numerous sexual partners. Young women thus find themselves in a bind: they are expected to be at once both sexually innocent and sexually sophisticated. They must appear self-confident, decisive, self-directed, and "together," and yet they must also retain some hint of the sexual innocence that maps them as "good girls" rather than "bad girls." Freitas describes how this impossible dual expectation translates into a bona-fide rift on college campuses, a social division of women into two types: those who are "datable" and, by contrast, those worthy only of a casual, commitment-free hookup. Alternatively, college women may choose to maintain two distinct personas: their "daytime" persona, where they appear respectable and successful, and their "nighttime" persona, where they may (or even must) dress and act in a highly sexualized fashion.[60]

Embedded within this complicated set of social expectations ultimately lies a deep ambivalence about women's sexual agency. Culturally speaking, women are typically framed as sexual gatekeepers: while men are characterized as "naturally" sexually aggressive and dominant, women are depicted as fundamentally more submissive and as bearing responsibility primarily for *reacting* positively or negatively to men's overtures.[61] Even while avoiding the label of "slut," women must appear nice, appropriately deferential to male desire, unaggressive when challenged, and not too pushy about their own longings. They are understood alternately as instruments of male desire, as responders, or even as victims—but not, primarily, as sexual agents in their own right. Moreover, whenever encounters become fundamentally nonconsensual, women are socialized within rape culture to blame themselves for "inviting" unwanted attention and "allowing" things to go too far. Indeed: damned if you do, damned if you don't. Against this toxic cultural backdrop, incentives abound for young women *not* to make clear what they do and do not want, sexually speaking. To claim their role as primary sexual co-agents is to risk social, cultural, and religious condemnation. It therefore comes as no surprise that so many college women relay that a hookup "just happened," absent any clear choice or indication of positive sexual desire.

The challenges of masculine sexual socialization are distinctly different. Sociologist Michael Kimmel is best known for his work in this field, and especially for his depiction of "Guyland"—a cultural world inhabited by teenaged and young adult men that is highly emblematic of US college campuses.[62] Guyland is characterized by a sort of hypermasculine suspended animation between boyhood and adulthood.[63] In Guyland, a competitive peer culture means that men's sexual self-esteem rests not on a passive quality of desirability but rather on a high degree of sexual prowess and achievement. Sex is something that young men are expected to "get" however they can. Men who are virgins are targets of mockery and shame, and "players" or "alpha males" are revered. Masculinity in Guyland is not just about having sex; it is about having as much sex as possible, with as many women as possible. Hence, such masculinity necessarily entails the objectification of women in service to men's heterosexual desire; women are, by definition, not treated as dignified, agential, or worthy of respect in their own right. Instead, men are fundamentally understood to be the desirers—and women the desired.[64]

It is not hard to see that this hypermasculine identity fails to square well with the vulnerability and relational intimacy embraced in this book. Spurred on by popular media imagery in which male sexual expression is readily characterized by violence, the act of caring emotionally for one's sexual partner makes one less of a man, by definition; a young man in an emotionally vulnerable relationship may be belittled as "whipped." Masculinity is fundamentally defined in opposition to what counts as feminine. From a young age, boys are taught not to cry, not to be weak, and not to display any vulnerability whatsoever. The ubiquity of porn—reaching more than 85 percent of all men by the time they are twenty-two years old—amplifies the problem. In mainstream heterosexual pornography, women generally are infinitely available and compliant and make few if any emotional or even basic relational demands.[65]

Of course, a hypermasculine ideal is a far cry from what many, if not most, actual boys and young men genuinely desire. After conducting scores of personal interviews with college men, Donna Freitas has concluded that what many men wish for are caring, respectful relationships—relationships substantially different from those called for by the norms of performative masculinity.[66] These young men face an uphill battle in the midst of college sexual culture. Even those men who appear to *embrace* social standards of hypermasculinity are not well served by them. This point is crucial to recognize: hypermasculinity not only harms the women whom it objectifies; it also harms the men—straight or queer—who are straitjacketed by its expectations. Along these lines, according to journalist Friedman, a 2016 meta-review of seventy-eight studies on masculinity and mental health concluded that men who place value on having power over women are more likely to suffer from depression, body image issues, substance abuse, and other psychiatric challenges.[67]

Within a Christian frame of understanding, such gendered sexual scripts are best characterized as social sin—that is, sin that transcends individual action and is located also in the collective. In social sin, cultural wrongheadedness functions to constrain possibilities for the flourishing of real individual women and men.[68] There is no question that such constrained possibilities are real—as well as urgent. The aggressive heteronormativity of hookup culture amplifies harmful and constricting gender stereotypes. This results in the deprioritization and cultural discouragement of women's genuine, positive sexual agency, as well as the promotion of a hypermasculine (detached, unemotional, objectifying, and even violent) understanding of what sex should look like. In this way, hookup culture's gendered power dynamics translate into psychological and physical danger for women, emotional stunting for men, and the depreciation of emotional intimacy, mutuality, and equal regard for all. It is not enough to articulate these normative qualities as distant ideals; we must be attentive to the ways our current cultural landscape, including the narratives of hookup culture, devalue and even block them.

Sexual Agency on Campus—Take Two

A full and holistic account of human agency—one that transcends a reductionistic focus on individual consent—must squarely challenge these cultural expectations, which implicitly (and sometimes explicitly) hinder both the genuine freedom and well-being of young adults today. It is clear that a simple focus on consent will not suffice. Amplifying individual consent surely must be part of our goal in the service of authentic human freedom. But a focus only on consent will largely leave in place the cultural objectification of women's bodies, an objectification too often internalized by individual women themselves who have come to equate their own worth with their sexual desirability. It will gloss over the ways in which women's sexual agency depends in part upon women themselves feeling internally free to make sexual choices in the first place—and to know that those sexual choices can find purchase, even amid a highly gendered and sexually violent cultural landscape. Finally, a narrow focus on individual consent will fail to beckon men (or anyone else) to an increased level of care, emotional engagement, or vulnerability—all qualities that are essential to human relational well-being.

Affirming genuine human agency as a dimension of human flourishing entails a rethinking of modern-day hookup culture. To this end, and against the dysfunctional cultural backdrop described above, I propose three normative "buckets" that build upon the insights of chapter 2 to characterize a more robust version of sexual agency in the context of hookup culture: *genuine* freedom of choice and desire; mutuality and equal regard; and emotional integrity.

Freedom, Reenvisioned

To be sure, an affirmation of personal agency, as described in the first few chapters of this book, does entail upholding the norm of individual consent—but only as it is recognized as embedded within a larger cultural landscape, one that encourages women to claim their own sexual choice-making and others to respect those choices. *This* sort of freedom is more than simply a choice to dress provocatively, or not; to have sexual intercourse, or not; or even to participate, or not, in hookup culture. It includes a profound affirmation of each person's capacity for self-determination, to choose not only her actions but also her ends, loves, and ultimately the meaning of her life. *This* sort of freedom roots itself in a deep recognition of one's own (and others') dignity and self-worth, a dignity in Christian tradition embedded in the *imago dei*.

Practically speaking, such freedom stems from both a sturdy self-confidence and a social environment that affirms the equal worth of all persons. It invites one not to lose oneself in societal expectation but rather to articulate and stand by one's values, one's desires and choices, and one's personal well-being and bodily integrity—and to respect the same in others. Moreover, authentic sexual freedom, it must be emphasized, depends upon a genuinely positive vision of human sexuality, one that unequivocally affirms sexual desire as part of what it means, for many, to live a full human life.

It almost goes without saying that the unspoken rules of hookup culture contradict such a robust understanding of human freedom. While in theory the choice of whether or not to hook up in any given instance belongs to each individual, thick cultures of sexual shame (especially for women), peer pressure, gendered expectations, sexual privilege, and even relational violence infringe upon sexual agency in real and disturbing ways—particularly for those who, by reason of age or personality, may feel especially socially insecure or ill at ease. Authentically free choice is unattainable in the face of such strong constraints.

Moreover, hookup culture's reliance upon a highly ambivalent understanding of sex—including the harmful "virgin/whore" dichotomy for women—contradicts a vigorous affirmation of sexual desire and pleasure as goods in their own right. And Christian tradition's nearly single-minded embrace of chastity as the primary regulatory norm for human sexuality practically speaking reinforces the virgin/whore dichotomy by bolstering a broader taboo approach to sexual morality. Such an approach fails to promote authentic sexual agency, instead encouraging a highly individualistic understanding of sex as "forbidden fruit," dangerous and best avoided, at least until (heterosexual) marriage. Thus even as the tradition may attempt to counter the hypersexualized demands of hookup culture, it also perversely entrenches those demands by integrating them into its own historically dichotomized understanding of female sexuality, such that the only morally acceptable route, especially for young unmarried women, is a resounding (and individually articulated) "no."

Conversely, hookup culture celebrates sexual accomplishment among men, measured by the number and social status of one's sexual partners. In addition to the obvious harm to the women—really, *all* women—who are objectified by this norm, those men (whether straight or queer) who underperform by the culture's standards or, alternatively, refuse altogether to play by its rules are marginalized as well. When particular Christian communities fail to challenge the hypermasculine norms that underlie this perverse celebration, they also fail to provide a meaningful alternative to hookup culture for boys and men who live in the real world. Taken as a whole, these dynamics amount to an enormous restriction of free choice and ultimately of genuine sexual agency for all persons. In diverse ways, they discourage young adults from identifying, articulating, and honoring their own deepest commitments with respect to sexuality.

Thus it is clear that a Christian ethical approach that aspires to promote human flourishing must take a different tactic. In lieu of a taboo approach to sex or an uncritical promotion of individual chastity, what is needed is a robust version of freedom that affirms authentic, confident, and value-driven sexual choice-making, undergirded by a strong and positive understanding of sexual desire itself as sacred and holy. Sexual freedom depends in part upon actively rejecting slut-shaming double standards, positively affirming the sexual decision-making capacity of young women as a whole, and calling society to support and uphold women's sexual agency as equal to that of men. It also requires denouncing those aspects of gender socialization that allow or even encourage men to devalue or dishonor the free choices made by their sexual partners. That is, all men must be encouraged toward a more inclusive exercise of their sexuality, one that resists the dominant temptation to assert their own desires at the expense of others. Moreover, heterosexual men in particular must be called to recognize and check their own sexual privilege, by actively seeking to respect and honor women's choice-making capacities—as well as by taking full responsibility for their own thoughtfully made choices.

Yet even as it does this, an honest view of sexual freedom will also acknowledge that sexual choice-making can be murky—and that decision-making is not always clear and straightforward for any given individual. Thus, women (as well as men) must be encouraged to take ownership over their "yes," their "no," their "yes to this and no to that," and even their "I'm not sure."[69] In other words, deeply respecting human freedom does not only involve affirming individual choices; it also includes empowering persons to recognize and give voice to their own values and goals, as well as to the nuanced and incremental steps involved in actualizing them. It requires acknowledgment that growing into one's sexual choice-making is a bit like learning a language, and that it will thus entail careful discernment, mistakes, and realignment.[70]

It must be quickly acknowledged that it is difficult for even the most self-actualized individual to enact such freedom in the absence of a society that fundamentally protects and respects it. As we have seen, social sin, once established, shapes and limits individual freedom. In other words, sexual empowerment is not *only* a matter of choosing to shrug off the gendered expectations and other social constructs that limit personal choice and constrain individual behavior. Also essential is a social context that is capacious and affirming enough to encourage growth in personal self-knowledge, confidence, and egalitarian respect for one another and for women as a whole. Such a context is akin to what Donna Freitas has called a "culture of consent": a social culture that maximizes the possibility that genuine freedom and justice will predominate among persons. Such a culture, according to Freitas, implies at a minimum the expectations of mutual care and respect, open communication, emotional and physical nonviolence, empathy and compassion, social justice, inclusiveness of sexual diversity, and education about personal consent.[71] Without this cultural moral scaffolding, authentic individual choice-making can scarcely conduce to genuine human flourishing.

Mutuality and Equal Regard

Even as we recognize that free choices, in order to genuinely be free, depend in large part upon cultural forces that envelop and codetermine them, we have stepped into the relational realms of human experience and their associated norms—including mutuality and equal regard. Hookup culture, with its strong reliance upon a backdrop of hyperindividualism and casual attitudes toward sex, presses against these norms and challenges their meaning at a fundamental level. Is hooking up capable of fostering mutual, equal sex that respects the shared quality of human dignity? Its proponents may claim just that. Superficially, at least, the prioritizing of individual consent in a casual hookup might solve the problem of equality, since an equal environment of explicit honesty and personal choice can theoretically bypass the hidden dysfunctional power dynamics that have long characterized sex.

Yet when we dig beneath the surface, the cultural and social analysis above reveals quite a different picture. Not only do gendered social scripts, compromised self-knowledge and self-esteem, and alcohol consumption make difficult the authentic expression of freedom. So too does the background of social injustice—the social and structural form of sin described in chapter 2—which lessens many heterosexual women's power to enter into truly egalitarian arrangements. Hence, despite the fiction of total and equal freedom of choice, hookups too often seem to "just happen," with little choice at all. And without genuine freedom of choice, mutuality and equal regard are emptied of their authenticity and normative power.

One might note here that same-gender sexual partners may enjoy a certain structural advantage in this regard. While power differentials can of course still exist, these may be lessened due to a shared gender-based social power enjoyed in same-gender hookups. That is, same-gender partners may in fact be less subject to the deeply gendered interpersonal power differentials that heterosexual couples de facto face. Many queer women students, for instance, emphasize that their own pleasure in hookups derives substantially from the emotional connection, intimacy, and trust that they experience with partners during and after sexual encounters. Still, it is imperative to recognize that LGBTQ+ students themselves are far from immune to the social pressures, influences, and gendered expectations that heterosexual students also experience, vis-à-vis hookup culture; nor of course should we assume that same-gender interactions entirely evade other forms of power inequity. Neat distinctions are, therefore, difficult to draw.[72]

Yet even apart from the ways the compromised freedom and heavily gendered norms of hookup culture decrease mutuality and equal regard, hookups are an uneasy fit with sexual reciprocity itself. True mutuality rules out the instrumentalizing of self and other that lies at the heart of hookup culture. That is, the fundamental intersubjectivity that characterizes mutuality depends upon a level of vulnerability not typically found in a casual hookup. Even when two parties *mutually* "use" one another, as in a fully honest and consensual hookup, such use entails an atomistic and invulnerable paradigm of the self. In hookup culture, I act upon or am acted upon by another. However, if I am playing by the correct rules, I do not allow myself to be fundamentally *changed* by that other. There exists little genuine give and take, and little or no deep mutual interchange. The careless attitude toward the other person—which, as we have seen, is an expected or even mandated element of hookup culture—discourages the sort of intersubjective vulnerability that is necessary for true mutuality to thrive.

Genuine mutuality entails a willingness to speak—sometimes loudly—one's own truth but also to listen carefully for the truths that others articulate. Perhaps more fundamentally, it involves a willingness to be impacted by those truths. Here, vulnerability is best understood not as individual weakness but rather as a critical ingredient to genuine intimacy, connection, and love; it represents our willingness to discard a guarded, false sense of self and instead to open ourselves compassionately to authentic interaction with the other.[73] Mutuality thus entails a deep level of intersubjectivity. Moreover, the kind of sexual agency to which it contributes is both more robust and more holistic than that called for by a simple ethics of individual consent.

Emotional Integrity

The final category I promote here as constitutive of human flourishing and bolstering authentic human agency is that of emotional integrity: that amorphous quality that integrates one's sexual choices, practices, and attitudes with one's values, beliefs, and broader life story. So described, emotional integrity invites persons to see themselves as centers of meaning, maximally thriving when all aspects of the self—interior and exterior; material, psychological, and spiritual; past, present, and future—are understood to be knit together into one whole, undivided cloth. Of course, people need not reach "wholeness" (in this more robust sense) before they can be said to exercise a baseline threshold of sexual agency. But there can be no doubt that integrating one's sexual actions with one's deeper sense of values and personal history contributes mightily to a sense of human well-being, including empowered choice-making.

The work of such integration is fundamentally emotional work. It therefore does not dovetail easily with the expectations of hookup culture, where emotional awareness is discouraged or even sidelined. To reflect upon the deeper meaning of sexual activity within the context of a supposedly meaningless hookup is (to state the obvious) a contradiction in terms. Moreover, the casual attitude of "chill" that is considered such an asset in a commitment-free hookup also quite naturally demands a high level of psychic *disconnection* and ultimately interpersonal mistrust among participants. People who are extremely active in the college hookup culture must learn to disconnect emotionally from their sexual partners, walling off the tenderest aspects of themselves from the interaction. Even some authors who accept hookup culture or promote it as beneficial to women's social achievement and well-being acknowledge that women in fact must embrace emotional *disconnection* in order to benefit by the standards internal to that culture.[74]

It is not only the casual ambivalence so characteristic of hookup culture, however, that contradicts the work of emotional integration. Emotional integrity as a value is also ill served by the gendered expectations for both women and men described above. As we have seen, women are too often culturally discouraged from making and taking ownership over their own sexual choices, or shamed for those choices once made—often by religious institutions themselves. In this context, honest and authentic integration of women's sexual decision-making with their larger life stories will remain difficult or even impossible. For their part, men are laden with hypermasculine expectations that they will engage in heterosexual sex competitively and frequently, without attending to their own emotional vulnerabilities, caring for their sexual partners, or even respecting those partners as full human beings. Needless to say, such constricting expectations work directly against the integration of one's sexual behavior with one's personality, values, and history.

By contrast, a Christian ethic that interests itself in fostering genuine sexual agency will promote an *environment* that encourages persons to integrate, not wall off, their sexuality with the rest of their identity. It will actively call people to consider their values, their histories, and their emotions as they make sexual choices, being honest with themselves about their fears, desires, and goals. Culturally speaking, it will reject taboo- and shame-based understandings of sex, marital or not, which effectively discourage young persons from taking full responsibility for their actions in the sexual sphere. Instead, a Christian ethic will seek to articulate and promote what might count as supportive, safe contexts for sex—contexts that foster human wholeness and therefore emotional, psychological, and spiritual well-being.

Attending to emotional integrity entails the recognition that sexual involvement makes us deeply vulnerable to one another—vulnerable to joy and sorrow, to ecstasy and pain. Here, a Christian directive toward sexual self-integration dovetails well with the emotional honesty that is required of many persons who identify as LGBTQ+ within a heteronormative campus environment. That is, queer students must in fact exercise enormous vulnerability if they are to live out their sexuality honestly under heterosexist social constraints—constraints that presume and privilege heterosexual sex as a matter of achievement for men and desirability for women. While few persons are thoroughly insulated from these gendered expectations, straight people may well be able to learn from the emotional and social vulnerability that is de facto asked of students identifying as LGBTQ+. In this way, straight and queer people alike are invited to a higher level of sexual honesty that rejects gendered stereotypes in lieu of a more integral expression of sexuality.

Suggestions for Moving Forward

It is no small task to change campus hookup culture in these ways. What is needed is not simply clearer understandings and guidelines related to individual consent, nor the reassertion of a Catholic or Christian moral culture that recommends and promotes the virtue of chastity. What is needed, rather, is a holistic call for justice in the context of hookup culture, an understanding of justice that serves human flourishing by promoting the freedom, relational health and well-being, and emotional integrity of persons and communities in the campus sexual environment. I intend the following as preliminary suggestions for how campuses might begin such an endeavor.

First, it is imperative that campuses begin actively to promote a culture that sexually *empowers* rather than shames young adults—men, women, or nonbinary; straight or queer. This begins with a vigorous rejection of a taboo morality approach to sex, including when it takes place outside the confines of heterosexual marriage. In a Christian context, it must be stressed, sex is fundamentally a holy endeavor, one that has the potential to connect us more closely with ourselves, with others, and with God. But in order for young persons to tap into this holiness, they must be allowed, invited, and empowered to explore their own desires and take charge of their own sexual decision-making in a safe and nonjudgmental environment.[75] They must be encouraged to discern their deepest values—including spiritual and/or religious values—and to articulate them in interpersonal contexts without apology or shame. In spite of its purported embrace of sexual liberation, hookup culture as it exists today provides no such environment. Neither does a single-minded emphasis on chastity as the primary Christian virtue used to express sexual flourishing. Campus-wide conversations about hookup culture as well as alternative relational practices must rather become honest, normal, staple features within student life programming, residence halls, campus ministry, and the classroom.

Second, anyone seeking to promote a change in campus sexual culture must squarely challenge the gendered and heteronormative social expectations that predominate within hookup culture (and beyond). This is a complicated and multifaceted but indispensable task. Above all, the slut-shaming norms that cripple women's ability to articulate their own sexual desires must be put to rest, and Christian campuses must reject these most vociferously of all. Women should not be portrayed in the least way as gatekeepers but rather as fully agential sexual persons, both active and receptive, with genuine needs, desires, and powerful—even if sometimes uncertain, ambivalent, or complex—voices. They must be encouraged to discover and claim the meaning of "yes," "no," and "maybe," and to understand their ambivalence not as an invalidation of their perspective but rather as an invitation to deeper discernment.

While this entails, in part, the encouragement of young women to more readily discover and assert their yearnings and needs, it also necessitates a profound social change: the replacement of a sexual script of male power, entitlement, and sexual privilege with one that prioritizes genuine relational equality and mutual interactivity among all persons. We must ask of boys and men not proof of sexual prowess but rather a strong demonstration of their commitment to value all persons, including women, as coequals, and to listen to, take account of, and be *changed* by their sexual partners' expressed needs and desires. A rejection of hypermasculinity entails a refocused emphasis, *by men*, on respect and care—sexually and otherwise. Boys and men must be called not to competitive sexual "achievement" but rather to accountability and responsibility in the sexual sphere, that is, to respect and care for others and to thoughtfully recognize the breadth of their own emotions. Further, boys and men must be actively encouraged to check their sexual privilege, by breaking the "culture of silence" that too often prevails on college campuses—a culture that protects the most violent or egregious male sexual behaviors, thereby bolstering rape culture more generally.[76] Not only does this silence profoundly harm women and queer people; it also hamstrings those straight, cisgender men who yearn for a healthier, more mutual, and humanizing sexuality.

From the perspective of Christian sexual ethics, one aspect of extending a more egalitarian posture into the realm of sex would be deprioritizing penile-vaginal intercourse as the central paradigm for normative sex. As ethicist Elizabeth Antus has rightly pointed out, following the thinking of Christine

Gudorf, a focus on penile-vaginal intercourse privileges heterosexual men's pleasure over women's—because it centers on a type of sex more conducive to the former, then creates a norm from that particular sexual activity. In this way, both women's and queer people's sexual needs, desires, and pleasure are effectively demoted in importance. By contrast, Christian ethics must in fact *decenter* such intercourse as the norm for "real" sex and begin also to embrace forms of sex more conducive to *all* people's pleasure and well-being.[77]

Third, campuses must actively challenge their students to reject an understanding of sex that promotes casualness to the point of not caring. The competitive ambivalence endorsed by hookup culture, and the emotional invulnerability that underlies it, threaten the well-being of those who take part. These qualities stand in direct opposition to the norms of kindness, trust, and investment in the other—indeed, neighbor love in action—that are central ingredients to a Christian vision of human flourishing. Those who continue to choose to engage in hookups in fact do themselves and others a disservice by pursuing a commitment to casualness for its own sake; instead, at a bare minimum, brief sexual encounters must be held to standards of thoughtfulness, respect, and a baseline of care and concern for oneself *and* one's partner.

Fourth, campuses must discover new and creative ways to temper the culture of binge drinking that supports and exacerbates the worst manifestations of hookup culture. As sociologist Elizabeth Armstrong and her colleagues have pointed out, a punitive approach to alcohol consumption has often *heightened* the symbolic significance of drinking, leading students to drink more while also pushing alcohol consumption into more dangerous private spaces. A creative approach might include, for instance, the intentional creation of more student-run community spaces that function as alternatives to fraternity and house parties.[78] As it stands now, binge drinking, and the accompanying expectation of hooking up, is often the only real social option on many campuses. Moreover, students frequently use alcohol to excuse bad behavior or relieve sexual responsibility ("the alcohol made me do it"). To change sexual culture such that it prioritizes genuine sexual agency means not that campuses "go dry" but rather that they nurture a greater sense of responsibility vis-à-vis alcohol consumption, no matter the age of the consumers.

Finally, and of crucial importance, insofar as *consent* continues to merit its status as a central sexual norm on college campuses, as it should, we must insist that such consent be continuous, enthusiastic, and mutual. As I have argued, consent by itself can become a truncated, narrow, and inadequate norm with which to evaluate the ethical contours of campus hookup culture. But, while consent alone is insufficient, it nonetheless remains absolutely necessary. A "yes means yes" standard for sexual consent constitutes an essential starting point for the exercise of genuine sexual agency. At a minimum, this standard demands that we probe beneath the surface of what passes for "consent" to unearth the psychosocial complexity of real persons—that is, persons who live real and complicated lives under imperfect and unjust social conditions. If genuine freedom, mutuality and equal regard, and emotional integrity are to become authentically possible norms for college sexual culture, our efforts will begin—though definitely not end—by thickening our understanding of consent, and finding creative new ways to implement that understanding on college and university campuses today.

Notes

1. Rosin, *The End of Men*, 44.
2. Freitas, *Sex and the Soul*. See also Freitas, *The End of Sex*; and Freitas, *Consent on Campus*.
3. See, respectively, Winner, *Real Sex*; King, "A Theology of Dating"; King, *Faith with Benefits*; Beste, *College Hookup Culture*.
4. Kalish and Kimmel, "Hooking Up," 141–42.
5. King, *Faith with Benefits*, 6–8.
6. Freitas, *The End of Sex*, 25–31.
7. Brown and Vanable, "Alcohol Use, Partner Type."
8. Beste, *College Hookup Culture*, chapters 1 and 2.
9. Kate Julian, "Why Are Young People Having So Little Sex?," *The Atlantic*, December 2018, https://www.theatlantic.com/magazine/archive/2018/12/the-sex-recession/573949/.
10. Centers for Disease Control and Prevention, "Trends in the Prevalence of Sexual Behaviors."
11. According to one 2014 study, college-aged adults overall are not experiencing more frequent sex or more partners than their counterparts from earlier eras, but sexually active college-aged adults are increasingly more likely to report sex within a casual date or friendship versus a regular partnership. See Monto and Carey, "A New Standard of Sexual Behavior?"; and Wade, *American Hookup*, 17.
12. Kalish and Kimmel, "Hooking Up"; Kimmel, *Guyland*, 195; and Bradshaw et al., "To Hook Up or To Date."
13. Bogle, *Hooking Up*, 71 and chapter 5.
14. Lisa Wade, "The Hookup Elites," *Slate Magazine*, July 19, 2013, https://slate.com/human-interest/2013/07/hookup-culture-for-the-white-and-wealthy.html. See also Lisa Wade, "Sex on Campus Isn't What You Think: What 101 Student Journals Taught Me," *The Guardian*, August 23, 2016, https://www.theguardian.com/us-news/2016/aug/23/sex-on-campus-hookup-culture-student-journals; and Spell, "Not Just Black and White."
15. Wade, "Sex on Campus."
16. As in other chapters, I use the term *queer* mindfully, though in this chapter more frequently. Again, I recognize that for some, the term retains a negative connotation. Many others, however, and especially younger persons—who make up the vast majority of hookup participants—utilize the term as both empowering and broadly inclusive of those whose sexuality or gender identity does not fall along heterosexual, cisgender lines.

17. See, for instance, Lamont et al., "Navigating Campus Hookup Culture," 1001; Rupp et al., "Queer Women in the Hookup Scene," 213; and Bogle, *Hooking Up*, 68–69.
18. Hamilton, "Trading on Heterosexuality"; and Rupp et al., "Queer Women in the Hookup Scene."
19. Kuperberg and Padgett, "Dating and Hooking Up."
20. Anderson et al., "The Virtues and Downsides of Online Dating." See also Kuperberg and Padgett, "Dating and Hooking Up"; and Watson et al., "What We Know."
21. Lundquist and Curington, "Love Me Tinder."
22. "Activity on Dating Apps Has Surged During the Pandemic," *Fortune*, February 12, 2021, https://fortune.com/2021/02/12/covid-pandemic-online-dating-apps-usage-tinder-okcupid-bumble-meet-group.
23. Mescher, "The Moral Impact of Digital Devices"; and Nancy Jo Sales, "Tinder and the Dawn of the 'Dating Apocalypse,'" *Vanity Fair*, September 2015, http://www.vanityfair.com/culture/2015/08/tinder-hook-up-culture-end-of-dating.
24. Lundquist and Curington, "Love Me Tinder."
25. Anderson et al., "The Virtues and Downsides of Online Dating."
26. Wade, *American Hookup*, 159–60; Kalish and Kimmel, "Hooking Up," 147. See also Snapp et al., "The Upside to Hooking Up"; Garcia and Reiber, "Hook-Up Behavior"; Fielder and Carey, "Prevalence and Characteristics of Sexual Hookups"; and Kenney et al., "First-Year College Women's Motivations."
27. Wade, *American Hookup*, 168–69; see also Grigoriadis, *Blurred Lines*, 33.
28. Beste, *College Hookup Culture*, chapter 2.
29. Barrios and Lundquist, "Boys Just Want to Have Fun?," 286. See also Kuperberg and Padgett, "Dating and Hooking Up," 519, citing Dean Klinkenberg and Suzanna Rose, "Dating Scripts of Gay Men and Lesbians," *Journal of Homosexuality* 26, no. 4 (1994): 23–35, https://doi.org/10.1300/J082v26n04_02.
30. Beste, *College Hookup Culture*, 121.
31. Wade and Heldman, "Hooking Up and Opting Out."
32. Wade, "Sex on Campus"; Beste, *College Hookup Culture*, 122–23; Bersamin et al., "Risky Business." See also Garcia et al., "Sexual Hookup Culture"; Freitas, *Sex and the Soul*, 154–55; and Friedman, *Unscrewed*.
33. Fielder et al., "Sexual Hookups and Adverse Health Outcomes"; and Julia Belluz, "5 Reasons Why 3 STDs Are Roaring Back in America," *Vox*, October 10, 2019, https://www.vox.com/science-and-health/2017/9/27/16371142/stds-syphilis-gonorrhea-chlamydia.
34. Fisher et al., *The Sexual Victimization of College Women*. See also Grigoriadis, *Blurred Lines*, 37–38.
35. Coulter and Rankin, "College Sexual Assault and Campus Climate." See also Adrienne Green and Alia Wong, "LGBT Students and Campus Sexual Assault," *The Atlantic*, September 22, 2015, https://www.theatlantic.com/education/archive/2015/09/campus-sexual-assault-lgbt-students/406684/.
36. Malamuth, "Rape Proclivity among Males," cited in Kimmel, *Guyland*, 224.
37. Wade and Heldman, "Hooking Up and Opting Out," 138.
38. Flack et al., "Risk Factors and Consequences."
39. Freitas, *Consent on Campus*, chapter 3.
40. King, *Faith with Benefits*, chapter 7.
41. Freitas, *Consent on Campus*, 82; see also Kalish and Kimmel, "Hooking Up," 142.

42. As Wade points out, poor and working-class students participate in hookups less often compared with middle- and upper-class students. See Wade, *American Hookup*, 95; and Wade, "The Hookup Elites."

43. In recent years, the promotion of affirmative consent (the presence of a "yes" rather than the absence of a "no") has begun to strengthen on college campuses, in part due to its promotion by the (now former) Obama administration.

44. Lamont et al., "Navigating Campus Hookup Culture," 1010–12.

45. Beste, *College Hookup Culture*, 147.

46. Friedman, *Unscrewed*, 9.

47. Sarah Watson, Shawn Hubler, Danielle Ivory, and Robert Gebeloff, "A New Front in America's Pandemic: College Towns," *New York Times*, September 10, 2020, https://www.nytimes.com/2020/09/06/us/colleges-coronavirus-students.html; and Danielle Ivory, Robert Gebeloff, and Sarah Mervosh, "Young People Have Less Covid-19 Risk, but in College Towns, Deaths Rose Fast," *New York Times*, March 2, 2021, https://www.nytimes.com/2020/12/12/us/covid-colleges-nursing-homes.html.

48. Phillips, *Flirting with Danger*, 17–18.

49. Wade, "Sex on Campus."

50. Joel Walkowski, "Let's Not Get to Know Each Other Better," *New York Times*, June 8, 2008, https://www.nytimes.com/2008/06/08/fashion/08love.html.

51. Freitas, *Consent on Campus*, 88.

52. Massey, "Against Chill."

53. Zimmerman, "In Control?," 60–61.

54. Freitas, *Consent on Campus*, 88, see also 56.

55. A deeper and more nuanced analysis is called for regarding the gender-related expectations experienced by queer persons engaged in same-gender hookups. While I cannot engage in such a full analysis here, I have hinted at how these expectations potentially complicate the college hookup landscape for LGBTQ+ students as well. For more on this, see, for instance, Lamont et al., "Navigating Campus Hookup Culture," in which the authors describe how many queer students position themselves against what they associate with "toxic masculinity" (expectations of aggressive, dominant, unemotional behavior) and yet sometimes reproduce many of those behaviors in their own same-gender hookups.

56. Butler, *Gender Trouble*.

57. King, "A Theology of Dating," 35.

58. Grigoriadis, *Blurred Lines*, xx.

59. Kimmel, *Guyland*, 247.

60. Freitas, *Sex and the Soul*, 130 and 5.

61. Armstrong et al., "Sexual Assault on Campus," 491.

62. In 2018 Michael Kimmel was publicly accused of sexual harassment by a former graduate student. He retired before any formal charges were made. I use his work here carefully; while I find his analysis of masculinity helpful, in no way do I wish to minimize the seriousness of the accusations made against him. For more, see Colleen Flaherty, "More Than Rumors," *Inside Higher Ed*, August 10, 2018, https://www.insidehighered.com/news/2018/08/10/michael-kimmels-former-student-putting-name-and-details-those-harassment-rumors.

63. Kimmel, *Guyland*.

64. McCabe, "A Feminist Catholic Response," 644.

65. Braun-Courville and Rojas, "Exposure to Sexually Explicit Web Sites," 158; and Kimmel, *Guyland*, chapter 8.
66. Freitas, *Consent on Campus*, 106. See also King, *Faith with Benefits*, 8; and Snapp et al., "The Upside to Hooking Up," 50.
67. Friedman, *Unscrewed*, 167.
68. McCabe, "A Feminist Catholic Response," 635–57.
69. Phillips, *Flirting with Danger*, chapter 7.
70. Genovesi, *In Pursuit of Love*, 125–26.
71. Freitas, *Consent on Campus*, chapter 7.
72. For an excellent study that examines these nuances, see Lamont et al., "Navigating Campus Hookup Culture," esp. 1013. More exploration of this topic is imperative, though it is beyond the scope of the present volume.
73. Beste, *College Hookup Culture*, esp. chapter 7.
74. Rosin, *The End of Men*, 28.
75. Freitas, *Consent on Campus*, 94.
76. Kimmel, *Guyland*, 280.
77. Antus, "Was It Good for You?," 628.
78. Armstrong et al., "Sexual Assault on Campus," 496.

CHAPTER FOUR

Teen Sexting, Objectification, and Justice for Women

In winter of 2010 in Lacey, Washington, a fourteen-year-old named Margarite took out her cell phone and snapped a full-length photo of herself, naked, in her bathroom mirror.[1] She then sent the photo to a potential new boyfriend, Isaiah, at his suggestion. A few weeks later, Isaiah forwarded the photo to another eighth grade girl, a former friend of Margarite's, who transmitted it (along with the text "Ho Alert!") to dozens of others on her cell phone contact list. Margarite became instantly (in)famous in her middle school; other kids began calling her a "slut" and a "whore," and she received sneers and ogles from peers she barely knew. Her friends were ostracized for hanging out with her. School officials soon discovered the situation, and the police were notified. Reaction was swift: the county prosecutor chose not to press charges against Margarite herself, but three students involved in the case, including Isaiah and two of the girls who forwarded Margarite's photo, were charged with distributing child pornography—a Class C felony. *All these students were in eighth grade.*[2]

Stories like this one are by no means an everyday occurrence, in spite of their notoriety. But neither are they a complete anomaly. In recent years, a few well-publicized cases of teen "sexting"—as I am using the term here, the sending of sexually suggestive images via mobile phones[3]—have inspired widespread fear on the part of parents and educators alike. And the dangers are not limited to middle schoolers like Margarite and Isaiah. In a similar case, Jesse Logan, an eighteen-year-old high school senior from Ohio, sent a nude photo of herself to her boyfriend, who then made the exquisitely bad decision to forward it to four other girls. The photo went viral, and Jesse was ostracized by her peers, taunted and labeled a "slut," a "whore," and a "skank," and she quickly spun into an emotional depression. Jesse Logan died by suicide at her home a few months later.[4] Unlike Margarite, Jesse was not a minor at the time of the incident; thus no child pornography charges were raised. But her case is undeniably tragic, and her death reminds us that teen sexting represents a far weightier act than a harmless youthful prank.

Sexting as a practice has grown exponentially in recent years and can be particularly troubling when carried out by minors, especially young teenagers—a demographic whose smartphone use has skyrocketed over the past decade, to the point where a full 95 percent of US teens now report that they have a smartphone or access to one.[5] Minors who send or receive sexual images often don't recognize the serious social, legal, and emotional and psychological implications of doing so. A further troubling aspect of sexting is that the images distributed are more commonly of young *women*, often without their consent. Hence, society's mostly fearful response thus far arguably contributes to the exercise of negative social control over women's sexuality. Without reverting to moral evaluations that extol young women's modesty or sexual purity—evaluations often promulgated by Christians and, as I demonstrate in previous chapters, propped up by historical anti-sexuality themes within Christian thought—we must nevertheless develop a freshly relevant moral and legal framework that discourages the practice of sexting while simultaneously empowering young women to claim primary control over their own sexual experience.

Along these lines, I here approach the topic of teen sexting with my overall normative framework in mind—that is, not only as a Christian concerned with what human flourishing requires but also as a feminist committed to expanding that understanding by taking more specific account of *women's* well-being in a real-world context. I bring these lenses to the question of sexting with particular emphasis on the concrete ways in which justice is frequently compromised by the practice. Relying upon an understanding of justice that attends to the concrete reality of the sexter, both individually and in social context, it is my contention that an adequate approach thus includes examining that person's social, emotional, and psychosexual experience. Moreover, for Christians, justice, addressed to the practice of sexting, must include attention to the sexual *injustice* that already structures the lives of so many young women—a backdrop that includes gendered objectification, coercive bullying, and sexual double standards that serve to punish women for being sexually active and often even for expressing sexual desire. In this context, rather than simply emphasizing free choice on the one hand or modesty and chastity on the other, an adequate understanding of justice promotes freedom, embodied well-being, relational intimacy, mutuality, and equal regard—qualities that, I argue, should in fact govern all sexual relations. I conclude with a few brief suggestions of concrete directions for an ecclesiastical and social response to the practice of teenage sexting.

The Prevalence of Teen Sexting

It is primarily teenagers and young adults who engage in sexting, and here I focus on teenagers. Analyses of the prevalence of sexting among teens vary dramatically. A 2008 study by the National Campaign to Prevent Teen and Unplanned Pregnancy, in conjunction with Cosmogirl.com, concluded that 20 percent of teens overall (22 percent of girls and 18 percent of boys) have sent or posted nude or semi-nude pictures or video of themselves (hereafter referred to simply as "nudes"). For young teen girls (age 13 to 16), the figure was 11 percent. According to the same study, 25 percent of teen girls and 33 percent of teen boys said they had had nude or semi-nude images—originally meant for someone else—shared with them.[6] A study conducted by the Pew Research Center in 2009 sampled teens aged 12 to 17 and found the numbers to be more modest: 4 percent of cell-owning teens said they had sent sexually suggestive nude or nearly nude images of themselves to someone else via text, and 15 percent said they had received such images.[7] Yet a large study published in the July 2012 issue of the *Archives of Pediatrics and Adolescent Medicine* found that a stunning 28 percent of public high school students aged 15 to 17 admitted to having sent a naked picture of themselves via text or email, while 31 percent had asked someone else to do so; and a full 57 percent had themselves been asked to send such pictures.[8] More recently, an April 2018 systemic review and meta-analysis published in *JAMA Pediatrics* revealed that among teens aged 12 to 17, about 1 in 7 (14.8 percent) had sent sexts, while 1 in 4 (27.4 percent) had received them—with rates increasing in more recent years, and as teens age.[9]

The variance in these numbers should cause us to pause before jumping on a media-fueled bandwagon that depicts sexting as a dominant feature of nearly every American teenager's life. However, even at the more modest figures, "sexting of explicit images involves a low percentage but still a considerable number of youth."[10] Moreover, the larger studies, if correct, reveal that US high school students consider sexting a relatively common practice and, further, that the *majority* of fifteen- to seventeen-year-old students have been urged at some point to take part in sexting. We simply cannot dismiss the practice as peripheral to modern teenagers' experience.

While some disagreement exists about how often it is *girls* whose images are sexted, most studies show that at least a slightly larger percentage of teen girls than teen boys have sent or posted nude or semi-nude pictures of themselves. According to the study by the American Academy of Pediatrics, 61 percent of those who created or appeared in sexted images were girls.[11] The latest 2012 study, while finding no significant difference between percentages of girls and boys who had *sent* a nude, found that girls were far more likely than boys to be *asked* for nudes; almost 70 percent of the girls polled had been asked to send a naked photo or video of themselves.[12] While both boys and girls, then, are transmitting sexted images, it seems that girls' bodies are more likely to be sought (and appear) as the subject of a nude. Further, according to Danah Boyd, a fellow at Harvard's Berkman Center for Internet and Society, although boys and girls both send nudes, "photos of girls tend to go viral more often, because boys and girls will circulate girls' photos in part to shame them."[13] Because girls and young women appear to be disproportionately impacted by the practice of sexting, it is imperative to examine the practice using the lens of gender analysis.

Legal, Social, and Emotional Ramifications of Sexting

What are the real consequences—legal, social, or emotional—for teenagers who engage in sexting? For teens sending or receiving a photo of someone under age eighteen, the legal penalties can be severe. Existing laws tend to address teen sexting under the rubric of child pornography, such that the transmitted images fall outside First Amendment protection. While the specific definition of child pornography differs from state to state, under federal law it is a felony to produce, possess, or distribute child pornographic materials. Receiving just one picture can carry a mandatory minimum sentence of five years.[14] Overzealous prosecution can lead to criminal charges, imprisonment, fines, and federally mandated sex offender registration—a designation that can drive teenagers from their parents' homes and haunt those teenagers decades into the future. Some states have begun statutory reform regarding teen sexting, but most have not.[15]

Many scholars agree that charging minors with child pornography offenses is not an appropriate or helpful response to teen sexting, especially for the original sexter and recipient. In numerous cases, these teenagers seem to have had little or no idea of the serious legal implications of their actions. Moreover, a teen sexter's experience is markedly different from victims of traditional child pornography; the intent of child pornography laws as they are written is to protect defenseless victims against being "manipulated and forced to participate in 'graphic sexual [activities]' against their will."[16] Admittedly, teen sexting does take place in a social context that may generally be characterized as exploitative of women and girls, but the level of direct manipulation involved in sexting is ordinarily lower than in the case of traditional child pornography.

Because penalties for child pornography are so severe, there is an obvious mismatch between these laws and the phenomenon of teen sexting. Legal scholar John A. Humbach points out the ridiculous consequences of applying such laws in blanket fashion:

> On the conservative assumption that, for each teen who photographs herself, an average of two or three classmates receive copies of the pictures, it is a plausible estimate that as many as forty to fifty percent or more of otherwise law-abiding American teenagers are already felony sex offenders under current law and as such are subject to long-term imprisonment followed by "sex offender" registration requirements for decades or for life. . . . There is certainly reason to suspect something is profoundly amiss when a system of laws makes serious felony offenders of such a large proportion of its young people.[17]

Not only does overzealous prosecution for sexting ruin young lives; the laws themselves can have profoundly negative effects on the broader public. For instance, the crowding of sex offender registries with convicted sexters would diminish the effectiveness of those registries vis-à-vis their original intent of alerting the public to predatory danger. As one legal scholar has argued, "The current system creates negative repercussions for the prosecution of traditional pornography, ruins the lives of the prosecuted children, and provides no long-term benefits for society."[18]

Of course, the negative consequences of sexting are not just legal; they also include profoundly important *social* and *emotional* penalties for many teens who engage in sexting. Harassment by peers can be debilitating and can dramatically impact a teenager's psychological well-being. In the American Academy of Pediatrics study, 21 percent of respondents appearing in or creating images reported feeling very or extremely upset, embarrassed, or afraid as a result, as did 25 percent of youth receiving such images.[19] Exacerbating the harm for girls who sext, a widely acknowledged sexual double standard too often labels them as "sluts" or "whores." The negative social stigma that results from sexting gone awry can remain with the sexter for a very long time, in an age where reputations spread virally and digital footprints seem immortal. Further, threat of parental and school punishment (including suspension or expulsion) can complicate emotional and psychological damage, with a teenager's future prospects for school, college, or employment severely compromised.

Why Teenagers Sext

If we are to take seriously the concrete reality of the sexter, it is crucial for us to try to understand: *Why* do teenagers choose to send nudes? What is it in a teenager's experience that inspires them to take part in an activity that may carry such dangerous legal, social, and emotional consequences? In fact, definite social benefits draw some teens to engage in sexting: social cachet and the craving for increased popularity, for instance, or the desire to draw closer to a boyfriend or girlfriend with whom one already shares an emotional relationship.

One of the most common reasons teenagers offer for sexting is simple "flirting": sexting represents a modern and high-tech version of the age-old flirtatious games that young people play as they grow and develop sexually. According to the "Sex and Tech" survey, 66 percent of teen girls and 60 percent of teen boys who have sent sexually suggestive content say that they did so to be "fun and flirtatious."[20] As an experimental stage of exploring and expressing one's sexuality, sexting can represent a playful invitation into not-yet-actualized relational and sexual activity. Sometimes either the original sender or the person asking for the nude is hoping to become romantically and/or sexually involved with the other party, and sending or requesting nude photos feels like a means to up the ante on a budding relationship.

Another reason that teens give for why they send nudes is to meet the requests or even demands of a significant other. Fifty-two percent of teen girls who engage in sexting send sexually suggestive content "as a sexy present" for a boyfriend.[21] The nude might indicate an openness to future sexual experimentation. Couples already sexually active might use sexting as an extension of their physical relationships. In some cases, though, one person might feel uncomfortably strong-armed into sexting; indeed, 23 percent of teen girls and 24 percent of teen boys in the same study said they were pressured by friends to send or post sexual content.[22]

Of course, not all sexters have benign intentions; some teenagers who sext do not send their own photos but rather maliciously forward the photos of another, in an act of high-tech bullying. Such "secondary" sexters may be motivated by the desire to mock or intimidate the primary sexter, or simply by the wish to gain a social leg up at another's expense. Or perhaps the secondary sexter is merely engaging in a thoughtless prank—albeit one with potentially serious consequences for all involved. It is noteworthy that it is not only teens who engage in such behaviors; "revenge porn," the nonconsensual posting on the internet of sexually explicit images, typically by a former sexual partner, is commonplace among adults, and it appears likely that the COVID-19 pandemic has only exacerbated the phenomenon.[23] Problematic as such adult behaviors are, however, the judgmental immaturity of many teenagers can have even more disastrous consequences when taking hurtful action requires nothing more than the tap of a Send button on a smartphone.

Regardless of their reasons, many teens do in fact get caught in the gap between their own intentions and an unforgiving societal response. Yet it would be incomplete to attribute their actions purely to individual bad judgment. Teen sexting does not exist in a social vacuum but rather is a part of a larger, gendered social system in which teen sexters—as sexual beings—replicate broader social behavior. As such, "when adolescents are taught, largely through the mass media, that sexual experience is a desired good, and these values are then perpetuated among their peers, it seems clear that portraying oneself as sexual would be a desirable strategy. Trying to save adolescents from themselves without understanding the roots of the behavior is misguided at best."[24] Thus, to better understand the reality of sexting, we must examine its place in the wider landscape of popular culture.

The Social Context of Sexting: Sexualized Media, Sexual Violence, and Purity Culture

In American popular media and advertising culture, it is no longer seriously in question that women's bodies are routinely hypersexualized, objectified, and demeaned. Even seemingly harmless advertisements for clothing, food or alcohol, and other consumer products often carry a subtextual message that women's personal identity and worth depend heavily on how physically attractive and sexy they appear. In a similar vein, women's sexual identities are frequently trivialized; sex is commonly presented as little more than a dirty joke or a titillating activity, divorced from any authentic human relationship or deeper personal identity. The idealized image of physical and sexual flawlessness—a fantasy that belies the reality of virtually every woman on the planet—is far from harmless; real women and girls measure themselves against these images every day, leading to untold (and largely unmeasured) damage to women's self-esteem and psychological well-being.[25]

The images are particularly shocking in the world of music videos, where women are generally presented in a state of perpetual sexual arousal, compliant with male fantasy and what has been termed the male "pornographic imagination."[26] Moreover, retrospective analysis reveals that the images themselves have become progressively more explicit over time, with increasingly shocking representations necessary to touch an overexposed and thus desensitized audience. The epidemic of eating disorders, cosmetic surgery, and violence against women and girls must be seen against the backdrop of the toxic media landscape in which women and girls find themselves.

So must the contours of the teen sexting debate. This pornification of popular culture functions to normalize teenagers' inclination to send nude or semi-nude photos of themselves to others. Indeed, teen super-idol Miley Cyrus (formerly Disney's tween star Hannah Montana) posed semi-nude at age fifteen for a controversial *Vanity Fair* photo spread in 2008. It is easy to see how many young teens would not hesitate to follow suit in such a culture of exhibitionism.

Along with a sexy media backdrop that demeans the feminine body and belittles human sexuality, body-related fear and shame are a dominant background experience for many (or arguably most) women and girls. Again, while accurate rape statistics are notoriously hard to obtain, at a minimum, one out of every six American women report having survived rape or attempted rape in their lifetime. For college and college-aged women, as we have seen, the number is significantly higher; these women are between three and four times (respectively) more likely than women in general to experience sexual violence.[27] Moreover, of women who are raped, 42.2 percent report that the rape happened before they were eighteen years old, and 79 percent report that it happened before age twenty-five.[28] Girls' developing sense of their sexuality must be set against this disturbing backdrop, one of clear misogynistic and objectifying practices and of violence directed specifically against women's bodies. Further, rape culture—aspects of popular culture that make sexual coercion and violence against women seem normal—does not merely serve to humiliate women vis-à-vis their bodies. As we have seen in the case of hookups, rape culture undermines women's sexual decision-making, such that "no means yes," or at least a flirtatious "maybe." Insofar as sexting invites the view that girls and women are the playthings of men, and that women's sexual "yes" can be assumed, the practice should be considered highly damaging and morally problematic.

Finally, an aspect of popular culture that is often overlooked—but should not be, especially by Christians—is what is sometimes termed "purity culture," described briefly in chapter 1. Purity culture, with its attendant purity balls and promise rings, pervades large swaths of North American society and is aimed in a particularly strong way at teenage girls, just on the cusp of sexual adulthood. In general, advocates of purity culture would like to return to what they see as a better, simpler era, when girls would "save themselves" for marriage—even as a "boys will be boys" mentality often releases teenage boys from similar expectations. As feminist critic Jessica Valenti points out, the message of purity culture is, ironically, not so different from our overly sexualized popular media culture: for both, a woman's worth lies in her ability, or her refusal, to be overtly sexual. Both approaches teach American girls that their bodies and their sexuality are what make them valuable.[29] While at times well intentioned, purity advocates perpetuate the same social rubrics that guide girls to understand their own sexual desire as a source of shame and embarrassment. Rather than encouraging girls to understand themselves as moral agents and sex as a moral and deliberate choice, purity culture encourages girls to think of themselves as moral children, in need of a father's or a husband's sexual protection.

In the midst of these social backdrops—an oversexualized, misogynistic culture of assault and rape on the one hand and a Christian-based purity culture where desire and pleasure are pathologized on the other—we must locate a helpful, life-giving, justice-based response to sexting, one that prioritizes both individual agency and relational well-being. To this end, society must empower young women to claim primary responsibility for their own sexuality while also avoiding the dangerous and unhelpful pitfall of treating teenage sexters as if they were adults engaged in child pornography. Yet, even as we seek to do this, we must acknowledge the cost to well-being that sexting exacts upon participants—that is, the alienating and debilitating impact that sexting too often exercises upon teen sexters.

A Christian Anthropological Understanding of Sexting

How, then, should Christians make sense of the practice of sexting? How do the elements of human flourishing articulated throughout this book come together, in the case of persons who digitally share sexual images of themselves? Put differently, what does justice—understood from feminist, Christian sensibilities—require, vis-à-vis teen sexting?

It is particularly useful to recall here Farley's articulation of justice—affirming persons according to their concrete reality, actual and potential—and the qualities of personhood, as both autonomous and relational. This understanding dovetails with the normative features of human flourishing articulated thus far in this volume. In the case of teen sexting, freedom, embodied well-being, relational intimacy, mutuality, and equal regard all have particular application and prescriptive force. In fact, these norms keenly illuminate the "concrete reality" of persons who sext—and thus, what justice requires.

If our normative analysis is to remain honest as well as invitational, it is imperative to honor the experience of sexting teenagers and also to invite them into a fuller understanding of sexual desire, one that challenges any practice that does not ultimately serve their well-being. In other words, a Christian sexual ethic must take care to challenge sexting where it harms or otherwise disrespects persons in their concrete, embodied realities—in their autonomy and their relationality. But it also must honor the joy and delight of human desire, and the way that human sexuality invites us to a transcendent experience of ourselves, of others, and even of the divine.

There exists another dimension of justice, however, that is vital to an honest analysis of sexting. An adequate account of justice and sexual flourishing must lift up the contextual and structural *in*justices that characterize a teenage sexter's world. I return here to Lebacqz, who maintains, "We cannot approach justice directly, because we already live in the midst of injustice."[30] Again, injustice is a lived reality central to human experience; as such, sexual injustice forms a backdrop to any theorizing about what exactly it is that "justice" requires. And as I argue throughout this book, it is insufficient to frame injustice as if it were purely a matter of individual or even institutional wrongdoing. Rather, as feminist philosopher Iris Marion Young has emphasized, injustice often transcends individual action and rather takes the form of *social* structures and processes—perhaps uncoordinated, and yet which together function to constrain choice and render some people vulnerable to domination.[31] Indeed, as we have seen, this same insight lies at the heart of the Christian concept of social sin. And it *must* inform any adequate account of justice that seeks to pay honest and sustained attention to women's well-being.

Addressed to teen sexting, this sort of structural lens on justice means that first and foremost we must recall the social context in which teenagers sext. That we live in a culture that disparages human sexuality and demeans the female body should be central to our moral analysis of sexting. Texting nude photos of a girl's body is not merely an individually wrongheaded act; it plays directly into this wider trivialization of sex and objectification of the female body. Insofar as sexted images function to portray women as sex objects lacking in full agency or self-determination, or as objects whose feelings and genuine experience need not be considered,[32] they support the sort of social injustice and constraint on women's opportunities that both Lebacqz and Young—and indeed an adequately revised Christian sexual ethics—call us to resist.

Moreover, the high incidence noted above of teenagers feeling compelled to send or post sexual content should profoundly disturb us in a world with such excessive rates of sexual violence. Sexting, when done by actual teenagers in the real world, often contains a subtle (or not so subtle) element of social pressure or manipulation that props up sexual injustices, characterized by fear and shame, that are already a part of our social reality. The fact that both girls *and* boys apparently experience such pressure at times does not diminish the very real price that sexting exacts specifically upon girls, who already live their lives with substantial awareness of the possibility of sexual violence. Whatever else a "just" response to sexting entails, it cannot overlook these harmful patterns or imagine that sexting exists in a sexually neutral setting.

In what remains of this chapter, I put forth a Christian sexual ethic specific to the practice of sexting. Such an ethic must take the context of injustice seriously, even while establishing what justice requires for human sexual flourishing. Drawing upon these insights, I elaborate the implications of freedom, embodied well-being, relational intimacy, mutuality, and equal regard as attributes that should guide us to an evaluation of the practice of sexting in today's world.

A "Sextual" Ethic for Christians

Perhaps the most troubling aspect of the story of Margarite, told at the start of this chapter, is that her *freedom* was completely disregarded by her boyfriend and classmates, such that she herself experienced real, tangible harm. As I argue throughout this book, freedom is of course an essential part of our human identity; our capacity for free consent, for self-determination, is in fact a central part of what it means to *be* human. Certainly some feminists—myself included—have rightly highlighted the ways in which a Western Enlightenment bias has at times led to the overemphasis of negative freedom as a defining characteristic of personhood, and in the realm of sexual ethics this has truncated our ability to offer a more robust version of sexual agency and well-being. But recognizing this overemphasis should not cause us to swing too far in the opposite direction, eviscerating the very real importance of freedom, particularly in the sexual realm and particularly for women. For many of us, our ability to *choose* our actions, our boundaries, and ultimately our loves is deeply connected to our identity and self-understanding.

When a boyfriend, girlfriend, or classmate passes along a nude that was intended as private communication, the freedom of the original sexter is most certainly violated—resulting in potentially deep psychological harm. But our analysis of freedom must also reach deeper than that violation, for freedom is transgressed on much more fundamental levels when one takes into account the manipulative culture in which sexting takes place. While it is important to resist evaluative discourse that removes all agency from teenagers who choose to sext, it also seems insufficient for a justice-oriented ethic to ignore the culture of exhibitionism and patriarchal power relations that heavily structure that very same choice. In other words, many girls send nudes (or are asked to send them) because our society tells them that their worth is to be found in their sexually desirable bodies. Many teenagers engage in sexting because our society tells them that sexual exhibitionism is a normal and socially acceptable way for adults to express their sexuality.

A choice driven by the desire to appear sexy or to increase one's popularity cannot be considered free in the fullest sense. It is no secret that the teenage years are often characterized by insecurity and the desire to be liked; teenagers, especially young ones, often do not have the inner strength and long-term judgment to make wise and confident choices. An ethic that promotes freedom in a more robust sense looks beyond mere *free choice* and embraces instead a vision of bodily self-possession, self-acceptance, and personal agency. This is particularly important for girls; teenage girls must retain primary control over their own sexual experience, refusing to let others—fathers, boyfriends, peers—dictate how they conduct their sexual lives. Sexual choices should be thoughtful, well-considered decisions—not choices made from social pressure, insecurity, or a lack of assertiveness.

While exhorting true and meaningful freedom in sexual decision-making, however, the feminist Christian ethic developed here also promotes and encourages a positive vision of sexuality: one in which bodies of various shapes and sizes are understood as beautiful and where human desire—even in teenagers—is considered a valuable part of an embodied creation. As crucial as freedom is to an adequate evaluation of sexting, a feminist approach must be quick to remind us that persons are more than free-floating centers of liberty. We are, once again, profoundly embodied creatures, and human sexual experience, identity, and self-understanding remain deeply connected to that embodiment. In other words, *being a body* is intrinsic to what it means to *be human*. My body is most certainly not all there is to me, but I cannot (and should not) understand myself as wholly separate from my body.

If we consider a strong body-self connection as an integral part of a good creation, there can be no doubt that we live under conditions of brokenness—for bodily objectification is a routine part of human, and especially *women's*, experience. Whatever else it achieves, the act of sending sexually explicit photos of oneself encourages girls and women to think of their bodies primarily as objects of male pornographic imagination. In this way, sexting can and often does forge a wedge between the sexter's experience of herself and her body. The practice thus contradicts the intimate link between body and self, potentially depersonalizing sexual self-experience. Decades ago—and long before the advent of sexting—Christian ethicist James Nelson described this sort of bodily alienation in detail:

> If the mind is alienated from the body, so also is the body from the mind. The depersonalization of one's sexuality, in some form or degree,

inevitably follows. The body becomes a physical object possessed and used by the self. Lacking is the sense of unity with the spontaneous rhythms of the body. Lacking is the sense of full participation in the body's stresses and pains, its joys and delights. More characteristic is the sense of body as machine.... When the body is experienced as a thing, it has the right to live only as machine or slave owned by the self.[33]

Nelson's portrayal here perfectly captures the bodily objectification that too often encapsulates the experience of sexting. Particularly when sexting takes place between two parties who do *not* share a high level of trust and emotional intimacy, the image of the sexualized body is essentially depersonalized in a nude photo. It becomes something to be *evaluated* in terms of socially determined standards of size, shape, or beauty. This depersonalization becomes heightened when the recipient passes along the nude to other, unintended recipients, as the original sexter's body is effectively walled off from her larger personality. Sexting of this sort constitutes a clear case of objectification, that is, "the failure to apprehend and respect [a] person in her or his whole reality."[34]

A Christian ethic concerned with justice and human flourishing must instead promote an integrated experience of body and self. The theological concept of the Incarnation, described in chapter 2, signifies that God affirms fleshly existence, that our bodies are not incidental to our identities but rather constitute an important part of *who we are*. As Nelson has beautifully articulated, "Beyond the dualistic alienations we experience the gracious resurrection of the body-self. I really am *one* person. Body and mind are one; my body is me as my mind is me."[35] Our bodies are inseparable from our souls, our spirits, our selves.

In the context of sexting, to affirm the moral value of human embodiment means that we must stop demonizing sexual pleasure and simultaneously challenge practices that segregate body from self. On the one hand, the mentality encapsulated in the various forms of purity culture is decidedly anti-body; it promotes shame and embarrassment and ultimately functions to deny the beauty of human sexuality as an instance of incarnation. On the other hand, an ethic advancing human well-being as necessary to justice should also insist on sexual practices that *unite* rather than *divide* a person's body from her larger personality. Sexting too often promotes this alienating division, particularly when it takes place outside of a more personal relational context. Theologically, it belies human dignity and thus denies the power of incarnation.

Freedom and embodiment, both key qualities that should govern the practice of sexting, are nevertheless insufficient on their own; these will be enabled and enhanced by a context of relational intimacy, mutuality, and equal regard. Intimacy highlights the emotional tenderness that potentially characterizes sexual interactivity, and the way that sex can draw its participants together at a level much deeper than the purely physical. In many ways, relational intimacy lies at the heart of what the tradition has called the *unitive* aspect of sex: the way sex has the power to draw persons into deep communion with one another. Moreover, the high level of mutual trust that ideally develops over time in conjunction with relational intimacy enables a profoundly life giving connection—one that is otherwise far less likely. To have that healthy relational intimacy and trust violated, then, is painful indeed. The depth of this emotional pain best explains the suffering experienced in instances of secondary sexting, such as in the case of Margarite and Isaiah.

Yet the moral problem lies not simply in the forwarding of sexual images to unintended recipients; even the *initial* act of sexting should prompt us to raise hard questions regarding relational intimacy and, further, mutuality. In many cases, sexting itself, even when freely undertaken, violates these norms. Recall that mutuality itself asks for a posture of both giving and receiving of sexual participants—that each engages in the interaction both by contributing to the interaction *and* by actively receiving the contributions of the other. Mutuality thus rules out the brute instrumentalization of one by another, that is, the pure *use* of a person to accomplish one's own sexual ends.

As is so often the case, context is crucial to evaluating whether or not sexting violates this norm. Sexting has a much different moral meaning when it takes place in the context of two people (especially two young teenagers) who barely know each other than it does in the context of a mature, emotionally close, mutual relationship between emerging adults or long-term committed partners. Why? In the first case, there can be little doubt that harmful objectification occurs. The recipient's gaze upon the nude image is divorced from a deeper appreciation of or respect for the sexter's identity. The subject of the nude becomes little more than a physical object to be admired, or in some cases mocked. When sexting takes place in the context of an emotionally close and mutually fulfilling relationship, on the other hand, it is at least conceivable that the recipient's gaze might be essentially a benevolent one, affirming the sexter's whole personhood within a broader perspective. In spite of this more humanizing possibility, however, such maturity and emotional grounding too often is lacking—especially in the case of young teenagers who engage in sexting as a means of flirtation, sexual experimentation, or in response to coercion.

A final quality that a Christian sexual ethic must promote vis-à-vis sexting is equal regard. Freedom, embodiment, relational intimacy, and mutuality are themselves arguably best achieved in relationships marked by equality. We know this most clearly by examining what happens under conditions

of relational *in*equality. That is, when one partner wields a disproportionate amount of power in a relationship, the other is more apt to feel forced or
manipulated into sexting, less able to retain a strong sense of the body-self connection, and unlikely to achieve deep relational intimacy, mutuality, or trust.

In a world where girls and women are routinely understood and portrayed
in the media as sex objects, true equal regard can be hard to come by. Insofar
as sexting is used to harm or further disempower girls or women, it must be
denounced. In fact, gender dynamics aside, we should be suspicious of *any*
instance of sexting that takes place within a relational context marked by a
power imbalance. Such imbalance is, of course, far more likely to take place
among teenagers, whose sense of personal identity and relational power is
still largely unstable. When sexting is used to bolster patterns of domination
and subordination—either by way of individual bullying and humiliation
or by furthering harmful gendered power dynamics—the practice severely
compromises human well-being and therefore must be roundly rejected.

Charting a Course Forward

I argue that an adequate response to sexting must squarely acknowledge that
it does not occur in a social vacuum. Rather, sexting as a practice reflects the
larger social patterns in which it takes place. Because these patterns are particularly debilitating toward young women's sexuality, we must remain keenly
alert to the ways in which our response can unintentionally exacerbate wom-
en's social and sexual disempowerment.

Along these lines, we must reject a purity-based response wherein we deny
the beauty of sexual desire, whether intentionally or inadvertently. Whatever
else we do, we must remind ourselves (and our youth) that sexual desire is
beautiful, delightful, and sacred. Indeed, it is *because* of this sacredness that
we must not treat sexual expression lightly. Rather than ignoring or denying
the beauty and power of human sexuality, our response to sexting must focus
on sexual well-being in the context of real human relationships, lifting up the
need to respect human freedom, embodiment, relational intimacy, mutuality,
and equal regard.

I briefly suggest here three directions in which these sexual norms point
us as individuals, as churches, and as a broader society concerned with justice
and human sexual well-being. First, and most importantly, a social response
to sexting must begin with and focus upon better education of ourselves and
our youth. Such education must include information about the dangers and
legal implications of sexting, but it must also extend to broader discussions

about gender stereotyping in the media and the cultural devaluation and instrumentalization of women's bodies and sexual agency. Without squarely addressing this educational component and broader social context, any response to teenage sexting risks harming the very children whose well-being should be our central concern.

Second, given the anti-body and anti-sexuality tenor of much of Christian public conversation, Christians concerned with justice have a particular obligation to go further: our conversations must incorporate and promote an understanding of embodiment that avoids harmful dualisms and affirms a profound body-self connection, particularly one that insists on a positive role for pleasure and desire. Churches must address the phenomenon of sexting head-on, not by condemning youth who send or receive nudes but rather through honest conversation about what it means to be sexual, embodied persons. Teens themselves need to be encouraged toward a deeper sexual self-understanding and equipped to identify the profound connections between their bodies and their deepest identities.

Finally, we as a society must revamp our legal approach to sexting. Treating sexting under the rubric of child pornography is thoroughly inadequate. Children are not adults. Child pornography laws were intended to protect children, not to punish them. Thus, federal laws must be revamped to account for the age and maturity of the sexter; the level of volition involved; and the frequency and scope of the sexting event(s). Sex offender registration, in the vast majority of cases, should be taken off the table, and criminal records for sexting should be expunged when minors reach adult status. Further, we must make a distinction between primary sexting and secondary sexting (passing along nude or semi-nude photos to others). In general, primary sexting, especially when engaged in voluntarily with one other person, should not be considered a legally punishable offense, and secondary sexting is best treated using remedies from civil, not criminal, law.

This response is not intended to suggest that the practice of sexting is morally acceptable in all or even most cases. In fact, it is my judgment that teen sexting is generally harmful to those who engage in it, particularly those who are young or immature, disempowered or insecure, or who engage in sexting apart from a relationship characterized by mutuality, equal regard, and trust. Such qualities are far less likely to characterize teenage relationships (particularly young teenage relationships) than the bonds that may exist between emerging or mature adults. Nevertheless, even in the case of adults, the relational and social context of sexting is not incidental to its moral status, and the topic deserves further consideration on its own merits. Such an assessment will, at a minimum, need to take account of the particular relational backdrop in which sexting takes place. Moreover, as I have argued, sexting exists within a sociocultural context that routinely objectifies and instrumentalizes women's bodies and normalizes sexual exploitation, and it thus potentially harms not only individuals but also the larger common good. These sorts of considerations must be accounted for in any larger evaluation of the practice.

Yet in our rush to highlight the myriad ways sexting can compromise human well-being, we must be careful not to revert to a heavy-handed legalism, particularly one that treats children as if they were adult criminals. Nor should we embrace an anti-body purity approach that demonizes sexuality more generally, negates the sexual agency of young women, or portrays women's sexuality in particular as dirty, dangerous, or shameful. Sexuality, desire, and pleasure are sacred, and at their best they connect us to a deeper, mysterious reality. In this sense, we might name sex as sacramental: it is a tangible sign of God's invisible grace, a window into the deepest nature of reality.[36] An adequate response to sexting affirms the sacred beauty of the body and of human desire, even as it insists that these are best expressed in the context of healthy personal agency and freedom, a well-integrated body-self identity, mutuality and relational intimacy, and equal regard. In this way, we can begin to inject a measure of sanity into society's response to sexting, thereby allowing for and encouraging a deeper conversation about the realities of the practice and its real impact upon today's youth.

Notes

1. An earlier version of this chapter appeared as "Mobile Porn? Teenage Sexting and Justice for Women" in the *Journal of the Society of Christian Ethics* 33, no. 2 (Fall/Winter 2013): 93–110.
2. Jan Hoffman, "A Girl's Nude Photo, and Altered Lives," *New York Times*, March 26, 2011, http://www.nytimes.com/2011/03/27/us/27sexting.html.
3. Sexting may be differentiated from internet pornography, which claims a quasi-permanent web presence. Sexting, as I examine it here, is ordinarily aimed at a private audience (at least initially) and, because it is accomplished via cell phone, lends itself to impulsivity.
4. Mike Celizic, "Her Teen Committed Suicide over 'Sexting,'" *Today*, March 6, 2009, https://www.today.com/parents/her-teen-committed-suicide-over-sexting-2D80555048; and "Jessica Logan Suicide: Parents of Dead Teen Sue School, Friends over Sexting Harassment," *HuffPost*, March 18, 2010, https://www.huffpost.com/entry/jessica-logan-suicide-par_n_382825.
5. Anderson and Jiang, "Teens, Social Media & Technology 2018"; see also Pew Research Center, "Mobile Fact Sheet," April 7, 2021, https://www.pewresearch.org/internet/fact-sheet/mobile/. Few studies have been done examining differences in sexting behavior across lines of race, class, and ethnicity, although it appears to be a practice that crosses racial and ethnic borders. See Peskin et al., "Prevalence and Patterns of Sexting."

6. Power to Decide, "Sex and Tech."

7. Lenhart, "Teens and Sexting."

8. "'Sexting' Teens Found to Be Up to 82 Percent More Likely to Be Having Sex Compared to the Non-sexting Teens," *New York Daily News*, July 4, 2012, http://www.nydailynews.com/life-style/health/sexting-teens-found-tos-82-sex-compared-non-sexting-teens-article-1.1107729.

9. Madigan et al., "Prevalence of Multiple Forms."

10. Mitchell et al., "Prevalence and Characteristics of Youth Sexting," 19.

11. Mitchell et al., 16.

12 "'Sexting' Teens Found."

13. Hoffman, "A Girl's Nude Photo."

14. Humbach, "Sexting and the First Amendment," 437.

15. McLachlan, "Crime and Punishment."

16. Ryan, "Sexting," 371.

17. Humbach, "Sexting and the First Amendment," 437–38.

18. Shah, "Sexting," 216.

19. Mitchell et al., "Prevalence and Characteristics of Youth Sexting," 16.

20. Power to Decide, "Sex and Tech," 4.

21. Power to Decide, 4.

22. Power to Decide, 4.

23. Jessica M. Goldstein, "'Revenge Porn' Was Already Commonplace. The Pandemic Has Made Things Even Worse," *Washington Post*, October 29, 2020, https://www.washingtonpost.com/lifestyle/style/revenge-porn-nonconsensual-porn/2020/10/28/603b88f4-dbf1-11ea-b205-ff838e15a9a6_story.html.

24. Lunceford, "The New Pornographers," 113.

25. Jean Kilbourne brilliantly examines these patterns in advertising in her series of four documentaries, *Killing Us Softly*. See especially *Killing Us Softly 4: Advertising's Image of Women*, directed by Sut Jhally (Northampton, MA: Media Education Foundation, 2012), DVD. I have chosen to focus here on the portrayal of *women's* bodies; however, it is crucial to recognize that the media's portrayal of *men's* bodies (and sexuality) also contributes to the problem by valorizing men's physical power and dominance over women.

26. *Dreamworlds 3.*

27. RAINN, "Victims of Sexual Violence."

28. "Sexual Abuse Statistics."

29. Valenti, *The Purity Myth*, 10.

30. Lebacqz, *Justice in an Unjust World*, 154, esp. chapters 5 and 6.

31. Young, *Responsibility for Justice*, esp. chapter 2.

32. Nussbaum, "Objectification."

33. Nelson, *Embodiment*, 39–41.

34. Farley, *Just Love*, 121. The morality of objectification in a sexual context is a key concept that deserves more treatment that I can offer here. For a provocative treatment of the concept, see Nussbaum, cited above. Nussbaum argues that, in the matter of objectification, context is everything—and that sexual objectification may be morally acceptable as a temporary phase in a relationship characterized by mutual regard.

35. Nelson, *Embodiment*, 79.

36. For a fuller discussion of sex as sacrament, see Elizabeth Myer Boulton and Matthew Myer Boulton, "Sacramental Sex," *The Christian Century* 128, no. 6 (March 22, 2011): 28–31.

CHAPTER FIVE

Commercial Sex, Well-Being, and the Rhetoric of Choice

Among those who consider themselves fierce advocates of women's freedom and well-being, there arguably exist few topics more controversial in nature than commercial sex. Like hookup culture and more impersonal instances of sexting, "sex work" or "prostitution," as it is alternately termed, ordinarily injects a high level of anonymity into the otherwise intimate sphere of sexual relationships. Yet, unlike other forms of anonymous sex, commercial sex is transactional in a distinctly *monetary* way: it makes sex itself into a commodity. Sex is here traded not implicitly under the auspices of mutual physical pleasure (as in hookup sex) or as a means of flirtation or gaining social cache (as in sexting) but explicitly in the marketplace, legally or illegally. The primary ethical questions that surface in an examination of such transactions include first the nature of the trade and, by extension, the agency of the sex workers who engage in it—most of whom are women. But a more complete moral inquiry necessarily extends further, to an examination of the way the practice affects both sex workers themselves and society more broadly. All of this must be undertaken with a keen awareness of the broad social and economic conditions under which commercial sex takes place, for, as with other topics taken up in this volume, attention to human agency and well-being is wrongheaded if it is not set into the context of the concrete reality, personal and social, in which real individuals actually live.

In this chapter I begin by setting forth a brief description of the concrete realities of sex workers, including demographic depictions of sex workers themselves as well as the people who purchase sex. I then engage in sustained analysis of sex workers' well-being—physical, psychological and emotional, and relational. Further, and as a complement to this analysis, I outline the legal frameworks and constraints of commercial sex, with a particular (though not exclusive) focus on the United States.[1] Underneath these legal models lie certain important philosophical assumptions, having to do with the nature of human agency as well as the underlying meaning of sex itself. Having laid this groundwork, I then turn my attention to what constitutes an adequate Christian response, taking account of these various dimensions of well-being and agency. Based in the theological anthropology embraced throughout this volume, I argue that while Christian ethics has tended to emphasize the themes of sin and chastity (or rather its violation) to scrutinize commercial sex, a sounder approach will instead utilize the language of justice, agency, and well-being (robustly understood) to promote human flourishing in a real-world context. After examining these moral contours using this more suitable lens, I conclude the chapter with a brief set of policy recommendations to guide real-world deliberations. These, I believe, can lead individuals, churches, and other social institutions in the direction of a more sexually just understanding of and approach to commercial sex in the contemporary US context.

Portraits of the Sex Trade

The terms *commercial sex, sex work,* and *prostitution* are broad and rather hazy in the specific activities they seek to describe. A wide range of sex-for-payment arrangements typically fall under the definitional umbrella, ranging from "street prostitution" that operates with or without facilitators (sometimes called "pimps"—a term I generally avoid using here), to brothel workers, to upscale mistresses who may do business on their own or through escort services, and to college students seeking sugar daddies to help pay for their education. Additionally, legal massage parlors, strip clubs, erotic theaters, and even dating services may serve as fronts for illegal sex work, though these same establishments may also deliver other, more socially legitimate services. The lines also blur between commercial sex-for-pay arrangements and pornographic filmmaking, webcam modeling, and phone-sex operation. In this chapter, I focus less on these affiliated practices and more on the forms of commercial sex where physical, in-person, and (on-balance) consensual sexual activities are explicitly exchanged for payment.

As in most matters, language here is not incidental. For reasons that become clearer through the chapter, those favoring the decriminalization of commercial sex tend more readily to adopt the term *sex work*, likening the sex-for-pay exchange to other forms of voluntary labor. By contrast, those favoring what is known as an "abolitionist" approach are more likely to use the term *prostitution* and sometimes to refer to the seller of sex as a *prostituted person*. My own approach lies somewhere in between these views. In general,

I favor the term *commercial sex* (versus *sex work*) to avoid conflating sex work fully with other forms of work, yet I do have a great deal of respect for the amplified agency that the term *sex worker* (versus *prostitute*) attempts to convey. I use all of these terms at different points, though my analysis tends to refer to the system or practice by the term *commercial sex* and to those actively engaged in it as *sex workers*. Admittedly, the term *sex worker* is often understood as broader than simply *prostitute*, yet I focus here more narrowly on those engaged in these systems of physical, in-person sex for pay.

Because commercial sex is such an expansive category, and, moreover, because it often takes place largely within the social shadows, it is difficult to render a clear and stable portrait of a sex worker. Sex workers *may* fit the stereotype of poor or undereducated young women with few or no other economic options. But this stereotype is at best only a half-truth. Sex workers also may be college students seeking a way to pay for their education or middle-class homeowners trying to stay ahead of their mortgages. While most sex workers are not rich, not all are desperately poor; some in fact earn quite a bit from their activities. For instance, Phyllis Luman Metal, describing her work for nine years as a paid mistress to a wealthy San Francisco Bay Area man, explains that her undertakings funded a fairly lavish lifestyle for herself as well as a European education for her children.[2] Of course, Metal's experience represents a level of empowerment and financial security closer to one end of the spectrum of sex work; thus while it should not be discounted entirely, it also should not distract us from the many sex workers who enjoy far less economically stable lifestyles.

Sex workers are diverse in other ways, as well. They may be of any age, race, or gender, though they plainly skew toward younger women. Although it is widely cited that the average age of entry into commercial sex is thirteen, this statistic has been largely discredited, and the murky nature of the sex trade makes it difficult to arrive at a solid figure.[3] In any case, the term *child prostitution* is in fact a legal misnomer; by definition a child is legally unable to consent to sex, and therefore such a child is better understood not as a child sex worker but rather as the victim of commercial sexual exploitation of children. In fact, it is generally acknowledged that children who turn to the sex trade are often runaways with access to few social networks or supportive services.

While the vast majority of sex workers are women, boys and men may also sell sex; indeed, some believe that between 35 and 40 percent of younger sex workers are boys, who, if they live long enough to "age out," often go on to become facilitators within the sex trade themselves.[4] Sex workers also may identify as any race or ethnicity, though BIPOC women are generally overrepresented among them.[5] Further, the *experience* of sex work does vary according to racial identity. BIPOC persons, for instance, are at particular risk for harassment and arrest, and while only 40 percent of street sex workers are BIPOC women, these account for 55 percent of those who are arrested and 85 percent of those jailed.[6]

Sex workers also may identify as straight or queer, cis or trans*. According to Amnesty International, cisgender women account for the majority of sex workers in most countries; however, cisgender men also engage substantially in commercial sex around the globe. At least in some areas, the trans* community appears to be particularly strongly represented among sex workers, especially when compared with overall population; for instance, one 2007 study found that engagement in sex work was reported by as much as 44 percent of the trans* population in Sydney, Australia. And in the United States, a different study estimated that trans* persons engage in sex work at ten times the rate of cisgender women.[7] For a societally marginalized community, this is perhaps unsurprising; as one former sex worker, a refugee in the United States from Argentina who is both trans* and undocumented, put the matter, "Let's be realistic. . . . For people like me, sex work is not 'one' job option. It's the *only* option."[8] Sex work itself is notably more dangerous for the trans* community; transgender sex workers report high levels of rights abuses and live with much higher rates of HIV than cisgender sex workers, male or female.[9]

A strong predictor of whether or not one engages in the sex trade is past childhood sexual abuse. Indeed, Andrea Dworkin, a scholar and opponent of legalized sex work, once famously declared incest to be "boot camp" for prostitution.[10] Between 65 and 95 percent of sex workers are survivors of sexual abuse, where such abuse has effectively groomed them for future engagement in the sex industry.[11] Such a chilling statistic indicates a *cycle* of victimization that lies at the heart of commercial sex, making the systems that are intrinsic to it particularly difficult to address, practically speaking. Tackling the forces that exacerbate childhood trauma and alienation is a complex task, but also a critical one, particularly for an approach that seeks to address sex work as more than a simple matter of individual choice.

Who are the purchasers of sex? As the moniker *john* implies, they are, by and large, *ordinary* men. The buyer of sex is the man who lives next door. He may be of any age, race, background, religion, ethnicity, or class. He may be a business executive, a student, a truck driver, a doctor, a construction worker, a teacher, a therapist. He may be married or unmarried—although, according to one Boston-based study conducted by psychologist and researcher Melissa Farley, the majority of sex buyers currently have wives or girlfriends.[12] In fact, in the same study, the buying of sex was found to be so socially pervasive in the United States that—if one includes pornography and services like phone sex and lap dances in the definition of sex work—it was found to be "shockingly difficult" to identify men who had *not* engaged in the purchase of sex in some form.[13] Other studies bolster Farley's conclusion here, revealing that between 16 and 30 percent of men in the United States have directly paid for sex at some point in their adult lives.[14]

Farley also has found a connection between the men who purchase sex and an overall aggressive posture toward women. According to her research, sex buyers most commonly view women with anger and contempt, lack empathy for their suffering, or relish the ability to degrade and inflict pain upon women. In addition, they are more likely than other men to understand sex as fundamentally separate from intimate personal relationships.[15] Farley has found that purchasers within the sex trade tend to sustain a fantasy that sex workers love sex and enjoy it with their customers—thereby avoiding the distinctly more complex conclusion that sex workers themselves are real (and thus multifaceted) people, with economic needs and struggles, desires and hopes, and personal relationships of their own.

Finally, an accurate portrait of sex work in today's world would be incomplete without underscoring the impact of the exponential growth of the internet in recent decades. This dramatic increase has led to an explosion of electronic methods of advertising, supporting, and carrying out sex work, making it far more readily available and transitioning it from a heavily outdoor (street-based) market to an indoor one. Economist Allison Schrager charges that the internet has radically altered supply and demand with respect to commercial sex, normalizing it and thereby expanding its economic reach and appeal: "Women who pre-Internet . . . wouldn't walk the streets or sign with a madam or an agency now can sell sex work, sometimes even on the side to supplement other sources of income."[16] Indeed, sites such as Backpage .com (now shuttered) or Craigslist have served as hubs for the proliferation of sex work in recent decades. Whether or not one interprets this development as making commercial sex physically *safer*—reducing the risk of physical attack and restoring more control to sex workers themselves—it undoubtedly has made the practice more easily accessible to those wishing to engage in it surreptitiously.

Commercial Sex and Women's Well-Being

The safety and well-being of sex workers—including their physical, psychological, and relational well-being—has been the subject of much research in recent decades. Although the diverse backgrounds and legal contexts of sex workers prevent easy generalization about their experiences, it is nevertheless imperative to recognize the most common threats that exist to sex workers' well-being. Most obvious is the physical danger that accompanies commercial sex. The homicide rate against female sex workers is the highest of any group of persons ever studied—and a full fifty-one times higher than that of the next most dangerous occupation, working in a liquor store.[17] Conservatively estimated, 2.7 percent of all female homicide victims in the United States between 1982 and 2000 were sex workers, and the majority of these homicides were committed by buyers.[18] There is often a larger pattern to such violence; one study suggests that as many as 35 percent of those homicides were perpetrated by serial killers, as was the case for example in the Green River murders in Seattle in the 1980s or the Long Island killings of the early 2000s.[19]

Short of homicide, sex workers are at extremely high risk for physical harm, disease, and abuse, including sexual assault. Sex workers also have a much higher probability than the general public of contracting sexually transmitted infections, tuberculosis, anemia, and hepatitis.[20] The threat of STIs is particularly elevated among street sex workers; in fact, one UK study estimates that the rates of STIs are between nine and sixty times higher among street sex workers than in the general population.[21] The industry is rife with manipulation, exploitation, and physical violence committed by both sex buyers and facilitators. In fact, much about sex work *relies* upon violent imagery for its "market" appeal. Sex workers frequently complain about the near-constant prevalence of hardcore porn in brothels, describing for instance the way such porn is used to stimulate the imagination of buyers, who then desire a reenactment of the violence.[22]

Violence against sex workers is not only perpetrated by buyers, of course. Popular understanding often attributes such violence also to facilitators. Certainly these third-party beneficiaries frequently do abuse and otherwise mistreat sex workers while simultaneously benefiting enormously from their work. However, the line between "pimping" and other relationships is often not an easy one to draw; by some definitions, anyone who lives off a sex worker's earnings may qualify as a pimp, legally speaking. In practice, such an understanding functions severely to limit sex workers' freedom to maintain personal relationships, including relationships with romantic partners, spouses, grown children, or even other sex workers. Thus, while laws against pimping may limit some abusive activity, they can also undermine families and friendships.

Further, police treatment of sex workers, while arguably improved in recent years, is often still far from benign. Sex workers attest widely to harassment, physical abuse, rape, sexual assault, and extortive treatment by policemen themselves.[23] Moreover, by some estimates, sex workers in the United States are arrested by police up to fifty times more frequently than are buyers— evidencing a double standard that is extraordinarily troubling from a feminist ethical point of view.[24] That statistic is even more disturbing when scrutinized under the lens of race; the high arrest rate of BIPOC sex workers effectively translates into a much greater degree of vulnerability to abuse from within the law enforcement system.

Government-regulated brothels may offer conditions that protect against such physical violence and other dangers, at least some of the time. The use of condoms, for instance, is generally required in such brothels, and sex workers there undergo regular health checks, are monitored using intercoms and panic buttons, and may call upon brothel owners and local law enforcement for protection. Of course, such measures may be imperfectly carried out or used to restrict rather than to empower sex workers, and they certainly do not solve the more socially pervasive problem of overall violence and discrimination against them. To take one example, the surveillance measures enacted upon sex workers in the name of enhancing their physical safety frequently extend to non-work hours; thus, rather than serving primarily to protect sex workers from harm, these measures in fact may function to restrict their movements and actions, even when they are not on shift.[25] Additionally, there may exist subtle pressure from brothel owners and managers, or even perverse financial incentives for workers themselves, to disregard or forgo certain of these health and safety measures. Nevertheless, it is reasonable to claim that legalized brothels offer at least the possibility of greater protection for sex workers against the worst physical abuses and dangers, even as they may do little to solve the heightened vulnerability of those workers on a larger social scale.

Beyond physical harm, frequent exposure to the violence and stress of sex work—even in regulated brothels—exacts a profound mental toll upon sex workers. Indeed, one study across five countries, including the United States, found that 67 percent of women engaged in sex work meet the criteria for a diagnosis of post-traumatic stress disorder.[26] The sense of disempowerment and lack of control that frequently accompanies commercial sex can engender feelings of fear and vulnerability, and the stigma attached to sex work often translates into a lowered sense of self and internalized negative social messaging.[27] Sex workers experience much higher rates of depression and suicide, and their habituation to pain is well attested in their own accounts. The resulting prevalence of substance abuse represents one way sex workers cope—that is, by further numbing their own emotional needs via illicit drug use, whether by personal choice or coercion.[28] Other tactics frequently employed by sex workers to maintain and protect some semblance of self-identity include explicit dissociation and the presentation of a false front while working. As "Gwynn," a former receptionist at a Melbourne brothel, describes, "Prostitution is all about being a good actress. The most popular girl at the brothel . . . was a charmer with the clients, but she actually hated sex."[29] Former sex worker Linda's words eerily echo this assessment: "I liked that none of the men could see the real me. I was always an aberration of myself."[30]

Finally worth highlighting is the frequently harmful *relational* impact of sex work. Sex workers have spouses, children, friends, and family. Yet these relationships themselves often suffer as a result of the everyday stressors entailed by sex work. Indeed, many former sex workers find it difficult to form and sustain healthy long-term relationships even after they leave the sex trade. Former sex worker Jade puts the matter bluntly: "It is hard to maintain relationships after you have been treated night after night with contempt."[31] The pain embedded in Jade's words indicate the depth of relational harm that often—albeit not always—results from sex work. Whether that harm traces back to specific treatment by buyers, facilitators, or police, or simply to the nature of the work itself, the impact of commercial sex on sex workers' overall well-being can be profound. As one former sex worker sums the matter up, "the physical intensity of working as a prostitute was like experiencing a car crash every single weekend. Mentally, your identity is messed with, you get another name, you become another person in prostitution. You shift from real you to fake you."[32]

Legal Responses to Commercial Sex

These hazards to sex worker well-being take place within the context of highly varied and complex legal frameworks around the globe. In many places, including nearly all of Asia, prostitution is fully illegal and prohibited. In other places, prostitution itself is legal, but the activities that make it possible—such as soliciting or pandering—are not. In the United States, prostitution is generally not legal, with the notable exception of the legalized, government-regulated brothel system in some rural counties of Nevada. Elsewhere—including New Zealand—sex work has been fully decriminalized and may thus be practiced without legal penalty. The Netherlands is particularly noteworthy for having legalized (and regulated) prostitution in place for many years; in fact, Amsterdam is globally known for its thriving sex tourism industry as well as for its red-light district.

Here I focus on two of the more recent clusters of legal strategies in response to commercial sex: full decriminalization on the one hand and partial decriminalization—commonly known as the Nordic model—on the other. These approaches are particularly noteworthy because they both avowedly seek to improve the lives of sex workers themselves, and they thus tend to be the only approaches widely advocated in those circles. By contrast, the alternative strategies of full legal prohibition (as practiced in most of the United States) and legalization and regulation (as in rural Nevada brothels) have tended to decenter the experiences and well-being of sex workers, decreasing their sense of agency and leading to their widespread abuse and/or control by governmental practices and representatives.

Full decriminalization—that is, the removal of criminal penalties for engagement in sex work, without, however, the addition of government regulation—is often favored by sex worker unions and other rights-based organizations, including, notably, Amnesty International, Human Rights Watch, and the World Health Organization.[33] Full decriminalization removes laws specific to prostitution so that the activities of sex workers, as well as those who frequent them or profit off of their earnings, become legal. Full decriminalization as a strategy generally frames sex work as legitimate employment—similar to any other occupation—and seeks to reduce the stigma associated with it. The approach is ultimately pragmatic: Amnesty, for instance, holds that gender equality as well as economic, social, and cultural rights, including education, employment options, and social security, are ill served by maintaining the illegal status of sex work.[34] Indeed, a direct correlation appears to exist between violence against sex workers and the illegality of the work.[35] Decriminalization is fundamentally designed to reduce this harm by allowing for a greater degree of sex worker agency and control, particularly when they are mistreated or otherwise exploited by third parties.

Yet critics of full decriminalization point out that the strategy leaves in place the legality of a fundamentally unjust system, one that exacts a particularly strong cost on sex workers from BIPOC communities. According to journalist Emily Bazelon of the New York Times, women who publicly argue for decriminalization tend to be white, and women of color often find it "harder . . . to get an audience."[36] Further, such critics charge that there is no solid evidence that decriminalization will in fact make the work safer or less exploitative. In New Zealand, for instance, where sex work has been fully decriminalized for some time, harsh employment conditions and violence against sex workers appear to have persisted.[37] Some opponents of full decriminalization worry that removing legal barriers to prostitution may result in an increased societal acceptance of women's sexual objectification and of their sexuality as an appropriate object of marketplace trade. Such opponents may also worry that the strategy in fact functions to increase demand for commercial sex more generally, thus also increasing the frequency of illegal sex trafficking, particularly of children.[38]

An alternative to full decriminalization that has become more prevalent in recent decades is partial decriminalization, frequently referred to as the Nordic model. This approach, spearheaded by feminists in Sweden with the 1999 Sex Purchase Act, has now also spread to Norway and, in modified versions, to other parts of the globe (including Canada and Northern Ireland). Partial decriminalization of sex work generally targets the *demand* side of sex work, making it illegal to purchase or advertise sex, but not to sell the sexual services of one's own body. Thus, buyers, facilitators, and brothel owners can be legally punished, but sex workers themselves ordinarily cannot. The Council of Europe and various women's rights groups have promoted this model, and the Swedish government itself has touted its success by pointing to a hefty 50 percent reduction in street prostitution—that is, to levels well below neighboring Denmark, for instance.[39]

Partial decriminalization has the distinct advantage that it aims to dismantle the *institution* of commercial sex without directly attacking sex workers themselves. In this regard, it arguably adopts a less individualistic posture, targeting the exploitation engendered by the system as a whole. The basic belief underlying partial decriminalization is that *systems* of sex work are incompatible with gender equality; thus, the goal is to shrink the practice of purchase while minimizing harm (wherever possible) to sex workers themselves. The approach generally includes a specific emphasis on providing exit strategies for sex workers who want them and enhancing the social supports necessary to enable such provision. The model also rightfully attends to the connection between sex work and sex trafficking; although these practices are conceptually different, the markets quite obviously overlap, such that some studies indicate that making sex work legal also functions to expand the reach of sex trafficking.[40]

Yet partial decriminalization also has its critics. Amnesty International, for example, points out that laws prohibiting only the buying of sex still in fact "force sex workers to operate covertly in ways that compromise their safety, prohibit actions that sex workers take to maximize their safety, and serve to deny sex workers support or protection from government officials."[41] In other words, by this account, partial decriminalization not only serves to make sex work itself more difficult to carry out; it also drives sex workers even further into the shadows, forcing them to seek out remote or otherwise more dangerous venues in which to carry out their activities. Along these lines, it is noteworthy that the drop in Swedish street prostitution appears to have been accompanied by a rise in online advertising for sex.[42] Others have charged that partial decriminalization may be strong on ideology but that its claims of success are unsupported and that it has been implemented haphazardly— making it more of a "policy irritant" than an effective practical strategy.[43]

Sex workers themselves appear deeply divided about these various approaches. Even long before partial decriminalization took shape as an inter- mediate global strategy responding to the sex trade, many sex workers' rights groups favored instead the strategy of full decriminalization, accompanied by public education to end the stigma associated with commercial sex. In their view, sex work constitutes bona-fide work, and arguments that condemn it as wrong do little more than perpetuate the separation of women into "good girls" and "bad girls," "whores" and "madonnas." This position was favored by COYOTE (Call Off Your Old Tired Ethics), the first organized sex workers' movement in the United States. COYOTE was founded in 1973 by Margo St. James, an ex–sex worker and a prominent leader in organized commercial sex who died in early 2021.[44] COYOTE's stated purposes included repeal- ing existing prostitution laws; empowering sex workers to bargain with their employers; informing the public about the reality, as opposed to the various myths, of prostitution; educating to prevent the spread of HIV and other sex- ually transmitted diseases; and ending the stigma associated with women's sexuality and earning power. Today's activist sex workers often maintain a similar position, rejecting the Nordic model in favor of full decriminalization, which they interpret to be an option that better empowers sex workers and protects their autonomous choice. For example, Pye Jakobsson, a Swedish sex worker and president of the Global Network of Sex Work Projects, cri- tiques Sweden's approach specifically:

> People think the Swedish state criminalized clients, and not us, because they cared about us, but that was not the case. . . . The law is about pro- tecting society, and we're seen as a threat. . . . Women who worked on the street used to have safe spots where they would tell the client to drive. Now clients say no, because of the police. They want to go some- place else remote. How can the woman be safe there?[45]

To Jakobsson's mind, the Nordic model's effort to protect sex workers by pun- ishing only customers is both misguided and directly harmful to sex workers' ability to safely earn a living.

Partial decriminalization is not without its vociferous defenders within the sex worker community, however. Many women engaged or formerly engaged in commercial sex take umbrage with the conclusion that this approach jeopardizes their interests and safety. In fact, as Australian feminist theorist Meagan Tyler puts it, "for every 'sex worker' rights organisation that opposes the Nordic Model, there is a survivor-led organisation that advocates for it." She argues that the Nordic model should not be blamed for what in fact amounts to the intrinsic lack of safety in commercial sex, no matter the legal context: "First things first, prostitution *is* unsafe. To suggest that the Nordic Model is what makes it dangerous is disingenuous." Tyler challenges studies that claim the Nordic model harms sex worker safety, charging rather that it is the strategies of decriminalization and legalization that have done little to protect women from physical, sexual, and psychological violence and trauma. Finally, she stresses that the Nordic model should not be understood apart from its critical reliance on developing comprehensive exit strategies from the sex trade; such exit programs are essential to a successful overall approach, so that sex workers have other, better options available to them as the industry shrinks in size.[46]

Underlying Philosophical Assumptions: What Is at Stake?

Underneath these contrasting legal strategies lie some clear philosophical fault lines, and unearthing these will nudge us toward a fuller analysis of sex worker agency and well-being, as well as a concrete pathway forward. At least two connected themes are at work here: the degree of genuine human agency and free choice that is present within commercial sex, and the nature of sex work itself, including whether or not it is helpful or even accurate to understand it as "work" in the first place. Let us consider both of these in turn.[47]

Agency and Freedom of Choice

Many advocates of decriminalizing sex work embrace the view that commercial sex in its "ideal" form must be viewed as a voluntary contract. According to this view, the adult sex worker and the buyer are best understood as two autonomous persons who agree to a mutually beneficial arrangement. That is, commercially traded sex is "entered into by each individual for her or his own benefit, each striking the best bargain that she or he is able."[48] It is only when the realization of this contract is hindered—for example, by intrusive laws, dishonest police, or buyers who fail to hold up one end of the bargain—that harm results.

Such an approach necessarily maintains the essential consent of the contracting individual sex worker. An extreme form of the argument holds that sex workers, as adult women, are perfectly free human beings who choose their work from an array of options not significantly different from the options available to most persons in our society. One need not go this far, however; many sex workers simply state that they had some options and that they freely chose among those options when they decided to enter the sex trade. As one Canadian sex worker emphasizes, "Let's stop the victim shit. . . . Let's recognize that we're not crippled as women in this industry. We are capable of exercising healthy control over our own environment."[49] Indeed, women are arguably no more forced into sex work than into any other stereotypically women's profession, such as social work, nursing, or childcare provision.

According to this line of reasoning, sex work is understood primarily as the autonomous choice of an individual person. One example of this approach can be found in Amnesty International's proposal, which relies heavily upon the framework of individual consent. Even as Amnesty acknowledges that states have obligations to protect individuals from exploitation, it holds that "states must also recognize and respect the agency and capacity of adults engaged in consensual sex work."[50] Indeed, many sex workers themselves powerfully insist upon equal recognition in this regard, targeting especially feminist theorists who ignore or downplay their agency. The Canadian Organization for the Rights of Prostitutes (now known as Sex Professionals of Canada), for instance, once demanded that feminists stop their "patronizing and condescending" behavior. "We want feminists to stop pimping our ass. We want them to start listening to us. We want them to stop looking at us as victims and see us as equals."[51]

By contrast, advocates of partial decriminalization are far less likely to embrace the idea that sex workers express uncompromised agency. Rather, undergirding this model is a view of sex work not as an empowered free choice that needs to be protected and made safer, but rather as a system of exploitation that is intrinsically violent and thus merits efforts at legislative reduction. Indeed, the Swedish government itself defends the success of its approach, reframing the shortcomings of partial decriminalization as a necessary by-product of combating systems of prostitution.[52] This understanding is echoed in the words of Sarah Wynter, a former sex worker and part of the WHISPER (Women Hurt In Systems of Prostitution Engaged in Revolt) oral history project. Speaking on behalf of that organization, Wynter describes prostitution not as freely chosen work but rather as a "crime committed against women by men," socially validated by a sexual libertarian ideology. She argues that portraying commercially traded sex as a free choice euphemizes men's perceived need and right to buy and sell women's bodies for sexual use:

> We, the women of WHISPER, reject the lie that women freely choose
> prostitution from a whole array of economic alternatives that exist
> under civil equality.... We reject the lie that turning tricks is sexual
> pleasure or agency for women. We reject the lie that women can and
> do become wealthy in systems of prostitution. We reject the lie that
> women control and are empowered in systems of prostitution.

Wynter thereby maintains that, far from choosing freely, women are *enslaved*
in systems of the sex trade—that is, commercial sex is founded on enforced
sexual abuse under a system of male supremacy, which itself is built along
a continuum of coercion. Moreover, women are deeply threatened by the
inherent danger of the sex trade; as Wynter notes, "every time a prostitute
climbs into a car or walks into a hotel with a strange man ... she risks her
freedom and her very life."[53] Commercial sex is here clearly expressed as a
case primarily of women's exploitation, not of women's freedom of choice.

This view highlights the differing degrees of social power that men and
women exercise more generally: in our society, men are assumed, expected,
and even encouraged to dominate women socially. Sex work both reflects and
exacerbates this inequality. Any understanding of commercial sex that frames
it purely as a contractual arrangement between equals fails to take into account
our larger patriarchal social reality. Carole Pateman, a feminist philosopher,
argues along these lines: "Prostitution has to be rescued from ... abstract con-
tractarianism and placed in the social context of the structure of sexual relations between women and men."[54] In other words, it is wrong to overstress the
primacy of individual agency; only when socioeconomic context takes center stage will the true character of commercial sex be revealed—as violence
against women. Such a view need not deny altogether the agency of sex workers, but it does indicate that "free" choice is in many cases heavily compromised by social location.

Taking greater account of that social location means an acknowledgment
that it is not possible in our society fully to divorce power from sex; sexuality
itself is constructed within relationships of domination and subordination. In
this way, commercially traded sex should never be understood as a fully free
act. Rather, it is an act expressing women's social (including economic) subjection. "To be able to purchase a body in the market," Pateman writes, "pre-
supposes the existence of masters. Prostitution is the public recognition of
men as sexual masters; it puts submission on sale as a commodity in the market."[55] Here, economic forces buttress male domination, since women, who
earn less than men, necessarily have a greater incentive to engage in sex for
payment. Legal theorist Catharine MacKinnon sums it up with characteristic

acerbity, "If prostitution is a free choice, why are the women with the fewest choices the ones most often found doing it?"[56] According to this view, consent to prostitution is, in fact, not true consent; it is submission, enforced not as much by individuals (though it indeed may be so) as by the socioeconomic power that men exert, particularly over less economically powerful women.

A closely related argument against commercial sex—one that also explicitly attends to social context—is that it reinforces male domination by *perpetuating* systems of inequality. Laurie Shrage, another feminist philosopher, argues that prostitution both depends upon and supports cultural assumptions that oppress not just sex workers but all women:

> Because of the cultural context in which prostitution operates, it epitomizes and perpetuates pernicious patriarchal beliefs and values and, therefore, is both damaging to the women who sell sex and, as an organized social practice, to all women in our society. . . . In short, female prostitution oppresses women, not because some women who participate in it "suffer in the eyes of society" but because its organized practice testifies to and perpetuates socially hegemonic beliefs which oppress all women in many domains of their lives.[57]

According to this view, while sex for money may not be inherently oppressive, it is so in our culture, where it reinforces harmful beliefs. Among these beliefs Shrage counts the conviction that all human beings share a potent sex drive. This, she holds, is a culturally determined assumption that is used to rationalize the existence of paid sex as a sexual outlet. Further, she points out that commercial sex in practice supports the myth of the "natural" dominance of men, since it caters to the sexual needs of an almost exclusively male clientele. Some theorists go a step further, highlighting the negative impact that such an underlying belief has on interpersonal relationships between men and women more generally; for instance, Yasmeen Hassan, the global executive director of the women's rights group Equality Now, considers: "If women are sex toys you can buy, think about the impact on relationships between men and women, in marriage or otherwise."[58]

What the above arguments share is a de-emphasis on individual agency (in some cases, to the point of gainsaying sex workers' freedom of choice altogether) and a corresponding stress on context—that is, the context of patriarchal sexuality and of women's socioeconomic subordination to men. The liberal strategy of decriminalization is not necessarily disputed here, but those who stress social context to this degree generally focus on opposing the practice of commercially traded sex as well as the patriarchal relations of which it is a part. In this way, they look beyond the issue of choice to the deeper concerns involved.

Sex as Work? The Underlying Meaning of Sex

A second thematic disparity that undergirds different legal and ethical approaches to the sex trade concerns the character of sex itself, and specifically whether its commercialization constitutes a bona-fide form of work, like any other practice of paid labor. Many proponents of full decriminalization argue that sex work is no less legitimate than other contractual business arrangements. While the state may have an interest in taxing and/or regulating it, the state has no business banning it. According to this view, sexual labor is similar to other, more socially accepted forms work that may seem particularly intimate or risky—for example, psychotherapy, modeling, massage therapy, or mining work. Simply because sex work may be at times unpleasant does not de facto mean that it is immoral. As one sex worker puts it, "Having a customer fondle a breast . . . may not be pleasant, especially if he's rough, but it doesn't feel like being violated. It's part of a job, and really no different than if he touched an elbow. It's not sexual; it's *work*."[59] And if sex work is simply work, it is hard to justify why it should merit different ethical or legal responses than other occupations.

By contrast, if sex work is best understood as part of a fundamentally exploitive system of social domination that falls along lines of gender and sexuality, then it is different, conceptually speaking, from most other forms of labor—including low-paid service labor. As journalist Katha Pollitt rhetorically poses in *The Nation*, "Maybe there's a difference between a blowjob and a slice of pie—one that is occluded when all types of service work are collapsed into one."[60] Philosopher Christine Overall traces the difference to the way that sex itself is socially constructed in today's world, within the socioeconomic context of patriarchy and capitalism. She argues,

> Unlike other forms of labor mostly performed by women, prostitution is dependent both for its value and for its very existence upon the cultural construction of gender roles in terms of dominance and submission. While women are taught to render sexual services for recompense and often to regard that rendering as part of what it means to be a woman, men are encouraged to seek and expect sexual services and, indeed, to regard the acquisition of sexual services as part of what it means to be a man.[61]

Here, it is the social construction of sexuality that is problematic; that is, insofar as paid sex takes place at the intersection of patriarchy and capitalism, it is inseparable from these problematic social structures. Put differently, an understanding of sex as purely transactional implicitly strips away sexual attraction itself from sexual activity, and what remains is a unique form of entitlement that allows and even encourages (primarily) men to expect sex from (primarily) women—so long as they have the means to pay for it.

This controversy itself pushes in the direction of an even deeper query, one having to do with the nature of sexual activity and its connection, or lack thereof, to more fundamental human emotions and, relatedly, experiences of personhood. As with many defenses of anonymous hookup sex, a contractarian justification of sex work often relies on an understanding of sexual good that is essentially individualist. That is, an emphasis on the sex worker as an autonomous agent, one who knows her own best interests and enters into a free contract, draws implicitly on a conception of the individual as primary. According to this view, each individual is uniquely equipped to determine her or his own best "good"; privately chosen goods supplant any overarching sexual values. It is therefore wrong to use the public arena to impose particular sexual agendas. Of course, such an approach dovetails well with a civil libertarian emphasis on the right of the individual to control her or his own body without unreasonable interference from the state. What we are left with is a relatively thin theory of sexual good, indeed of any bodily good; determination of good is left up to each person.

Some publicly visible sex workers, however, have taken this argument a step further, promoting the view that bifurcating sex from emotional affection is not only acceptable but desirable. Embracing a certain sort of sex positivity, this approach maintains that sexual expression, like other forms of human interaction, benefits from variation and thus should not be limited by love or commitment. The Canadian Organization for the Rights of Prostitutes, for example, once asked, "Since when is sex only acceptable and valid and good sex if it's linked to love or linked to someone that they're interested in, in terms of a relationship? . . . There's an excitement that goes with a new person, a novelty. . . . Is our sexuality so one-dimensional that we have no need for other ways of expressing it?"[62] In this view, unaffiliated and impersonal sex is by no means ethically wrong, and it may even be desirable on aesthetic grounds. Significantly, sexual expression here is taken to be no different from other human interactions; that is, there is nothing intrinsic to sexual behavior that merits special treatment or requires particular ethical guidance, beyond the contract itself.

The problem with such a view, of course, is that it leaves precious little room for a shared and more substantive understanding of sex. Whether one posits that sex bears a deeper intrinsic meaning for most people (as the Christian tradition has generally held) or that sex is socially constructed along problematic lines—or both—it is difficult to escape the conclusion that, for many sex workers, sexual activity *is* connected to a profound sense of self. To wit, many sex workers describe the great lengths to which they must go in order to keep their emotions in check. Emma Marcus, for instance, writes of her unwillingness to indulge a buyer's desire for conversation and kissing during sexual intercourse: "Talking dirty . . . seemed the most compromising act of all, involving as it did my imagination as well as my body. . . . I turned my head to my side so he wouldn't try to kiss me."[63] This avoidance of personal interaction is relatively common in sex workers' accounts, as they seek to protect their sense of self in frequently dehumanizing situations. Judy Edelstein, another sex worker, describes the loss of self that sex workers too often must resist: "Mostly the job is okay. . . . [But sometimes] I think about strangers sucking my breasts. And sometimes I wonder how I can let the men do that. I wonder what there is left for me. I wonder where I am."[64] Finally, one former sex worker known only as J speaks more consciously about her feeling that sex work directly attacked her human dignity. Her moving words merit quoting at length:

> The worst part about it is that you're obliged not to sell sex only, but your humanity. That's the worst part of it: that what you're selling is your human dignity . . . in accepting the agreement—in becoming a bought person. . . . That's why it's not as easy as just saying "Prostitution is selling a service." That's why it's selling your soul and not selling a service. . . . There's a special indignity in prostitution, as if sex were dirty and men can only enjoy it with someone low. It involves a type of contempt, a kind of disdain, and a kind of a triumph over another human being. . . . You've got to have tremendous defenses. You've just gotta turn off, somehow. . . . You are selling a lot when you are being a whore. You're giving up a lot. . . . As a prostitute, you're alienated, isolated even, not only from yourself but from the rest of society because you can't talk to people about it. . . . When I was a prostitute it wasn't me somehow.[65]

It is unclear whether this experience of alienation and dehumanization is best attributed to an inherent connection between sexuality and selfhood or to a socially constructed understanding that sex work is degrading—or both. What does seem clear is that paid sexual interaction is fraught with meaning for many, though certainly not all, sex workers themselves.

Christian Theological Responses to Commercial Sex

When legal theorists, policy experts, and even sex workers themselves are so deeply divided about how to understand and address commercial sex, it is no small task for Christian ethics to do so. Yet Christian sexual ethics—and in particular an approach that seeks to articulate the normative contours of sexual flourishing *broadly* understood—can ill afford to ignore this thorniest of problems. In fact, the ethical outlines espoused in this volume do yield insight and perspective into human well-being, and specifically women's well-being, in the context of the sex trade.

Before addressing commercial sex with what I consider to be an adequate Christian and feminist response, however, it is useful to take a brief look at how the Christian tradition, including the Bible itself, has generally approached the issue. As in so many matters related to sexuality, the tradition has been quick to default to a perspective grounded in the individual *sin* of sex workers. As Rita Nakashima Brock and Susan Brooks Thistlethwaite maintain, "When Christian theologians have reflected at all on prostitution, they have made the 'prostitute' into the archetypal sinner."[66] Indeed, Christian thought too often has emphasized the ways sex workers "tempt" others as well as harm themselves and society more generally. Perhaps the clearest ecclesiastical perspective can be found in the teachings of the Catholic Church, where prostitution is categorized as an offense against chastity. The *Catechism of the Catholic Church* does label prostitution as both "gravely sinful" and a "social scourge," yet it frames the practice primarily as one of individual fault that "does injury to the dignity of the person who engages in it, reducing the person to an instrument of sexual pleasure."[67] Pope John Paul II's *Letter to Women* emphasizes certain aspects of the sociocultural context of commercial sex and yet clearly circles back to the sinful actions of sex workers themselves; in his words, the church must "condemn the widespread hedonistic and commercial culture which encourages the systematic exploitation of sexuality and corrupts even very young girls into letting their bodies be used for profit."[68] Noteworthy here is that, while men and buyers are not entirely absent from the discussion, the unfortunate weight of the judgment once again falls the women and girls who *allow* their bodies to be "used for profit."

Biblically speaking, the issue is more complex. There are, of course, many references to prostitution in the Bible. Yet there also exists a great deal of confusion and disagreement about how exactly to interpret those accounts. In the Hebrew Bible, prostitution is often referenced as a metaphor for unfaithfulness to God, as in many of the prophets; in those cases the central point of the term translated as "harlot" or "whore" (*zonot* or *zanah*) is unfaithfulness toward God, not sexual behavior per se. In the book of Joshua, the character of Rahab is often popularly understood to be a "prostitute" (*zanah*)—though scholars disagree about the designation.[69] Modern readers are likely to focus on this status as indicative of Rahab's personal shortcomings or, at a minimum, her social marginalization. And while indeed Rahab was likely to have been socially marginalized within her own town, she nevertheless bravely and creatively came to Israel's aid in seizing Jericho, outsmarting the authorities and saving her own family in the process. Many groups of organized sex workers in today's world in fact highlight this personal strength and expression of agency, viewing Rahab as fundamentally a positive figure rather than as someone to be criticized.

As for the New Testament, there are actually relatively few interactions between Jesus and people named as "prostitutes," although Jesus famously declared in Matthew 21:31 that "prostitutes" were among those who would first enter the "kingdom of God," ahead of religious authorities. The clearest example of a direct interaction between Jesus and someone often *interpreted* in this way is in the Gospel of Luke, where Jesus prominently allows a woman who was considered a "sinner" to anoint his feet with tears and perfume, subsequently forgiving her for her "sins" (Luke 7:36–50). This "anointing woman" may or may not actually have been intended in the original story to be someone engaged in sex for pay; yet, importantly, sex workers today frequently elevate her as a most visible example of Jesus's solidarity with them, as well as a validation of their worth and identity.[70] Further, because alternative, similar versions of the story identify the anointing woman as Mary of Bethany, she is frequently confused in popular understanding with Mary Magdalene; yet there is in fact no biblical support for the identification. Still, as a result of the confusion, many sex workers venerate Mary Magdalene as their advocate and an empowering example of "legitimation for their inclusion in the church, as well as self-esteem."[71] Thus a theme appears: in many instances, it seems, the biblical witness is not entirely clear about whether particular women in fact *were* engaged in the sex trade; however, sex workers themselves often find these women to be powerful figures who symbolize inclusion, and who function to validate their own fundamental worth and power.[72]

It would seem that a clear and unanimous perspective around commercial sex in the Christian tradition is somewhat elusive. On one hand, the tradition has tended toward a condemnation of sex work based upon the virtue of chastity and the overall association of prostitution with sin. On the other hand, the biblical evidence condemning sex workers is far less clear than one might assume, and even where scholars do appear to come to consensus, as in the case of Mary Magdalene, sex workers themselves may find solace in nonscholarly perspectives. What *is* clear, however, both throughout the Bible and in the tradition more broadly, is God's strong call toward justice, mercy, neighbor love, and liberation from oppression as a posture of faithfulness. Any Christian response that takes seriously the person and teachings of Jesus will be less concerned with an individualized or behavioral critique of sex workers and more concerned with the ways that sex work itself may compromise the freedom and well-being of all persons, including women and others who are societally marginalized.

A Feminist Christian Assessment of Commercial Sex

In the face of such a multiplicity of theological and non-theological interpretations about commercial sex—including, notably, a diversity of views among sex workers themselves—how might a feminist, Christian account of sexual ethics proceed? Once again, the task here is to affirm human flourishing in all its fullness—including the authentic freedom of choice of those directly involved, but also other aspects of human well-being, robustly understood. And, as with the other topics taken up in this volume, this task involves taking account of *real* persons as they exist in *real* interpersonal and societal context—and therefore in all their beauty, in all their messiness, and in all their possibility.

The concrete realities of sex workers, individual and social, must therefore take center stage. As we have seen, these include first and foremost the economic constraints and social (racist, sexist, and otherwise limiting) restrictions within which so many sex workers find themselves. The comparatively limited employment options for women, especially many BIPOC women or women who grew up in poverty, form an inescapable and critically important backdrop to commercial sex. Simply put, the economic options available to women are more constrained and generally involve lower pay than those available to men, for a variety of complex reasons. Thus, to consider persons contemplating sex work—the vast majority of whom are women—as if their choice-making calculus were akin to that of men is a serious *mis*-reading of reality.

Along similar lines, the widespread incidence of explicit violence against women—whether in the form of domestic or relational violence, stalking, assault, sexual coercion, or rape—shapes the societal milieu of commercial sex in significant ways. The violation of women's physical, psychological, and emotional well-being is simply not accorded the serious social attention that it merits, and in the absence of that social attention, it is dishonest to speak of sex work, with its accompanying astronomical rates of violence, as if it is analogous to other low-paid labor. Suspicion in this regard is vital when we consider the particularly high rates of violence directed toward trans* sex workers, since an uncritical acceptance of "free choice" exercised within this community can function to discount the larger social forces at work that structure and constrain such choice. Likewise, widespread homophobia and transphobia—often taking place within families and frequently directly bolstered by the teachings of Christianity—pave the way for an easy entry into sex work as well as for the societal marginalization of sex workers, a disproportionate number of whom identify as LGBTQ+.

Finally, the practice of sex work takes place within the odious context of institutional and systemic racism, where Black and brown bodies have been and continue to be violated with stunning regularity and often with legal sanction. Whether under the auspices of chattel slavery, Jim Crow laws, police violence, mistreatment by legal systems, the school-to-prison pipeline, or mass incarceration, the racially based violence perpetrated against BIPOC persons is also reflected in the disproportionate arrest rates of BIPOC sex workers. Further, the unfortunate and wrongheaded but nevertheless widely held belief that a sex worker "cannot be raped" takes on a particularly ominous tone in light of these more widespread racist social patterns.

Taken together, this societal backdrop reminds us that the sex trade does not exist in a vacuum. Rather, the social, historical, and economic context of commercial sex deeply impacts the shape it takes—who is involved, how they are involved, and how the impact upon them intersects with broader patterns of marginalization and oppression. As we revisit questions of agency and well-being, it is critically important to bring these analytical lenses to the task.

Sex Worker Agency, Revisited

Within these contexts, describing sex work as a perfectly free choice is more than simply painting an incomplete or naïve portrait; it assumes a certain economic, social, and racial privilege that belies the concrete reality of many or even most sex workers themselves. Likewise, theories that narrowly focus on individual *rights* are insufficient, for they fail to critique economic, gender, sexual, family, legal, and racial structures that intersect with (and exacerbate) the *institution* of commercial sex. Such approaches ultimately rely on a constricted definition of the self, divorced from social context and mischaracterized as a fully empowered and relatively free-floating choice-maker. It is not the case that sex workers have no agency; rather, sex workers enjoy a form of agency uniquely shaped by the intersection of *sex* with these various forms of personal, institutional, and social oppression that characterize their world. Hence *choice* should be understood not as an assumed, abstract baseline quality exercised by individuals but rather as falling along a spectrum and deeply impacted by patriarchy, racism, classism, transphobia, and heterosexism.

I hasten to add, however, that even when the decision to engage in commercial sex is better understood as a survival strategy rather than a full-hearted choice, such a decision nevertheless represents and expresses a vital form of human agency. That is, even as they are acted *upon*, objectified and victimized by others, sex workers are, simultaneously, *actors*, exercising genuine agency in resilient fashion—albeit in ways that may fail to conform to what broader society deems moral or even acceptable. One sex-industry worker, a stripper who works in Boston's Combat Zone, illustrates well the courage of survival that exemplifies this agency: "Beyond meeting the basic necessities for food, clothing and shelter, working in the Combat Zone is the only way [sex workers] can afford the symbols of success that society has dangled in front of them all of their lives. Compared to the alternatives—slinging hamburgers for minimum wage, assembly-line drudgery, or trying to subsist on paltry government subsidies—putting up with the groping hands of a few drunk men looks pretty good."[73] Such analysis implies that sex-industry work (including sex for pay) is neither an act of complete freedom nor one of complete slavery. Rather, in commercial sex, genuine personal agency confronts social limitation, and sex workers must make difficult choices that most people never face or understand.

The task before Christian ethics, then, is to affirm and enable not simply sex worker agency but the *fullness* of that agency. This includes taking seriously their voices and their needs, thus refusing to classify them solely as victims. Meagan Tyler defends a qualified understanding of sex workers' agency; she argues, "When anyone practicing radical politics points out that free choice is a fairy tale, and that all our actions are constrained within certain material conditions, this does not equate to saying that we are all infantilized, little drones unable to make decisions for ourselves. It only means we are not all floating around in a cultural vacuum making decisions completely unaffected by structural issues like systemic economic inequality, racism and sexism."[74] Rather than highlighting the ways sex workers fail to incarnate some individualistic, abstract version of free choice, we do better to move in a more realistic direction, one that centers the courage, resourcefulness, and resiliency that sex workers express from within their own challenging social location. These virtues are themselves worthy of enormous respect and affirmation— even in the context of simultaneously critiquing the *institution* of sex work.

Yet an honest accounting of the fullness of sex worker agency will go beyond simply affirming their resiliency and survival skills; it will also critique any model of work that frames humanizing work as merely a matter of individual consent to a paid transaction. Here, Catholic social teaching offers a particularly sharp corrective to a typically "thin" Western liberal understanding of labor. Rather than framing legitimate labor as simply a matter of an agreed-upon transaction, Catholic social teaching has long understood labor itself to be grounded fundamentally in the dignity of the worker. That is, work is a means for the individual to both share and participate in the common good, a realization of human dignity within the broader societal context. The measure of good work is not its productivity per se but rather the subjective dignity of the worker. As Pope John Paul II articulated in *Laborem Exercens*, "Each sort [of work] is judged above all by *the measure of the dignity* of the subject of work, that is to say the person, *the individual who carries it out*."[75] Economic arrangements must ultimately affirm worker dignity and conform to the common good; thus the basic well-being of workers supersedes the terms of any given transaction if those terms result in unjust arrangements. A living wage (for the well-being of self and family) and a dignified livelihood are intrinsic to this vision of work, and, importantly, labor unions are understood as a valid tool to help achieve this vision of human dignity and the common good.

The question then becomes whether or not *sex* work can support and affirm the human dignity of the sex worker as an expression of human agency—especially given the racist, sexist, classist, transphobic, and heterosexist realities in which sex work is embedded and the compromised nature of consent upon which it relies. There exists no simple answer to that question; even as some sex workers insist that their work represents a positive, life-affirming, and dignified choice, others, as we have seen, flatly deny that characterization and instead understand commercial sex to be more a matter of exploitation. What is clear, however—especially when viewing sex work in the context of other forms of employment—is that sex work understood *as work* is far more physically dangerous, psychologically fragmenting, and emotionally challenging than nearly any other form of labor. That is, it threatens embodied well-being in a way that surpasses most human activities. This alone should cause us to be skeptical about its potential as a form of work that safeguards human dignity. The mere fact that sex workers desiring to leave the sex trade ordinarily require a carefully considered exit strategy to do so should serve as a sobering reminder that the analogy between sex work and other forms of work is at best imperfect, and at worst misguided and harmful.

In navigating this divide, then, a Christian ethical approach must draw upon its own most basic insight that erotic encounter amounts to *more* than simply a matter of consensual transaction, whether paid or not. By contrast, erotic encounter potentially connects to the self in the various deeper ways described in this volume. A feminist Christian account indeed must challenge, on a personal and societal level, harmful stereotypes that identify women's sexual virtue with chastity. However, we must also avoid too quickly trading in one stereotype (i.e., purity or even chastity as an ideal) for another that may be equally harmful (for instance, sexual libertinism). Instead—and as I argue throughout this volume—a feminist Christian vision of sexual flourishing must take the power of human sexuality seriously without retreating to harmful ideals that function practically to fence in women's behavior. As with other matters, this includes attending to the importance of the body in the experience of selfhood and personal identity—with a particular focus on mutuality and equal regard as well as emotional integrity and relational intimacy. In other words, even as we seek to affirm the many ways in which sex workers rightfully exercise their agency, this should not cause us to normalize commercial sex in such a way that we lose sight of the challenges it poses to a more robust account of human dignity.

Sex Worker Well-Being, Broadly Construed

Christianity's affirmation of a connection between the body and the deeper aspects of human personality serves as an important source of insight into what too often proves to be dehumanizing about commercial sex. Part of what it means to be human is to live as an *embodied* self, that is, a self whose body is not incidental to what gives life meaning or purpose—and thus whose body imposes an implicit obligation upon others not to exploit or disregard its well-being. If sex were absolutely no different from other activities, then sexual violence would be no different from battery. But we know that generally it is so, experientially speaking, for most persons who find themselves objectified by sexual violence. How much of this "felt difference" is due to a wrongheaded social construction of sexuality and how much to the deeper, more intrinsic meaning of sex that Christianity affirms is, finally, an unanswerable question. Regardless, it is incumbent upon Christians concerned with genuine human flourishing to seek out ways of amplifying the well-being of sex workers beyond simple questions about free choice and agency.

One of the clearest ways commercial sex contradicts the norms of sexual flourishing espoused in this volume lies in the near-impossibility of mutuality and equal regard as components of paid sex. The commercialized trading of sex—at least in the way it is practiced in the vast majority of cases—thrives on power differentials. In other words, commercial sex too often both depends upon and reinforces fundamentally inegalitarian or patriarchal (even misogynistic) paradigms and stereotypes. As we have seen more generally in contemporary US society, women tend to be sexually socialized to understand

themselves as passive or even dominated, and men, by contrast, are socialized to assume a more sexually aggressive posture. These binary gendered
patterns show up powerfully in sex work, which generally exploits the stereotypes for economic purpose. Thus, as Christian scholars Rita Nakashima
Brock and Susan Brooks Thistlethwaite point out, "much of what passes for
transgressive sex—for example, pornography, rape, sadomasochism, and
prostitution—may rely on socially entrenched assumptions about hierarchical power and puritanical notions of sexuality for their power to shock or
stimulate. . . . Sex, in a variety of forms, is used far more often to reinforce
structures of power and dominance than to undermine them."[76] In this light,
what might otherwise be defended as a form of "sex positivity" instead functions to mask the normalized objectification of, and even violence toward, sex
workers. According to investigative journalist Leslie Bennetts, for instance,
buyers often see their payment as purchasing the right to degrade and assault
sex workers. As one interviewed sex buyer put it, "You get to treat a ho like
a ho. . . . You can find a ho for any type of need—slapping, choking, aggressive sex beyond what your girlfriend will do."[77] Such a posture of domination
squarely contradicts the dignity of the sex worker; her dignity is subsumed
into the monetary nature of the transaction.

To be sure, in certain cases a sex worker may in fact feel *more* rather than
less powerful in relation to a sex buyer. That is, at times, sex workers appear to
take pleasure in the sense that their sexual attractiveness affords them a measure of dominance over the buyer. As one former sex worker explains, "Being
sexually desired was the fix I needed to feel in control, to feel powerful."[78] In
this case as well, arguably, the value of equality is not well served. In other
words, to use Kantian language, one or the other participant is in danger of
becoming a mere means to the other's ends, valued only in relation to the
sense of domination and control conferred upon the more powerful party. The
empowerment of women is a vital concern, both from feminist and Christian
standpoints; however, empowerment should always serve the larger goal of
creating humanizing relationships marked by mutuality and equal regard. Our
status as dignified persons worthy of respect is a shared status. Insofar as commercialized sex denies this status, it runs counter to human well-being.

Framed more positively, genuine mutuality and equal regard call for a
common respect and decisional authority among participants that is nearly
unheard of in most forms of commercial sex. Even the monetizing of the
exchange itself undermines this, since whatever mutual exchange takes place
entails values (i.e., sexual activity and money) that are vastly disparate in kind.
Further, the anonymity that accompanies the vast majority of commercially
traded sex renders genuine mutuality extraordinarily difficult; most sex

workers and buyers simply do not develop the sorts of longer-term connection that makes way for and encourages a reciprocal exchange of desire or emotion. In fact, only rarely is this sort of mutual exchange present at all in sex work; the sex worker's feelings, emotions, wants, and needs are almost always subordinated to those of the purchaser. Whether this baseline non-mutuality would theoretically be different under more egalitarian, non-patriarchal, and perhaps non-capitalist social conditions is not entirely clear. What is clear, however, is that the present realities of commercial sex, so deeply characterized by personal and social patterns of domination and submission, simply do not conduce to patterns of mutuality and equal regard, individually or socially.

Neither do they conduce to relational intimacy. The deep and authentic connection between persons that is so central to a Christian understanding of sex is not easily achieved when sex becomes monetized. As Brock and Thistlethwaite put it, "Sex for money is business; intimacy is not part of the transaction."[79] Moreover, the vulnerability that is so central to more profound forms of human flourishing—that is, love, emotional health, tenderness, and wholeness—is elusive in most forms of sex work. Instead, commercial sex is generally typified by an anonymity and a spirit of concealment that run counter to genuine intimacy and preclude the development of trust over time. While it is true that some sex workers *do* build up trust and a degree of intimacy with long-term buyers, this is hardly the norm of the industry. More commonly, sex workers necessarily develop a thoroughly impersonal attitude toward their work, one that stands in marked contrast with the contours of relational intimacy.

Closely related to relational intimacy is the norm of emotional integrity. Again, this norm insists that human sexuality is most life-giving when it is well integrated with our personal narratives and relationships. Integrity hints at wholeness, completeness, and a self-awareness that encourages the interlacing of one's sexual experiences with one's larger life story and value system. Emotional integrity in the realm of sex calls forth a willingness to live one's sexual life in a wholehearted fashion, to understand one's sexual choice-making as deeply connected to one's dreams, hopes, and fundamental values.

As we have seen, commercial sex makes this difficult. Insofar as sex work divorces sex from one's larger personality and sense of relationship, it violates one's integrity as a whole person. Sex workers frequently engage in dissociation and detachment as survival strategies—for example, by assuming false names or engaging in substance abuse while working—as a means of numbing or perhaps bifurcating their "real" identities from their identities within the sex trade. Moreover, this lack of personal integration may have a significant long-term impact on sex workers' relational capacities. Many former sex workers, as we have seen, find it difficult to maintain healthy and trusting intimate relationships even after they leave the life. The former sex worker J, quoted earlier, also writes, "I just can't stand it when people touch me. . . . I'm getting so I hate men. I'm getting so that I avoid men. What I am is I'm becoming aware of how much I always hated it. And I know now how it has ruined my relationships with men. . . . I'm becoming aware of how the whole experience just freaked me out."[80] Here it is clear that the prevalent sexual patterns of commercial sex can have devastating relational implications.

Taken together, these deeper relational, psychological, and emotional aspects of sex-worker well-being function symbiotically within a robust account of human agency. No person is free who is alienated from others and denied meaningful relationships. Rather, honest, just, and caring relationships foster and enhance our freedom, allowing us to live and choose well. They also help pave the way for more humanizing social patterns characterized by mutual respect and care.

Yet even as we affirm this robust set of sexual norms, we must remain deeply cognizant of the unquestionable challenges faced by sex workers in the real world today. Hence, this final and brief turn to concrete policy strategies must reflect both a utopian vision of women's (and other sex workers') agency and holistic well-being *and* a relentlessly practical commitment to reduce the harms that have come to characterize so acutely the lives of persons engaged in commercial sex.

Policy Strategies: A Way Forward

It should be apparent from this chapter that continuing with the present US strategy of simply prohibiting and criminalizing commercial sex is inadequate. Such an approach serves to disempower and endanger sex workers further, while doing next to nothing to address the cultural and socioeconomic challenges that give rise to the sex trade in the first place. However, legally speaking, it is not entirely clear which is the most effective way forward. Fully decriminalizing sex work, as organizations such as Amnesty International have proposed, may be likely to result in generally safer working environments for sex workers—though exactly how much safer is a source of some dispute, as we have seen. Criminalization deprives sex workers of meaningful control over their livelihood and makes it difficult for them to access law enforcement and other social services without risking disrespect, imprisonment, or even abuse at the hands of those tasked with helping them. Moreover, decriminalization, minimally, would frustrate buyers, facilitators, and even those law enforcement officials who are currently able to exploit sex workers more effectively as a direct result of sex work's shadowy legal status. It also would free sex workers openly to organize themselves, to seek improved working conditions, and to avail themselves safely of legal aid and social services.

Yet full decriminalization itself leaves in place the basic system of commercial sex, and, as I have argued, that system sinks its roots into highly problematic socioeconomic patterns and cultural expectations—patterns and expectations that harm sex workers as well as women more generally. The violence that is so emblematic of the sex trade is extremely unlikely to disappear under a policy of full decriminalization; in fact, it may even find new sources of strength as third-party beneficiaries operate with newfound legal freedom and protections. Further, the conceptual line between sex work and fully illegal sex trafficking is far from a thick one, and, as noted, there is some evidence that decriminalizing the former can in fact bolster the latter. Even in the cases in which a sex worker does enter the sex trade with a high degree of personal agency, it is clear that psychosocial factors (for example, emotional dependency upon a facilitator) as well as poor economic alternatives may compromise the ongoing nature of that choice. In fact, sex workers who *truly* and *ongoingly* choose to stay in the life appear to compose a small minority. Thus, the approach of full decriminalization is inadequate insofar as it leaves in place the various socioeconomic systems and dynamics (including racism and sexism) that function to compromise sex worker choice. Full decriminalization by itself will do little to attend to those larger systems and dynamics, nor will it foster long-term social patterns that bolster women's personal or social well-being.

By contrast, partial decriminalization (the Nordic solution)—by making illegal the purchase of sex but not the sale of one's own sexual services—aims to capture some of the advantages of full decriminalization while avoiding some of the pitfalls. As we have seen, the degree to which this model has achieved its goals is unclear. While some (including the government of Sweden) claim substantial success, others challenge that characterization, arguing instead that partial decriminalization simply forces sex workers further into the shadows to carry out their work. It is beyond the scope of this chapter to render a conclusion about this controversy, and, at a minimum, more complete empirical evidence would be needed in order to do so in a meaningful way. It is important to note, however, that in spite of its flaws, partial decriminalization does have the advantage of reducing the *appeal* of sex work while also relieving the legal burden currently placed too often upon the shoulders of sex workers themselves. Moreover, the Nordic model's explicit promotion of socially supported exit strategies for sex workers points in the direction of a more robust and holistic solution than full decriminalization can offer.

Legal strategies, however, are a rather blunt instrument to solve such a complex social problem, and decriminalizing sex work—whether fully or partially—is certainly not an end in itself. Rather, an ethical approach concerned to amplify sex worker agency and well-being while also attending to the common good of society more generally must propose other tactics, tactics that move the debate beyond the territory of the law. Instead, we must turn to the realm of support services, employment and housing policies, and educational campaigns that explicitly promote well-being while also addressing more effectively the root causes of commercial sex. Any approach that normalizes sex work—for instance, by equating it to other, less oppressive forms of labor—runs the risk of diverting attention away from the exploitation and harm that so many sex workers endure, while simultaneously diminishing the political will to expand more humanizing forms of work for women, LGBTQ+, and other socially vulnerable people. Also problematic, however, is an approach that denies sex workers their income without aggressively bolstering the social safety net necessary for unemployed sex workers to thrive. The question finally comes down to this: How can we maximize sex workers' personal agency and well-being while also seeking more humanizing relational and social patterns for them, and for all people?

It is not necessary to defend the moral licitness of systems of commercial sex in order to insist upon strategies that allow those who engage in sex work to do so safely. Thus, an adequate approach will necessarily involve greater crackdowns on violence perpetrated by facilitators, buyers, and police. But it will also involve a dramatic expansion of social services designed to aid and empower sex workers, including condom distribution, addiction services, and drop-in support centers. Those who work to provide legal, social, and law enforcement support on behalf of sex workers must be alert to and adequately trained about the long-term effects of trauma, vulnerability, and fear; the abuse of drugs within sex work; and the lingering consequences of childhood or other domestic abuse upon sex workers' well-being. Indeed, according to Rachel Lloyd, founder of nationally renowned Girls' Educational and Mentoring Services, society's emphasis must be squarely placed upon reforms like these—reforms that actually benefit girls and women—and not upon increasing legal penalties for men.[81]

Employment, childcare, and affordable housing policies must also be recognized for their connection to the socioeconomic realities that drive so many women into sex work in the first place. Persistent wage disparities between women and men as well as the erosion of labor laws that protect a living wage for all workers doubtless contribute to the appeal of sex work for women (or anyone) with few other options. The widespread lack of affordable housing and childcare, too, pave the way for economic choices that might not otherwise be necessary. In other words, social and economic interventions that strengthen the social safety net and better ensure a baseline level of well-being for *all* persons would go a long way toward amplifying the choices available to those who currently perceive sex work as their best available option. Further, these interventions would allow sex workers better to guard and protect the well-being of family members, especially children, who may otherwise be physically or psychologically at risk. Finally, an imperative part of any social proposal for change must be a robust and comprehensive exit strategy, including job retraining, for sex workers seeking to leave the sex trade.

A systemic approach to commercial sex will not stop with ramping up social services and overhauling employment policies, however. To truly address the complex dimensions as well as the root causes of sex work, we must take steps in personal, social, and, for Christians, ecclesial settings—steps to fortify the agency and confidence of women, girls, and especially trans* and other LGBTQ+ persons. This entails the development of self-esteem and relationship training for all young persons, including robust, ongoing educational campaigns to combat domestic, dating, and relational violence. Serious and sustained attention to child abuse, *especially* (but not exclusively) within ecclesiastical settings, is a critical element of preventing the dysfunctional cycles that too often lead young persons into commercial sex. Schools, social organizations, and churches must fund broad educational programs to empower adults to parent their children in non-abusive, non-homophobic, and non-transphobic fashion. Churches also must reject models of sex education that play upon gendered stereotypes of purity or chastity or that erase LGBTQ+ forms of sexual experience while failing to promote mutuality and justice in sexual relationships. Rather, churches as well as society more broadly must challenge—in education, advertising, policy, and doctrine—constructions of masculinity that inadvertently promote sexual entitlement and dominance and constructions of femininity that encourage helplessness and dependency. Anti–toxic masculinity training for boys and men, including within law enforcement settings and as a required element of the sentencing of buyers, is an imperative element of long-term, meaningful change.

Conclusion

It is tricky indeed to support and respect sex workers while highlighting injustices intrinsic to the activities in which they engage. The interventions outlined in this chapter aim to promote women's agency and well-being—and indeed the agency and well-being of all persons—while simultaneously highlighting how systems of commercial sex too often degrade and humiliate those exploited within them. It is time for Christian ethical formulas to stop condemning sex work from a posture that emphasizes sin and chastity and instead to start accentuating justice, authentic agency, and well-being in the service of human flourishing. It is also time for society to cease to consider consent alone as the only meaningful criterion to describe ethical sex, thereby enabling the persistent exploitation of sex workers. Rather than continuing to stigmatize sex work and alienate sex workers on the one hand or to falsely claim that sex workers exercise perfectly free choice on the other, Christian ethics must instead bring to the table a commitment to support the dignity and equal worth of all persons, including sex workers, and to labor for their empowerment in such a way that they may both flourish and become authentically and meaningfully free.

Notes

1. I focus in this chapter primarily on the sex trade as it exists in the United States and, to a lesser extent, other Western societies. Obviously, this is a limited lens. However the cultural assumptions of the United States—emphasizing, for instance, individual freedom of choice—lend themselves in a particular way to the quandaries engaged here regarding how best to foster the well-being of women while also honoring a robust version of their agency.
2. Phillis Luman Metal, "Bohemia Ho . . . Ho Ho Ho," in Delacoste and Alexander, *Sex Work*, 85–87.
3. Chris Hall, "Is One of the Most-Cited Statistics about Sex Work Wrong?" *The Atlantic*, September 5, 2014, https://www.theatlantic.com/business/archive/2014/09/is-one-of -the-most-cited-statistics-about-sex-work-wrong/379662/.
4. Brock and Thistlethwaite, *Casting Stones*, 181.
5. Farley, "Prostitution and the Invisibility of Harm."
6. Brock and Thistlethwaite, *Casting Stones*, 152.
7. Amnesty International, *Amnesty International Policy on State Obligations*, citing Victoria L. Hounsfield et al., "Transgender People Attending Sydney Sexual Health Services over a 16 Year Period," *Sex Health* 4, no. 3 (August 23, 2007); and citing Jaime M. Grant, Lisa A. Mottet, and Justin Tanis, *Injustice at Every Turn: A Report of the National Transgender Discrimination Survey* (Washington, DC: National Center for Transgender Equality and National Gay and Lesbian Task Force, 2011).
8. Jasmine Garsd, "Should Sex Work Be Decriminalized? Some Activists Say It's Time," *National Public Radio*, March 22, 2019, https://www.npr.org/2019/03/22/705354179 /should-sex-work-be-decriminalized-some-activists-say-its-time.
9. Amnesty International, *Explanatory Note on Amnesty International's Policy*, citing UNAIDS, *The Gap Report* (Geneva, Switzerland: UNAIDS, 2014).
10. Dworkin, "Prostitution and Male Supremacy," 4.

11. Moloney, "Prostitution Legislation," 17. See also Brock and Thistlethwaite, *Casting Stones*, 174; and Farley, "Prostitution and the Invisibility of Harm."
12. Farley et al., "Comparing Sex Buyers."
13. Leslie Bennetts, "The John Next Door," *Newsweek*, July 25, 2011, 60–63, at 61.
14. Cunningham and Shah, "Decriminalizing Indoor Prostitution," 1683, citing "General Social Surveys (1992–2010)," National Opinion Research Center, dataset; and Gary Langer, Cheryl Arnedt, and Dalia Sussman, "Primetime Live Poll: American Sex Survey," *ABC News*, August 16, 2007, https://abcnews.go.com/Primetime/News/story?id=156921.
15. Bennetts, "The John Next Door," 61.
16. Garsd, "Should Sex Work Be Decriminalized?" See also Cunningham and Shah, "Decriminalizing Indoor Prostitution," 1683.
17. Potterat et al., "Mortality in a Long-Term Open Cohort."
18. Brewer et al., "Extent, Trends, and Perpetrators," 1101.
19. Brewer et al., 1101. See also Rachel West, "U.S. PROStitutes Collective," in Delacoste and Alexander, *Sex Work*, 279–89, at 287.
20. Shively et al., *A National Overview*.
21. Jeal and Salisbury, "A Health Needs Assessment."
22. Linda, "Saved by Horses," in Norma and Tankard Reist, *Prostitution Narratives*, 31–42; and Jacqueline Gwynn, "I Was a Pimp," in Norma and Tankard Reist, *Prostitution Narratives*, 197–206.
23. Karen, "Police as Pimps," in Delacoste and Alexander, *Sex Work*, 58; Gloria Lockett, "What Happens When You Are Arrested," in Delacoste and Alexander, *Sex Work*, 39–40; and West, "U.S. PROStitutes Collective," 283.
24. Bennetts, "The John Next Door," 63.
25. Brents and Hausbeck, "Violence and Legalized Brothel Prostitution."
26. Farley et al., "Prostitution in Five Countries," 405. See also Dempsey, "Sex Trafficking and Worker Justice," 81
27. Gorry et al., "Selling Your Self?," 495.
28. Gorry et al., 496.
29. Gwynn, "I Was a Pimp," 203.
30. Linda, "Saved by Horses," 35.
31. Jade, "The Fake You," in Norma and Tankard Reist, *Prostitution Narratives*, 43–49, at 48. See also Linda, "Saved by Horses," 41.
32. Jade, "The Fake You," 46.
33. Amnesty International, *Amnesty International Policy on State Obligations*; Human Rights Watch, "Why Sex Work Should Be Decriminalized"; and World Health Organization, *HIV Prevention, Diagnosis, Treatment and Care*.
34. Amnesty International, *Amnesty International Policy on State Obligations*. Amnesty's position has been criticized by many, including some who charge that its policies and positions in this regard have been shaped by specific individuals who have benefited personally from the illegal exploitation and trafficking of others involved in sex work. See, for example, Kat Banyard, "Why Is a Pimp Helping to Shape Amnesty's Sex Trade Policy?," *The Guardian*, October 22, 2015, https://www.theguardian.com/commentisfree/2015/oct/22/pimp-amnesty-prostitution-policy-sex-trade-decriminalise-brothel-keepers.
35. Brock and Thistlethwaite, *Casting Stones*, 145; and Brents and Hausbeck, "Violence and Legalized Brothel Prostitution," 270–95.

36. Emily Bazelon, "Oppression or Profession?" *New York Times Magazine*, March 8, 2016, 34–43 and 55–57, at 38.
37. Moloney, "Prostitution Legislation," 12–21.
38. Meagan Tyler, "Ten Myths about Prostitution, Trafficking and the Nordic Model," in Norma and Tankard Reist, *Prostitution Narratives*, 213–25, at 219; and Kristof and WuDunn, *Half the Sky*, 26 and 31–32.
39. Bazelon, "Oppression or Profession?," 40.
40. Tyler, "Ten Myths."
41. Amnesty International, *Amnesty International Policy on State Obligations*.
42. David Crouch, "Swedish Prostitution Law Targets Buyers, but Some Say It Hurts Sellers," *New York Times*, March 14, 2015, https://www.nytimes.com/2015/03/15/world/swedish-prostitution-law-targets-buyers-but-some-say-it-hurts-sellers.html; and Bazelon, "Oppression or Profession?," 40.
43. Kingston and Thomas, "No Model in Practice," 435.
44. COYOTE itself no longer exists, though many of its functions were later absorbed into the National Task Force on Prostitution, and the organization itself transitioned into St. James Infirmary, a peer-run health and safety clinic for sex workers in San Francisco.
45. Bazelon, "Oppression or Profession?," 40.
46. Tyler, "Ten Myths," 217 and 220–21.
47. Here I draw partially upon my earlier, though differently organized, analysis of these themes. See Peterson-Iyer, "Prostitution."
48. Jaggar, "Prostitution," 262.
49. Bell, *Good Girls, Bad Girls*, 181.
50. Amnesty International, *Amnesty International Policy on State Obligations*.
51. Bell, *Good Girls, Bad Girls*, 212. See also Margo St. James, "The Reclamation of Whores," in Bell, *Good Girls, Bad Girls*, 81–87.
52. Bazelon, "Oppression or Profession?," 40–41.
53. Sarah Wynter, "Whisper: Women Hurt in Systems of Prostitution Engaged in Revolt," in Delacoste and Alexander, *Sex Work*, 266–70, 269.
54. Pateman, "Defending Prostitution," 563.
55. Pateman, 564.
56. MacKinnon, "Prostitution and Civil Rights," 28.
57. Shrage, "Should Feminists Oppose Prostitution?," 352.
58. Bazelon, "Oppression or Profession?," 38.
59. Peggy Morgan, "Living on the Edge," in Delacoste and Alexander, *Sex Work*, 21–28, at 25.
60. Katha Pollitt, "Why Do So Many Leftists Want Sex Work to Be the New Normal?," *The Nation*, April 2, 2014.
61. Overall, "What's Wrong with Prostitution?"
62. Bell, *Good Girls, Bad Girls*, 206. Margo St. James, a now-deceased leader in the sex worker unionization movement, famously echoed this depersonalized understanding of sex: "Why should the women be considered deviant because they're separating sex and love? I think separating sex and love is a good thing personally. I think romance may be oppressive. . . . I've always thought that whores were the only emancipated women. We are the only ones who have the absolute right to fuck as many men as men fuck women." St. James, "The Reclamation of Whores," 83–84.
63. Emma Marcus, "Hong Kong Massage," in Delacoste and Alexander, *Sex Work*, 43–49, at 48.

64. Judy Edelstein, "In the Massage Parlor," in Delacoste and Alexander, *Sex Work*, 62–69, at 63.

65. Millett, "Prostitution," 104, 106, 108, 116, and 119.

66. Brock and Thistlethwaite, *Casting Stones*, 236.

67. *Catechism of the Catholic Church*, 2355.

68. John Paul II, *Letter of Pope John Paul II to Women*, 5.

69. For an excellent discussion of the disagreements surrounding the figure of Rahab, see Ipsen, *Sex Working and the Bible*, chapter 3.

70. Ipsen, 142.

71. Ipsen, 24.

72. See especially Ipsen, 122–24.

73. Morgan, "Living on the Edge," 24.

74. Tyler, "Ten Myths," 215.

75. John Paul II, *Laborem Exercens*, 6, italics in original.

76. Brock and Thistlethwaite, *Casting Stones*, 157.

77. Bennetts, "The John Next Door," 62.

78. Judy Helfand, "Silence Again," in Delacoste and Alexander, *Sex Work*, 99–103, at 101. Notably, this same author goes on to describe this sense of power in retrospect as a false one, ultimately preventing her from recognizing her oppression.

79. Brock and Thistlethwaite, *Casting Stones*, 186.

80. Millett, "Prostitution," 66.

81. Bazelon, "Oppression or Profession?," 18.

CHAPTER SIX

Sex Trafficking, Rescue Narratives, and the Challenge of Solidarity

As we saw in chapter 5, the difficult question of what constitutes genuine free-dom of choice lies at the heart of how to interpret commercial sex, including how to respond to it in a way that amplifies human flourishing and women's well-being, broadly construed. When we move more specifically into the realm of sex trafficking, questions of freedom become even more compli-cated; for, unlike sex work by choice—even choice that may be limited or imperfect—sex trafficking represents a deprivation of agency of a different magnitude. A sex-trafficked person's capacity for self-determination may be compromised by physical or psychic force from a third-party intermediary (a facilitator, boyfriend, or even a family member), or because the so-called sex worker is actually a minor, or both.[1] Either way, the stage is set for a profound denial of agency by severe economic and social precarity, virtually driving vulnerable persons into the hands of traffickers. Indeed, sex trafficking rep-resents one of the most damaging and inhumane sexual violations a person can experience.

Twenty years ago, public consciousness about sex trafficking was almost nonexistent, and sex-trafficked persons themselves were often dismissed as "prostitutes." The Polaris Project—one of the most widely respected anti-trafficking organizations in the United States—was founded in 2002 by two Brown University graduates when they discovered so little awareness of and resources to help fight modern-day slavery, including not only sex trafficking but also other forms of human trafficking.[2] Since the passage of the Traffick-ing Victims Protection Act in 2000, US attention on the topic has steadily grown to the point of a virtual explosion of interest today. In 2007, the US Senate designated January 11 as National Human Trafficking Awareness Day, and in 2011 then president Barack Obama declared January as National Slav-ery and Human Trafficking Prevention Month.

Unsurprisingly, churches and parachurch organizations, both Protestant and Roman Catholic, have taken a keen interest in the topic, and in many cases they are on the forefront of efforts to fight human trafficking. A cursory internet search reveals scores of religious organizations seeking to raise awareness about the practice. From the evangelical Protestant–supported International Justice Mission to Pope Francis's 2014 pledge (and subsequent advocacy) alongside other world religious leaders, and from Roman Catholic diocesan task forces across the country to the local and national arms of various mainline Protestant denominations, Christians of diverse stripes have come to recognize the importance of addressing human trafficking and the moral mandate to work for its end. Disproportionately visible among these efforts has been the attention given to *sex* trafficking as opposed to other forms of human trafficking.

Often, responses to sex trafficking, including and perhaps especially Christian responses, make heavy use of the paradigm of *rescue*: that is, the urgent need to rescue the victims of human trafficking from those who imprison and exploit them. At times drawing upon Christian narratives regarding the "liberation of the oppressed," Christians seek to encourage other Christians —often those in economically privileged and stable circumstances—to take action to become modern-day "emancipators" or "abolitionists." In the face of the profound suffering associated with human sex trafficking, these theological themes are powerfully motivating.

Yet in spite of their ability to inspire, rescue-identified frameworks are also problematic, especially when taken in isolation. Well intentioned though they may be, such frameworks are excessively individualistic, deny authentic human agency, and perpetuate a top-down, dichotomous, and overly simplistic understanding of the relationship between "victims" who are trafficked and those who wish to "free" them. Further, they inadvertently draw upon an older paradigm of sexual ethics that too closely aligns sexual virtue with discrete "right" sexual choices, taken in a social vacuum. This is particularly knotty when examined through a feminist lens seeking to promote the understanding of women as embodied, relational subjects of their own liberation rather than as objects of others' actions.

The victimization of trafficked persons, while real, does not tell the whole story. Well-meaning Christians who envision an adequate response as the need to swoop in and rescue poor, helpless girls and women misconstrue the problem and do little to facilitate long-term solutions. In fact, they arguably make the matter even worse by subtly encouraging an understanding of trafficking victims (primarily girls and women) as lacking in full and complex humanity and relational moral agency, as well as by failing adequately to highlight the structural socioeconomic and cultural contributors to the explosion of human trafficking worldwide.

The feminist Christian lens embraced throughout this book seeks a different angle and yields more promising results. Scrutinizing sex trafficking through a feminist Christian anthropology mandates that we understand sex-trafficked persons not as victims but rather both as genuine sexual agents, possessing intrinsic dignity and self-determination, and as multifaceted persons in all their relational complexity. Thus, justice for sex-trafficked persons becomes a matter not of simple rescue nor even of liberation but rather of collaborative restoration to a more honest and complete version of moral agency. Moreover, a heightened attention to social context as a core part of promoting human flourishing necessitates an examination of the economic and gender injustices that lie at the foundation of sex trafficking. That is, contextualizing and historicizing the lives of trafficked persons is an integral part of treating them justly.

Understanding women as subjects of their own liberation rather than objects of others' actions, a feminist appraisal must therefore reject a simple rescue methodology and instead promote a framework centered on positive agency, characterized not only by freedom but also focused particularly upon the norm of mutuality—individually and, as it manifests socially, as solidarity. Mutuality, as I describe it throughout this book, lies at the heart of human identity; our humanness is defined not only by our autonomy but by the shared quality of our human dignity and by our capacity to be profoundly changed by each other. As I have developed it, this is the element of sexual flourishing that perhaps most incisively illuminates the controversies and questions embedded in sex trafficking. Further, solidarity, defined by Pope John Paul II as "a firm and persevering determination to commit oneself to the common good," represents a social manifestation of mutuality and inspires a vision of our global interconnectedness.[3] Together, these norms move us away from a one-way paradigm of rescue and toward a more complete response, one that is empowering and liberating both for those who are trafficked and for those seeking to help them.

Sex Trafficking Defined

The National Human Trafficking Hotline—a nationwide hotline and resource center founded to serve victims and survivors of human trafficking and the anti-trafficking community—defines sex trafficking as a form of modern-day slavery in which individuals perform commercial sex through the use of force, fraud, or coercion—noting that under federal law, however, any minor under the age of eighteen years induced into commercial sex is a victim of sex trafficking, regardless of whether or not force, fraud, or coercion is present. Sex traffickers frequently use tactics such as violence, threats, lies, false promises, debt bondage, and other forms of control and manipulation to keep trafficked persons involved. Although the conceptual line is fuzzy between sex trafficking and sex work practiced by choice (however imperfect), most would agree that such a distinction does, in fact, exist. That is, where sex workers may experience compromised choices due to economic or social precarity, sex-trafficked persons suffer a more direct violation of their agency by way of force or manipulation, whether physical or psychological. Sex-trafficked persons may be induced into selling sex by way of physical violence or force or the threat thereof. However, they may also be lured by friends, family members, or "Romeo pimps," who fraudulently recruit their targets by offering gifts, romantic enticements, or other false forms of affection.

Like commercial sex more generally, sex trafficking takes place in an enormous variety of settings: fake massage parlors, escort services, residential brothels, truck stops, hotels, strip clubs, and city streets.[4] In the United States, where many women enter into the world of commercial sex while still teenagers, runaways make up an enormous percentage of trafficked persons; in fact, the National Center for Missing and Exploited Children estimates that one in six of the reported runaways in 2020 likely became sex trafficking victims.[5]

It is widely agreed that human trafficking is among the fastest growing and most lucrative criminal industries on the planet.[6] It takes place in virtually every nation, including all fifty US states. Contrary to a common misperception, human trafficking, including sex trafficking, does not necessarily involve migration across borders. Worldwide, it is difficult to pin down hard numbers for the prevalence of human trafficking, since as a whole it exists in the shadows of society and often goes unreported. The 2018 Global Slavery Index, produced by the Walk Free Foundation (a global human rights organization), estimates that in 2016 there were 40.3 million enslaved persons worldwide, and the International Labour Organization echoes that number.[7] It remains a matter of dispute what percentage of these would be classified under the rubric of sex trafficking, but the United Nations Office on Drugs and Crime in its 2020 report estimated that over 50 percent of trafficking in persons worldwide is for purposes of sexual exploitation.[8]

Persons who are sex-trafficked are at enormously increased risk of harm, including contraction of HIV and other STIs, drug addiction, and violence or murder at the hands of traffickers and purchasers of sex. Siddharth Kara, in a study of prostituted women in Mumbai, India, claims that most do not survive past their mid-thirties. Since sex-trafficked women are the most exploited and least empowered within the category of so-called prostitutes, they fall into the highest physical risk category within this population.[9] Indeed, sex-trafficked victims are generally considered by traffickers to be "disposable"—fully replaceable once they have become worn out in their profit-maximizing capacity.

The "Rescue" Paradigm as a (Failed) Response to Sex Trafficking

In the face of the horrifying reality endured by victims/survivors of sex trafficking, it is little wonder that caring observers, including Christians of many backgrounds, are deeply motivated to provide help. And if the broadly popular tropes about trafficking are to be believed, the most immediate way to do so is to support the *rescue* of sex trafficking victims. Responses from within the US government and from many anti-trafficking activists, not to mention from Hollywood and the media more generally, commonly depict a fitting response to sex trafficking as the rescue of poor, innocent, vulnerable victims (usually cisgender women) from "bad guys," bringing the latter to justice— what I am here calling a "rescue paradigm."

Nicholas Kristof and Cheryl WuDunn's important book and documentary, *Half the Sky*, illustrate this approach, even as they raise widespread and vital awareness about the prevalence of trafficking. In one example from the book, Kristof and WuDunn describe the story of Srey Momm, a teenage girl in Cambodia who is trapped in a brothel in Poipet. They portray Momm pleading with Kristof to be purchased, freed, and taken back to her home. Kristof indeed purchases Momm's freedom and returns her to her family on the other side of Cambodia. While she was apparently welcomed back with open arms and subsequently began a new life as a meat seller (with the help of Kristof and another aid organization), Momm soon returned on her own to the Poipet brothel. It seems that she was addicted to methamphetamines and (the authors tell us) thus felt compelled to return to the site of her meth supplier. Kristof and WuDunn use this story to illustrate the ambiguities of choice and the difficulties of "rescuing" sex-trafficked girls.[10]

Yet in spite of its power to inspire, Kristof and WuDunn's approach draws upon—and arguably replicates—many of the stereotypes found in the rescue paradigm. Kristof's stories, narrated both in his book and frequently in his *New York Times* column, recount case after case of women in developing nations suffering at the hands of their captors, and the documentary based upon the book contains dramatic rescue attempts spearheaded by Kristof himself alongside an array of famous actors and other prominent public figures. At times Kristof's detractors are extremely sharp in their criticism of the white savior mentality of which they accuse him. For instance, deconstructionist theorist Yasmin Nair argues that Kristof's "over-sexed stories place women not as their own agents, but as abject creatures always in need of rescue from white saviours and the broader state apparatus." She goes on to label Kristof's accounts "trafficking porn" and to ask, sarcastically, "What could be easier—and sexier—than saving lovely young brown women from sexual servitude?"[11]

Similarly well-intentioned, explicitly Christian responses to sex trafficking frequently rely on analogous frameworks and stereotypes. Christian mandates to liberate the oppressed or to take a preferential option for the poor—arguably the most justice-oriented mandate within a Christian framework—are utilized in the cause of enabling the immediate emancipation of people enslaved within the sex trade. In fact, Christians are very often urged to become modern-day "abolitionists."[12] Concerned Christians, often from more economically developed regions such as the United States or Western Europe, thus are called to support interventions that rescue girls and women from their tormentors, oppressors who are almost always portrayed as male and sometimes as incarnating the very forces of evil itself.[13]

Such rescue-oriented tropes may be observed in a variety of Christian-inspired organizations, books, documentaries, and Hollywood movies about sex trafficking. More often than not, gender stereotyping is employed in the effort to draw people in. For example, the Defenders USA, a wing of Shared Hope International, is targeted specifically at men who wish to engage in the fight against human trafficking. Their promotional materials urge such men that it is "time to man up" to help end the demand for bought sex.[14] In a similar vein, Truckers Against Trafficking ran a campaign in 2017 advertising for "everyday heroes" needed to fight for "young girls" who are "forced into sexual slavery."[15]

David Batstone, founder of the Not for Sale Campaign and author of a book by the same title, describes the "fascination with rescuing victims" as a "natural response to want to save individuals who fall into captivity." He points out how this has led to a tendency in the media to romanticize rescue efforts.[16] One case in point may be found in the example of International Justice Mission (IJM), a Christian-inspired organization founded by Gary Haugen. IJM has gained media notoriety—and an enormous amount of financial backing from US evangelical Christians—for its international efforts to rescue victims of human trafficking and to work through criminal justice systems to stop traffickers. To be clear, IJM does important work; it seeks not *simply* to engage in "sting" operations (though it does indeed do that) but also to bring criminals to justice, restore and heal survivors, and strengthen local justice systems to help prevent such exploitation. Yet IJM is best known for its well-orchestrated, well-publicized, and dramatic rescues, rescues that arguably tell an overly simplistic story about both trafficked and traffickers. Moreover, its emphasis on criminal justice does precious little to point toward the underlying social and economic factors that contribute to sex trafficking in the first place. From a theological anthropological viewpoint, therefore, IJM has not done nearly enough to challenge a top-down paradigm whereby Christians with more means are tasked with "saving" those with less.

On the face of it, it is difficult to argue that there is anything wrong with rescuing sex-trafficked persons out of exploitive and harmful (even deadly) situations. Indeed, one might consider direct intervention on behalf of trafficked persons to be one important prong in a necessarily multipronged solution to the problem of sex trafficking. However, peeling back the surface of the problem, a rescue-oriented approach is at best insufficient and at worst perpetuates harmful stereotypes about the nature of and solution to sex trafficking. Feminist scholar Carrie Baker has incisively pointed out how this approach taps into "patriarchal and orientalist tropes of passive, ignorant, or backward women and girls who are trafficked and of their powerful and/or enlightened male rescuers."[17] Its anthropological assumptions fall short, distorting the human person, specifically the relationship between rescuer and rescued, and relying heavily on gendered and racialized stereotypes. Moreover, the paradigm's analysis tends toward the individualistic; even when it hints at a social response, that response is most often centered on the criminal justice system—punishing bad persons rather than addressing the underlying structural concerns.

Anthropological Considerations

There can be little doubt that an approach that focuses on rescue relies upon and reinforces a now-popularized image of trafficked women first and foremost as quintessential *victims*. As women's studies scholar Gretchen Soderlund has put it, rescue discourse "casts women as victims in need of protection from harm rather than as subjects deserving of positive rights."[18] The rescue paradigm trades on an understanding of freedom that is primarily negative in tone: the freedom *from* imprisonment, force, coercion. Yet it does little to promote the fuller, more robust interpretation of freedom embraced in these pages, one more consonant with a feminist and Christian construal of the human person. Drawing on the work of Joseph Raz, Catholic moral theologian Cathleen Kaveny has advocated for an expanded, positive understanding of human freedom—autonomy understood as the opportunity to become "part-author" of one's own life.[19] This version of autonomy requires more than a simple emphasis on rescuing victims. It requires a social commitment to stand with and empower women and other trafficked persons to reclaim their own lives and futures—that is, to help *restore* survivors via aftercare and rehabilitation. As Kaveny puts the matter, citing Raz, "Coercion and manipulation are not the only threats to the exercise [of] autonomy; a lack of a sufficient array of positive options also undermines it."[20]

US public policy itself has generally promoted the image of trafficked persons as helpless victims who must rely on law enforcement to claim any sort of real agency. Protestant ethicist Yvonne Zimmerman observes in her thought-provoking *Other Dreams of Freedom* that the Trafficking Victims Protection Act itself is framed in such a way so as to object not primarily to the *state* of trafficked persons being victimized, but rather to the *abuse* of women who are nonetheless conceived as powerless and vulnerable on the basis of gender.[21] In order to secure a T visa (a visa reserved for trafficking survivors), trafficked persons must be willing to cooperate with law enforcement to prosecute their traffickers (or be formally excused from doing so); in other words, to get long-lasting help, survivors must become "perfect victims" who seek help from others, even at great risk to their own personal safety.

A model that emphasizes the helpless status of trafficked persons is incomplete. It is not that trafficked persons are not victimized; they are. But to pigeonhole them as *only* victims—and, in the context of rescue, as vulnerable dependents—risks defining them not in terms of their agency but rather in terms of the lack of such agency. Describing the different but somewhat analogous situation of migrants, moral theologian Kristin Heyer argues that "an exclusive focus on constrained agency . . . misses crucial aspects of [migrants'] experience."[22] The same is true for trafficked persons. Indeed, these categories of persons are not entirely mutually exclusive. The precariousness inherent in the situation of migrants is heightened in the case of women; for instance, more than 70 percent of women attempting to cross the Mexican border become targets of sexual exploitation.[23] Many of these women may themselves become trafficked in the course of such migration.

A model that exclusively stresses the victimhood of those who are trafficked fails to pay sufficient attention to what women (and even children) are doing to resist, to help themselves, or simply to survive amid extremely dehumanizing circumstances. It paints a flat, non-nuanced portrait of trafficked persons, understanding women primarily as the *objects* of change rather than as the *agents* of change. As Zimmerman puts it, "Women who have been trafficked are commonly depicted as passive, helpless, and inept. The concept of 'trafficking victim' is often used in a way that ideologically locates the trafficked person as helpless and pitiful, thereby robbing 'her' of agency or subjectivity and creating a very one-dimensional picture of who trafficked persons are and what they are like."[24]

Not only are victims/survivors themselves portrayed unidimensionally in the rescue paradigm; so are both traffickers and outsiders wanting to help. Trading on imagery of male aggression, traffickers are depicted as fearsome bad guys, uncomplicatedly pernicious. Rescuers, on the other hand, are ordinarily pictured as strong, power-wielding law enforcers or, alternatively, as educated and enlightened saviors. In either case, the stereotypes are limiting to men themselves and do little to foster an ideal of egalitarian relationships between genders. Indeed, the rescuers are trapped in a patriarchal and/or colonial self-image that almost completely evades the norms of mutuality and equal regard.

These tendencies are particularly problematic from the perspective of a Christian moral mandate not simply to consider the generalized other but also *particular* persons. Part of the problem with maintaining a vague, uncomplicated portrait of trafficking victims is that it allows well-meaning Christians to self-identify as religious white knights on steeds, ultimately reinforcing an us/them mentality that further dehumanizes those who have been trafficked in the first place. Indeed, for Christian interventionists, a passive portrayal of trafficking "victims" paves the way for a "savior" self-understanding, as self-defined Christian abolitionists lead "fallen" women to new lives of sexual purity.[25]

Trafficked persons who do not neatly fit into the profile of the "perfect" victim—because they are male, drug addicted, formerly promiscuous, or identify as LGBTQ+, for example—are easily overlooked in this paradigm. In fact, anyone not appearing completely innocent or physically chained up in a dark room risks portrayal as somehow deserving of—or even complicit in—his or her own victimization. The danger is particularly troubling in the case of LGBTQ+ youth, who make up a substantial proportion of homeless teenagers in the United States and thus constitute a population at particularly high risk for being trafficked. A paradigm that ignores this reality is insufficient and problematic from any justice-based approach, especially a Christian one.

Resisting such stereotypes, we need instead to take honest account of the textured social reality of trafficking survivors. Contextualizing and historicizing their lives is an integral part of treating them justly. For instance, romanticizing the heteronormative nuclear family as a safe haven for "rescued" trafficking survivors fails to acknowledge that such families may well have contributed to the reasons for the trafficking in the first place. High rates of domestic (including child) abuse in the United States, the all-too-common failure to provide love and support to teens identifying as LGBTQ+, and, at times, familial complicity in the trafficking of children—these tendencies should collectively make us suspicious of efforts to equate "success" for rescued trafficking survivors with family reunification or with finding boyfriends or husbands.[26] Letitia Campbell and Yvonne Zimmerman have argued as much. "No matter how thoroughly romanticized or broadly defined, home and family are not able to fully offset the effects of the market. Home and family do not solve the problem of economic vulnerability."[27] To put the matter differently, trafficked persons must be seen not simply as discrete, distinctly unlucky individuals needing rescue and reunification with their families but rather as a category of persons located squarely in the crosshairs of economic marginalization and gender injustice. It is to these forms of vulnerability that we now must turn.

Structural and Social Concerns

Not only does a rescue-oriented approach to sex trafficking, along with an attendant focus on its primarily criminal nature, impoverish our understanding of human freedom and rely upon a distorted understanding of the human person. It also fails spectacularly to get at a central aspect of the trafficking problem: the broader structural injustices at its root. A focus on deviant captors (or even criminal networks) and heroic rescuers is fundamentally individualistic and truncates long-term solutions. As women's studies scholar Baker argues, a rescue framing "obscures structural factors and the social, economic, and political conditions that create vulnerability to trafficking, such as wealth inequality and poverty, gendered cultural beliefs that devalue women and girls and commodify sex, and the denial of human rights based on race and/or nationality."[28]

Poverty and economic inequality are undeniably related to the prevalence of sex trafficking. Most often, trafficked persons are not one-dimensional "innocents" who are kidnapped in dark alleyways but rather women, girls, or boys who are economically vulnerable or who have few reliable social support networks on which to fall back. Sometimes daughters who are valued less than sons are sold to traffickers in order for an impoverished family to make ends meet or to purchase consumer goods that it otherwise could not afford. Other times, runaway and affection-starved teens fall in with so-called "Romeo pimps" who promise to love and protect them in exchange for their financial "help." Still other times, economically struggling women and children, chasing after the dream of financial stability, find themselves duped by traffickers into more than they bargained for.

Whatever the specific pathway, it is important to recognize that socioeconomic forces lie at the root, both internationally and domestically. Globally, neoliberal economic policies that encourage the free flow of capital and restrict the flow of labor, combined with an emphasis on growth and profit by global financial institutions, have led to extreme economic inequality, among and within nations. The terms of structural adjustment loans and austerity programs, again pushed by global financial institutions, ultimately deprive countries of the capital needed for economic development, medical care, and education, and they force the elimination of social services and safety nets that could keep economically struggling populations out of poverty.[29] It is worth emphasizing that within these populations worldwide, women on the whole have far less access to cash income, economic assets, and financial decision-making power. Moreover, approximately half of the world's poorest persons are younger than eighteen.[30] For these women and children, harmful neoliberal economic policies have unquestionably paved the way for increased vulnerability to human trafficking, including especially sex trafficking. Indeed, the idea of "disposability" itself seems intrinsic both to a neoliberal economic system that values free trade and low-cost consumer goods *and* to the expectations of modern-day sex traffickers, who understand trafficked persons as themselves disposable—easily replaceable from an enormous pool of the economically desperate.

Domestically, too, economic policies tell an important part of the story of human sex trafficking. Beginning at least with the Reagan/Bush era, the shrinking social safety net in the United States over the past forty years has created an ever-increasing population of impoverished people with fewer and fewer economic options. At this point, increasing levels of inequality are old news, as are the 16–18 percent of all American children (including 30 percent of Black children, 29 percent of American Indian/Alaska Native children, and 24 percent of Hispanic children) who live in poverty and 39 percent who live in low-income families.[31] Moreover, shrinking social supports for those poor and often homeless children and youth mean that sex trafficking, from their perspective, can seem like the "best" available option from a severely constricted list of possibilities. Race and sexuality complicate these vulnerabilities further, such that large swaths of BIPOC youth or youth who identify as LGBTQ+ are at disproportionate risk of being trafficked.

Added to these socioeconomic realities, of course, are the gendered cultural beliefs and practices that devalue women worldwide. As Siddharth Kara observes, "The particular ascension of sex slavery resides at the intersection of the socioeconomic bedlam produced by economic globalization and a historic, deeply rooted bias against females."[32] Foremost among these patriarchal cultural patterns lies the devaluation of women and girls in religious dogma and practice. To take Christianity as one example, in both Catholic and Protestant traditions—and in spite of a fair amount of egalitarian rhetoric, as described in the earlier chapters of this book—the exclusion of women from positions of leadership in public settings and the subservient status of women in private, familial settings contribute to the widespread devaluation and disempowerment of females in both. It seems that, in an adaptation of the famous words of George Orwell, "some are more equal than others."[33]

Gendered cultural patterns are particularly apparent, and extremely troubling, in the sexual sphere. As we have seen, religiously inspired ideals of sexual "purity" set up a well-known virgin/whore dichotomy wherein some women are considered "good girls" (sexually pure, innocent, blameless) and others are "bad" (fallen, dirty, sexually available). This religio-cultural anxiety about women's sexuality serves to fan the flames of harmful stereotypes and practices within sex trafficking. One stark example lies in the large financial premiums routinely charged for sex with virgins, who often command prices several times higher than non-virgins.[34] According to these dichotomous patterns, if girls and women who are trafficked are seen somehow as "fallen," they are on the one hand easier to ignore—tolerated as a socially "necessary" evil—and on the other hand may be seen as appropriate targets for salvation by Christian rescuers/guardians. Any suggestion that a trafficked person is less than virginal or innocent before her oppression potentially complicates the picture, for it seems far preferable to understand her as a one-dimensional victim. As Baker has argued, analyzing images of sex trafficking in governmental and nonprofit materials as well as in popular media, "rescue narratives require a worthy victim, and traditional sexual and gender ideologies heavily influence what makes a victim worthy: she is virginal and never complicit in her sexual commodification."[35]

A Christian approach with justice at its heart can do better. Older, less adequate versions of sexual ethics—with their tendency to portray "good" sex as primarily a matter of making right choices, as well as their attendant emphasis on chastity and sexual purity—are ill equipped to uncover the realities at the heart of sex trafficking. These more individualistic methodologies conduce to an approach that paints sex trafficking's nuanced realities in black and white terms: victims and victimizers, good girls and bad girls, innocent children and heroic rescuers. Moreover, when sexual ethics is primarily a matter of making right choices, it becomes all too easy to treat trafficked persons as if they are merely the appropriate objects of pity rather than as bona-fide moral agents caught in systems of oppression.

Thus, in the midst of the victimization of trafficked persons that surely *does* exist, we must simultaneously understand these persons in fuller, more complex, and ultimately more hopeful terms. This will involve being more (not less) attentive to the concrete social, cultural, and economic realities that function to keep trafficked persons in conditions of material precarity. Under an adequate response to sex trafficking, supporting trafficked persons looks less like a one-way heroic rescue and more like a process of empowerment, rooted in the Christian and feminist ideal of mutuality and its social manifestation as solidarity.

A New Lens: Mutuality and Solidarity

Mutuality, as I have described it, and solidarity are concepts closely intertwined in Christian ethics. While solidarity rightly points us toward collective social responsibility, mutuality highlights an extremely "particular" facet of human interaction: the ways in which individuals give and take, are both active and receptive, bind and are bound one to another. We humans are, it seems, inescapably interconnected, and true change is never only one way. Christine Gudorf, in her celebrated challenge to Christian accounts of *agape* that privilege "disinterested" or purely self-sacrificial love, argues instead that *all* love aims at mutuality. When we overemphasize the altruism in loving actions and underemphasize the ways our actions fortify ourselves, we can "seriously damage the other, distorting his/her real needs and desires."[36] Accordingly, one might argue, "loving" the oppressed other as someone solely in need of our one-way help or rescue is an inaccurate and insufficient way to love. Instead, genuinely loving action aims at, and even requires, acts that ultimately transform both the lover and the beloved.

Mutuality cannot remain on an individual level, however, particularly in the context of human trafficking; it *must* include a public dimension if it is to escape reduction to a rather vague and sentimental feeling. Accordingly, *mujerista* theologian Ada María Isasi-Díaz has called mutuality the strategic aspect of solidarity, implementing solidarity and providing the theoretical ground for its continued elaboration.[37] So understood, mutuality is an intrinsic part of the struggle for liberation. Under a framework of mutuality, solidarity itself becomes less of a vague commitment ideologically to support the struggling other and more of a concrete endeavor to engage with that other in a mutually transformative process. For her part, Isasi-Díaz describes a posture of dialogue between those who are oppressed and those who stand alongside them as "friends" and partners; the former challenges the latter to question the structures that oppress, and thus invites them to become co-creators of new, more liberating structures.[38]

In a similar vein, Christian ethicist Rebecca Todd Peters has described a continuum of moral agency that privileges mutuality and the recognition of interdependence over postures of sympathy or one-way responsibility.[39] According to the progression Peters describes, people respond first to the suffering of others with the moral intuition of sympathy, which, while well intentioned, nevertheless maintains a fundamental divide between the self and the other. Sympathy is often followed by a stage of responsibility, wherein the privileged recognize their status as such and experience accountability to care for the less fortunate. While this represents progress beyond the first stage, Peters points out that the danger at this level is the inequality embedded in paternalism, whereby the "helpers" come to understand the "helped" as fundamentally lacking in agency. Theologically understood, "God did not endorse an ethic of paternalism by telling people to love their neighbors as they love their children; rather, the commandment to 'love your neighbor as yourself' is a commandment of equality, which forms the foundation of an ethic of solidarity."[40] Peters's third stage of moral agency is that of *mutuality*, where the moral instinct to help emerges from a recognition of true human interdependence. As I have elaborated earlier in this volume, mutuality is based in partnership and respect, and, theologically speaking, in the ubiquitous presence of the *imago dei*. It is this egalitarian relationship and motive for action that lies at the heart of solidarity.

Solidarity as a concept takes the interdependence highlighted by the notion of mutuality and extends it in the direction of broader social currents and relationships. Indeed, the concept of solidarity squarely affirms the intrinsically social nature of beings and, as Kaveny points out, presses us "to transcend consideration of the justice of our actions in isolation and to evaluate their larger effects and currents of influence."[41] Thus standing in (perhaps creative) tension with Western individualist tendencies, solidarity, understood as an extension of mutuality, points toward our constitutive relationality: we were not created by God to be alone, and, further, individual good is inescapably linked to the common good.

In recent years, there has arguably been a discernable tendency in popular usage of the term *solidarity* to mean a sort of warm, like-minded, and charitable affirmation of another person's or group's goals. The not-uncommon desire to travel to a far corner of the earth to "help" those less fortunate than oneself, while certainly preferable to moral apathy, is nevertheless problematic. Such an instinct too often functions to reinforce culturally dominant narratives that describe poverty and oppression as problems that mostly occur somewhere *else*. Moreover, it invites imbalanced relationships and fails to challenge us, personally and collectively, toward the deeper cultural and structural changes necessary for long-term and more profound justice-oriented change.[42]

Understood as a norm of Christian ethics, solidarity pushes beyond charity toward the more radical purposes of liberation and empowerment. Such an approach is characterized by an undeniable dialogical and egalitarian thrust. Instead of maintaining an us/them divide, solidarity aims rather to break down the thick walls between "oppressor" and "oppressed," moving to a model of love whereby engaging with each other enriches *both* parties in mutual transformation. This involves not simply a feel-good warm-heartedness toward those one is trying to help but also and especially a recognition of the complicated relationship between privilege and oppression.

This dialogical aspect of solidarity has also been elaborated by Latin American liberation theologian Jon Sobrino, summarized well by Catholic ethicist Mark Potter. Potter describes five "movements" of solidarity, from the perspective of the one seeking to stand with those who are suffering or oppressed: a praxis of humble presence; a compassionate and merciful response to the suffering of others; a recognition of accountability for, and often complicity in, the dehumanization of others; a transformation via the gracious acceptance (of the non-oppressed) by the oppressed themselves; and an ongoing mutual collaboration in practices of presence and service in the real world.[43] In this way, solidarity becomes not so much a "doing for" others as a "being with" others[44]—and, importantly, being with others in a way that not only challenges oppressive behaviors and structures but also affects both "helper" and "helped" in profound ways, through a praxis of encounter and mutual transformation.

This understanding of solidarity is much more in line with an incarnational Christian theology than it is with the triumphalist theological vision sometimes hinted at in rescue narratives. That is, the God of the Incarnation is not a hero who "swoops in" to save humanity from on high but rather one who makes God's self *vulnerable* in the broken body of Jesus Christ. Hence, we find God not in *saving* (rescuing) others but in genuinely standing alongside those who are suffering, responding to their needs, and simultaneously allowing ourselves to be transformed in the encounter. To be truly *for* another in this way is a humble, and humbling, endeavor.

Beyond this more personal dimension of solidarity lie important institutional dimensions. For many Christian faith communities, solidarity will entail a noteworthy shift in fundamental priorities: a movement *away* from a centeredness in privilege, with its concomitant posture of "outreach" toward vulnerable persons and communities, and *toward* standing squarely alongside such communities as equals. For many churches, this will entail a disruptive relocation—similar to the witness of Jesus himself, in his scandalous rejection of religious and social barriers and identification with those who suffer. As Mary Doak asks in her incisive ecclesial response to trafficking, "Rather than building communities among the privileged and then occasionally reaching out to the enslaved, abused, and oppressed, should the church not embrace the risks involved in locating itself primarily among the despised and rejected of society with occasional outreach to the powerful and secure?"[45] In this way, churches can enact the demands of mutuality on a corporate level, contributing to the empowerment of trafficking survivors while also paving the way to the sort of mutual transformations articulated in this chapter.

Even more broadly, on a national and international level, solidarity ultimately demands that nations take collective responsibility for international order and make a deepening commitment to the common good.[46] Lines of solidarity thus extend beyond individual relationships to the postures and actions of political organizations and governments, addressing broad socioeconomic patterns and policies that function to oppress. Such an approach thus points toward an inescapably economic dimension to solidarity: the economy forms the material basis of human reality, and economic analysis that unveils the shared interests between affluent and poor people is essential to the doing of justice.[47]

Theologically understood, such a move involves the recognition of the *structural* (versus individual) dimensions of sin elaborated earlier in this volume. Persons who are marginalized are not so simply because of the actions of "bad" people. They are, rather, marginalized in large part because society's patterns and policies are structured in ways that effectively mute their voices and compromise their access to material goods. "Sin" itself has become embedded into unjust social structures, making it difficult for individuals to recognize the varied and often hidden ways in which they maintain, cooperate with, or otherwise participate in it.

Attention to this complex nature of sin, including especially the social dimension of sin, is fortified by a Niebuhrian theological perspective that recognizes the paradoxes at the heart of human nature and experience. As considered in chapter 2, Niebuhrian awareness guides us away from a naïve or starry-eyed dismissal of our complicity in structural sin. Instead, we must be clear-headed about group egotism, including how it can mask our own involvement in subtly vicious patterns of action, patterns that individual members of groups often fail to admit—even to themselves.[48] Crafted as a theological response to these forms of structural oppression, institutional solidarity seeks to affirm human agency, both by recognizing and amplifying the voices of the "voiceless" *and* by challenging the social and economic structures that keep these same people marginalized. These strategies are in fact interrelated; for any challenging of social structures must take place in a way that both empowers and amplifies the previously muted perspectives of those who have been marginalized by those very structures. Along these lines, in her analysis of immigration, Heyer (drawing on the work of David Hollenbach) elaborates a response of institutional solidarity, pointing out that it demands in part the "development of structures that offer marginalized persons a genuine voice in the decisions and policies that impact their lives."[49] Even as this call to empowerment is true for migrants, it is similarly true for trafficking survivors.

Mutuality, Solidarity, and Sex Trafficking

Examining sex trafficking from this new perspective, elaborated by way of the twin concepts of mutuality and solidarity, leads us away from a posture of one-way rescue and into a posture of accompaniment with, and empowerment of, trafficked persons. Specifically, three broad but concrete implications surface for those motivated to respond to sex trafficking while relying upon a fuller account of human agency, thereby promoting genuine justice for trafficking survivors.

First, it is essential that those wishing to help end the scourge of human sex trafficking redefine a simplistic victim/rescuer divide and recognize the needs and complexities of both trafficking survivors and anti-trafficking activists. In general, trafficking survivors have by definition been operating in a realm of severely constrained options. Part of an adequate response to their need will be to stand alongside and empower them, not simply rescue or liberate them, such that they can begin making their own choices more fully and freely. Kevin Bales has pointed this out in his lengthy account of modern-day slavery: "Liberation is a bitter victory if it leads only to starvation or re-enslavement. . . . If slavery is to end, we must learn how ex-slaves can best secure their own freedom."[50] Along these lines, resources and promotional materials must be aimed not simply at the "rescue" of trafficked persons but, more holistically, at the fulfillment of their ongoing needs so that they may take control over their own recovery. Moreover, taking seriously the concrete complexity of trafficked persons requires that we cease making distinctions between "deserving" and "undeserving" recipients of aid—for such distinctions are both hollow and irrelevant. Rather, survivors seeking to retake control over their lives deserve—as a matter of justice—to be respected in their human dignity, their agency, and the particular complexities (the *messiness*) that characterizes their lives.

Sex-trafficked persons, as noted, ordinarily are not young girls snatched from dark street corners—though certainly that does occur on occasion. More often, they are individuals who find themselves marginalized by social or familial structures and attitudes that disempower and alienate them from supportive community. These survivors may develop complicated emotional relationships with their traffickers, becoming not only fearful of them but also psychologically reliant upon them, therefore disinclined to leave abusive and exploitive circumstances. Rather than to further ignore or denying the personal agency of such a survivor, anti-trafficking activists must promote her holistic and long-term rehabilitation and empowerment. This may mean helping her to develop her voice, identify her personal strengths and recognize her basic worth and dignity, or begin the long psychological journey of reclaiming her emotional integrity and forging a personal identity separate from her traffickers. It may mean celebrating the ways that such a survivor has, in fact, *survived*—itself an action strongly indicative of human agency. It may even mean temporarily accepting the choice of a survivor to return to her trafficker. As Doak avers, "When trafficked victims are too traumatized to leave the sex industry, Christians must respond with patient solidarity and accompaniment in hope of healing rather than with condemnation of what is perceived as immoral sexual behavior."[51] In this way, rather than assuming a posture of (seemingly) benign but fundamentally patronizing assistance, churches instead adopt a primary stance of respect and long-term support for trafficked persons. Implicit is the recognition that healing and restoration take place as a process, not a single action—and especially are not accomplished with a single dramatic rescue.

In a related vein, anti-trafficking activists who aim to help those who have been trafficked must be called to recognize their own complex motivations and complicities, and that they are perhaps not so "other" from persons who have been trafficked. Along these lines, it is imperative to avoid the white savior mentality that has so readily characterized Euro-American intervention in problems around the world. The disastrous history of colonialism, if it does nothing else, should remind us that a top-down strategy of intervention fails genuinely to liberate or empower. Insofar as anti-trafficking efforts base themselves upon a non-mutual understanding of right, just, or loving action, the ghost of such colonialism will haunt them. An adequate understanding will aim instead at a more egalitarian relationship, recognizing the ways that those who wish to help are in fact *themselves* changed, humanized and transformed by the process of being welcomed in solidarity alongside those who are struggling.

Second, a lens that privileges solidarity rather than rescue will emphasize the need for cultural, social, and religious empowerment of females and LGBTQ+ persons. This entails addressing head-on the discrimination that these groups face in our world today. Homophobia, transphobia, and heteronormative social patterns and expectations function to disempower those identifying as LGBTQ+, ultimately making these youth far more likely to end up homeless and economically vulnerable. We also must challenge sexist or misogynistic practices that harm or otherwise incapacitate women in ways both obvious and subtle. Devaluation of girls around the world is now quite well established. As Amartya Sen famously pointed out in 1990, more than 100 million of the world's females could in fact be considered "missing": vanished, dead, or never born due to economic, cultural, and social neglect.[52] In the face of such a horrifying statistic, social policy and religious practice should urgently aim at empowering, educating, and trusting women, affirming them as full human persons with authentic human agency. Until women and girls enjoy coequal social valuation with men and boys, they will remain particularly vulnerable to exploitation and oppression via sex trafficking.

Likewise, we must be quick to challenge any cultural belief systems that allow (or encourage) a sense of *entitlement* to sex in men and boys. As described in chapter 3, such a belief is manifest in the nearly ubiquitous "boys will be boys" mentality used to justify rape culture and sexual exploitation, as well as in the victim-blaming that characterizes sexual violence both domestically and abroad. The explosion of demand for commercial sex—the same demand that has led to an exponential increase in sex trafficking worldwide— undoubtedly draws upon this mindset. These forms of gender-based sexual entitlement not only stunt the emotional development of boys and men; they contribute immeasurably to the emotional and physical disempowerment of girls and women around the globe.

For Christians, such challenges are both pressing and poignant. The history of discrimination, devaluation, and downright harm toward females and LGBTQ+ persons within the church is scandalous. Both explicit and implicit patterns of misogyny, homophobia, and transphobia have made churches some of the most *unwelcoming* places on the planet for these populations. Christian reliance on sexual purity codes—disproportionately applied to girls and women—as central measures of morality have in fact functioned to shame and effectively link self-worth to sexual activity. Further, the failure to extend the boundaries of Christian community to be genuinely welcoming toward sexual minorities ultimately drives countless persons identifying as LGBTQ+ into more economically and socially precarious circumstances.

Christians must therefore urgently call out sexism, homophobia, hetero-sexism, and transphobia within and outside the church. They must promote the development of genuine resources to reach out to and empower LGBTQ+ youth, who make up such a large proportion of runaways. Moreover, once again, Christians must vigorously challenge religiously based norms that elevate purity as a positive understanding of girls' and women's sexuality. These exacerbate the problem of sex trafficking, giving religious sanction to gendered dynamics that elevate male heroes (or saviors), and ultimately deprive women of control over their own lives, including their sexuality.

Third, and in some ways most importantly, an adequate response to sex trafficking will reframe the issue *not* primarily in terms of a criminal justice and security model, or a "good-guys-versus-bad-guys" standoff, but rather as a call to oppose political and socioeconomic practices and structures that pave the way for sex trafficking to take root. Putting an end to sex trafficking will require that we squarely face and begin to address the structures of global capitalism and political conflict that contribute to poverty, inequality, and displacement because those patterns make people vulnerable to being trafficked. Politically, the explosive worldwide refugee crisis constitutes a moral emergency of mammoth proportions, in part because persons who are displaced are far more vulnerable to trafficking than they would otherwise have been. So understood, sex trafficking becomes one of the many costs of war and political conflict; we cannot address one without also addressing the other.

Economically, the financial collapses of 2008 and 2020 have wreaked havoc on the US economy, to be sure, but they also have created misery around the world. Reexamining policies such as the North American Free Trade Agreement in light of their specific impact on the world's most vulnerable must be an integral strategy in fighting against all human trafficking, including sex trafficking. To use the ethical language of rights: understanding *economic* rights as *human* rights, and fostering such rights that genuinely enhance full human agency, are crucial to any long-term strategy that seeks to address sex trafficking in an effective way.

Along with a broad questioning of economic structures, we must also examine patterns of Western consumption that reverberate around the globe and contribute to human trafficking, generally speaking. Western consumers chasing low prices often do not contemplate why indeed some prices can be *so* low, and it is now well established that enslaved labor is frequently a part of that equation.[53] Too often, Western privilege functions in economic life to mask the ways that Western actions and patterns of consumption are interlinked with the well-being of faraway others. While this reality indicts forced labor trafficking more clearly than sex trafficking, the links between the two phenomena, and the ways labor-trafficked women and children easily become targets for sex trafficking, make it a critical consideration. Additionally, practices that exacerbate harmful patterns of consumption—that is, patterns that exploit cheap laborers in the pursuit of inexpensive consumer goods—ultimately invite a mindset that accepts some persons to be lacking in human dignity: "disposable" for the sake of the transitory pleasure of others less vulnerable.

Rather than blindly continuing an unquestioned allegiance to consumerist and profit-and-growth-oriented models of development, well-intentioned societies must instead refocus their efforts on the social changes necessary to support women and children. Specifically encouraging initiatives that concretely empower women and girls are an important step toward protecting them from involvement in sex trafficking. Microcredit loans, community investment, educational initiatives, and support for women's cooperatives all function to guard against the socioeconomic vulnerabilities that enable sex trafficking. Domestically, support for laws and programs to ameliorate poverty is in fact crucial to providing pathways for women and children to avoid being trafficked—or, once caught up in trafficking, to minimize financial and emotional dependence on their traffickers. Such programs must address wage disparities, the availability of health care, affordable housing, labor rights, paid parental leave and quality childcare, child support enforcement, and better access to quality education for all. While it is tempting to dismiss this as a "laundry list" of liberal demands, it is also easy to see how strengthening the socioeconomic safety net in these ways discourages the sex trafficking of vulnerable populations.

The above propositions do not eliminate the need to use the criminal justice system to help remove disempowered persons from exploitive situations. But "rescue" in this way is only *part* of an adequate solution to sex trafficking—and a dubious one at that, insofar as it trades on stereotypes of trafficked persons as well as those wishing to help. The intertwined ideals of mutuality and solidarity provide a better guide for a Christian approach to sex trafficking, paving the way for genuine empowerment and thus more accurately pointing us toward long-term solutions. Rather than slipping into a neocolonial posture of rescuing the innocents, our focus must center itself on solidarity and the mutual transformation that takes place therein. Taking history itself as our guide, one might compare current abolitionist responses to sex trafficking—as well as to all modern forms of slavery—to nineteenth-century abolitionist movements. Even then, an abolitionist response was problematic and insufficient when it sought to rescue enslaved persons without *also* seeking to empower them with the tools necessary to rebuild their lives, or to challenge the racist and socioeconomic practices and assumptions that underlay the practice of slavery to begin with. We as a nation continue to struggle, right up to the present day, with slavery's terrible legacy. In our modern efforts to put an end to sex trafficking, it is imperative that we learn from these mistakes, and instead seek solutions that are characterized less by heroism and more by respect, empowerment, and authentic justice.

Notes

1. Minors in these circumstances are better characterized as commercially sexually exploited children. The terms *child sex worker* and *child prostitute* are, by definition, misnomers.
2. It is important to emphasize that sex trafficking is indeed only one subset of human trafficking. Other forms of trafficking, sometimes overlapping in nature, include forced labor (sometimes involving domestic servitude), forced begging, the selling of children, forced marriage, trafficking in child soldiers, and organ trafficking.
3. John Paul II, *Sollicitudo Rei Socialis*, sec. 38.
4. National Human Trafficking Hotline, "Sex Trafficking."
5. One oft-cited statistic is that the average age of entry into commercial sex (generally) is thirteen. Significant controversy surrounds this statistic, however, and the Polaris Project now places the average age of entry into sex trafficking within the United States at seventeen. See US National Human Trafficking Hotline/Polaris, "2019 Data Report." National Center for Missing and Exploited Children, "Missing Children Statistics." A two-year study from January 2011 to December 2012 in Alameda County, California, identified 84 percent of sexually exploited minors as runaways ("Human Trafficking 101," training materials obtained privately from Freedom House San Francisco [https://www.sfcaht .org/freedom-house.html]).
6. United Nations Office on Drugs and Crime, *Estimating Illicit Financial Flows*.
7. Walk Free Foundation, *Global Slavery Index 2018*; and "New ILO Global Estimate of Forced Labour: 20.9 million victims," International Labour Organization, June 1, 2012, http://www.ilo.org/global/about-the-ilo/newsroom/news/WCMS_182109/lang —en/index.htm. This figure includes roughly 25 million cases of forced labor and 15 million cases of forced marriage. Anti-trafficking author and activist Kevin Bales, founder of Free the Slaves, defends the widely cited number of 27 million victims of modern slavery worldwide. See Bales, *Disposable People*, xxiv n3.
8. The global figures here are taken from the 2020 *Trafficking in Persons* Report by the United Nations Office on Drugs and Crime, citing 2018 figures. See United Nations Office on Drugs and Crime, *Global Report on Trafficking in Persons, 2020*.
9. Kara, *Sex Trafficking*, 15.
10. Kristof and WuDunn, *Half the Sky*, 37–39.
11. Nair, "Somaly Mam, Nicholas Kristof."
12. See, for example, Bales, *Disposable People*, 258ff; and Batstone, *Not for Sale*, 259–60.

13. One stark example of this imagery may be found in the subtitle of the evangelically inspired documentary *Nefarious: Merchant of Souls*, directed by Benjamin Nolot (Grandview, MO: Exodus Cry, 2012), DVD.

14. Shared Hope International, "About the Defenders," accessed August 12, 2020, http://sharedhope.org/wp-content/uploads/2013/12/About-the-Defenders_UPDATE.pdf.

15. Truckers Against Trafficking, accessed December 21, 2017, www.truckersagainsttrafficking.org. The campaign has since concluded, and Truckers Against Trafficking now identify their mission in perhaps less self-centered although no less militaristic terms as "raising up a mobile army of transportation professionals to assist law enforcement in the recognition and reporting of human trafficking." See "What We Do," Truckers Against Trafficking, https://truckersagainsttrafficking.org/what-we-do/, accessed August 12, 2020.

16. Batstone, *Not for Sale*, 63–64.

17. Baker, "Moving beyond 'Slaves, Sinners, and Saviors,'" 2.

18. Soderlund, "Running from the Rescuers," 82, cited in Baker, "Moving beyond 'Slaves, Sinners, and Saviors,'" 20.

19. Kaveny, *Law's Virtues*, 7.

20. Kaveny, 26.

21. Zimmerman, *Other Dreams of Freedom*, 28.

22. Heyer, *Kinship across Borders*, 24.

23. Heyer, 50 and 61–98, esp. 64.

24. Zimmerman, *Other Dreams of Freedom*, 11.

25. Zimmerman, 11.

26. Examples of these sorts of romanticized accounts are widespread and span both Christian and non-Christian sources. See, for example, Batstone, *Not for Sale*, 68, 237; and Kristof and WuDunn, *Half the Sky*, chapter 2.

27. Campbell and Zimmerman, "Christian Ethics and Human Trafficking Activism," 162.

28. Baker, "Moving beyond 'Slaves, Sinners, and Saviors,'" 17.

29. Shelley, *Human Trafficking*, 46.

30. United Nations Department of Economic and Social Affairs, Statistics Division, *The World's Women, 2015*; within this document see especially chapter 8, "Poverty," including a helpful summary at https://unstats.un.org/unsd/gender/downloads/Ch8_Poverty_info.pdf. Further, according to UN Women, 60 percent of chronically hungry people are women and girls: UN Women, "Facts and Figures." The figures for poor children are from a 2016 joint World Bank/UNICEF study; see UNICEF, "Nearly 385 Million Children Living in Extreme Poverty."

31. US Census Bureau, "Income, Poverty and Health Insurance Coverage"; National Center for Children in Poverty, [Table on children in low-income families, by state]; and Children's Defense Fund, "The State of America's Children, 2020." According to recent US Census Bureau statistics, 32.6 percent of poor people in the United States in 2016 were younger than age eighteen.

32. Kara, *Sex Trafficking*, 30.

33. Orwell, *Animal Farm*, chapter 10.

34. Bales, *Disposable People*, 56.

35. Baker, "Moving beyond 'Slaves, Sinners, and Saviors,'" 6.

36. Gudorf, "Parenting, Mutual Love, and Sacrifice," 182, 185.

37. Isasi-Díaz, *Mujerista Theology*, 93.

38. Isasi-Díaz, 95–96.
39. Peters, *Solidarity Ethics*, esp. 37ff.
40. Peters, 40.
41. Kaveny, *Law's Virtues*, 54.
42. Peters, *Solidarity Ethics*, xiii.
43. Potter, "Solidarity as Spiritual Exercise," 835.
44. Isasi-Díaz, *Mujerista Theology*, 86.
45. Doak, "Trafficked," 56.
46. Steck, "Solidarity, Citizenship, and Globalization," 164. See also Heyer, *Kinship across Borders*, 115.
47. See Hobgood, "Solidarity and the Accountability," 139.
48. Christine Firer Hinze has offered a nuanced examination of the intersection between Niebuhr's perspective on social sin on the one hand and Catholic social teaching's approach to structures of sin and solidarity on the other. See Hinze, "The Drama of Social Sin."
49. Heyer, *Kinship across Borders*, 114–15; and David Hollenbach, "The Life of the Human Community," *America* 187, no. 14 (November 4, 2002): 7, https://www.americamagazine.org/issue/410/article/life-human-community.
50. Bales, *Disposable People*, 253.
51. Doak, "Trafficked," 59.
52. Amartya Sen, "More Than 100 Million Women are Missing," *New York Review of Books*, December 20, 1990, http://www.nybooks.com/articles/archives/1990/dec/20/more-than-100-million-women-are-missing/.
53. Bales, *Disposable People*, 238.

Concluding Reflections

In the course of this volume, I have sought to build the contours of a refreshed framework for sexual ethics—that is, to reenvision how the Christian tradition might better serve the contemporary individual as well as the common good in the realm of sexual personhood. I have also sought to illustrate why this *matters*. My effort has been in part to paint a more complete portrait of the distinctive sexual struggles, yearnings, and limitations that characterize particular lives, especially younger lives, in contemporary US society. Individuals, churches, universities, and civic institutions can ill afford to diminish or avoid the sexual themes addressed herein. And yet, by and large, Christian sexual ethics has not adequately and honestly addressed these subjects in a way that promotes justice, especially for women, and an expansive understanding of human flourishing. This lacuna translates into an all-too-common ethical vacuum, one filled by a cultural individualism and even, at times, a drift toward solipsism. Not only does this tendency function to dismantle human well-being in real ways; it also fans the flames of injustice against women, LGBTQ+ persons, and various other marginalized communities.

To elucidate these challenges more specifically, including how we might better address them, I have examined various topics and cases of pressing concern within the US sexual-cultural landscape. On college campuses, foremost among these are the sexual minefields of hookup culture, which many students are forced to navigate without a clear idea of what matters to them with respect to sex, personally and spiritually speaking. For these students, the sexist (and heterosexist) constraints, gendered expectations, and superficial, uncaring attitudes imposed by hookup culture itself too often come across as non-negotiable. Yet absent an alternative, justice-minded sexual framework—one genuinely responsive to today's social realities—the only tool available to them is the vital but philosophically thin tool of individual consent. This has proven to be necessary but also insufficient. Instead, I have attempted to refocus that conversation away from the hyperindividualistic assumptions of campus sexual culture and, more positively, toward norms of full, empowered agency and freedom, mutuality and equal regard, and emotional integrity. Notably, these norms do not focus on the form of chaste heterosexual marriage as a sexual ideal. While I in no way seek to diminish the value of a marriage commitment, the more pressing, relevant, and holistic need here is to promote justice in *all* sexual relationships, married or not.

Similarly, in chapter 4, I introduced the complicated social ecosystem of teenagers who engage in sexting, such as Margarite and Isaiah. These not-quite-adults, in the awkwardness of adolescence and the desire to be flirty and to fit in with their peers, too frequently make sexual decisions that lead to confusion, disenchantment, public shaming, and even legal penalties. It is not enough simply to offer these teens an ethical model of purity or even chastity, for their social environs present a relentless and far more enticing portrait of human sexuality: one that substitutes pornographic self-objectification for genuine sexual agency and self-care. Instead, Christian ethics can and must offer more robust tools of sexual justice, tools that affirm the beauty of human sexuality and the importance of freedom while also promoting emotional health, holistic intimacy, and more mutual, egalitarian patterns of relational well-being.

Chapters 5 and 6 elaborated the stories of both sex workers and sex-trafficked women and children, whose agency is often severely compromised in obvious as well as not-so-obvious ways. Taken as a whole, the moral imperatives articulated in these two chapters urge and endorse justice for individual sex workers, for trafficked persons, and for women and children in society more generally. In the case of sex work, women (and sometimes men) all too frequently are driven by genuine financial limitation, leading them voluntarily to subsume their own safety, authentic desires, and emotional needs to the impersonal demands of the marketplace. Here again, the rhetoric of pure individual choice falls short—largely because it attributes the entirety of sexual flourishing to the mere existence of that choice itself without attending more robustly to the way choices intersect with other, more textured aspects of human well-being. My aim in that discussion has been squarely to promote sex workers' empowered agency and well-being, holistically understood, against a backdrop of capitalized sex and limited job options for far too many people, especially many cisgender women and trans* people.

A narrow cultural focus on individual choice leads to a similarly inadequate analysis of sex trafficking. To be sure, a serious lack of personal freedom does indeed lie at the heart of the profound physical and emotional violation experienced by sex-trafficked women and children. But a simplistic narrative of rescue—with its attendant goal of restoring liberty of movement and choice—belies the far thornier realities of human trafficking and those caught up in it. This unfortunate rescue narrative thus effectively patronizes trafficking survivors, minimizing or even erasing their agency, and distracts from the unjust social realities that too often lead to trafficking in the first place. Again, it is incumbent upon Christian ethics to provide an alternative and more full-bodied ethical approach, one that promotes the positive agency of trafficked persons by way of the concepts of mutuality and solidarity.

All told, then, to respond to these multifaceted struggles equipped only with the ethical tools of individual free consent and chastity is to respond in a woefully inadequate manner. To do so not only downplays the authentic psychological, spiritual, and relational needs of concrete persons and groups; it also ignores the multiple ways our social location and circumstances in fact *impact* our freedom as well as our deeper sense of possibilities, both personal and communal. As we have seen, freedom and well-being are closely intertwined, and we cannot afford to ignore either in the quest to promote authentic and holistic human flourishing. Alternatively, reifying chastity as *the* central sexual norm has served to entrench the individualistic, act-oriented quality that characterizes far too much of Christian sexual ethics. Still more troubling, it distracts from or even fortifies existing injustices against women and queer people, thereby further diminishing their genuine sexual agency and compromising their well-being.

As a means of expanding and reenvisioning the ethical picture, then, I have developed in these pages a framework of flourishing more broadly construed, one that in fact pays serious attention to women's concrete well-being as well as core questions of individual agency. Moreover, I have done this while foregrounding socioeconomic and gender justice, interpreted theologically as instances of social sin. In this way, I have sought to remain attentive not simply to the flourishing of bodies and persons but rather to the flourishing of *historically situated* bodies and persons—in all of their socially embedded messiness. Importantly, the framework I propose includes a strong affirmation of human freedom and agency, as well as of physical health and pleasure, emotional integrity, relational intimacy, and mutuality and equal regard—all understood in the context of social injustices that constrain what it means to thrive as a human being in today's world.

This fuller vision of human flourishing pushes Christians (as well as others sympathetic to a Christian approach) in new directions—beyond the individualistic tropes that are far too characteristic of modern Western culture and that also, unfortunately, have come to typify some segments of Christian sexual ethics. Here, I have sought to ground this thicker, societally attentive, and more liberatory ethical posture in the most life-giving insights that the tradition has to offer. The various domains I have examined within these pages represent, to my mind, places where we as a society have clearly failed to extend ourselves beyond the limitations of a largely individualistic approach. In each of these areas, a primary challenge has been to reject the culturally casual attitude toward sex that has come to predominate in US society—one that sets few normative boundaries around sex other than to affirm the privacy of choice—without defaulting to a dated, chastity-focused methodology that diminishes or elides the demands of justice. If we are to take seriously the challenges inherent in contemporary sexual life, we must also take seriously the authentic struggles and desires of real, historically shaped persons and communities today. Doing so entails the reclamation of a certain "sex positivity" —that is, a strong affirmation of the joy, delight, and goodness of sex—while simultaneously refusing to limit that goodness to social arrangements that too often prove to be sexist and heteronormative.

Importantly, while the illustrative chapters in this volume form a kind of collection of Christian and feminist case studies focused on sexuality and justice in concrete societal contexts, neither the topics themselves nor the norms I propose in each setting are entirely separable from one another. Because each social practice takes place on gender-unequal terrain, each also in some way replicates the harm and injustices that characterize that terrain more broadly. And while each case spotlights specific challenges as well as qualities of human flourishing, the justice-minded lenses that they assemble invite creative cross-fertilization across the topic addressed and beyond. To take but one example: the value of solidarity, here elaborated primarily in the context of sex trafficking, also begins to illuminate how differently situated moral actors may learn from and stand alongside each other regarding the challenges and pressures present in campus hookup culture, sexting, and sex work. In this way, justice is elaborated here less as an *ending* than as a *beginning*: an invitation to the hard work that lies before Christian sexual ethics today.

The move to broaden the ethical conversation in the direction of less individualistic and more justice-focused norms is both timely and urgent. Not only is personal well-being ill served by a near-exclusive focus on individual choice; a narrow focus on personal decision-making also tends to efface the very real public health challenges and gendered communal struggles that form the complicated backdrop of these choices. To wit: the devastating COVID-19 pandemic has highlighted the ways that traditionally gendered social roles—such as the primary identification of women as wives and mothers and the related expectation that women will perform the bulk of caregiving work—serve to place many women into positions of extreme economic and social instability. Not only have domestic violence rates against women and queer people skyrocketed under pandemic-related economic shutdowns; so too has women's overall economic precarity. Black and Latina women have been the hardest hit, facing historically high unemployment rates since the pandemic began.[1] After the widespread March 2020 shelter-in-place order, working mothers were particularly impacted by school and childcare closures, ultimately resulting in a massive exodus from paid work. In fact, a December 2020 report from the Bureau of Labor Statistics revealed the stunning truth that women were leaving the workforce at four times the rate of men, provoking one group of prominent women soon thereafter to petition President Joe Biden for a "Marshall Plan for Moms"—that is, a plan to provide mothers with basic income and to address pay inequities, the need for affordable childcare, and parental leave.[2]

If Christian (or any other) analysis focuses solely on personal decision-making as the locus of sexual ethics, it will fail to address these very real sexual injustices and the systemic undercurrents they reflect. Our choices are structured in large part by our social location. The norms we privilege must therefore not simply consist in maximized freedom or even individual well-being; they must instead suggest flexible sensibilities that further justice on a real and historicized level while squarely accounting for the various sorts of social injustice women face.

Concretely, where do these commitments lead us? As I have explicated in the context of each topic, this way of conceiving human flourishing suggests particular educational and public policy steps and commitments. The task falls not simply to individuals but also to families, churches, schools and colleges, civic groups, legal scholars, and policymakers. Educationally, we must take better care to open up both public and private spaces wherein sex can be openly discussed—not as a taboo subject to be approached sheepishly or, worse, summarily dismissed but rather as the subject of frank yet profound conversation. This is imperative in faith communities, where shame and fear currently predominate far more than honesty and empowering exchange. Along these lines, Christian sexual education must also refuse the continued erasure of queer sexual experience, instead proposing more authentic and justice-based norms as the guideposts for what counts as humanizing sexual expression. Faith communities are well positioned to highlight and explicate these dimensions of justice. Moreover, they are ideally suited to provide the groundwork that underlies them, including strong reassurances regarding basic dignity and self-worth.

In a related vein, families, churches, and schools must dramatically increase explicit efforts to uncover, address, and prevent future instances of childhood trauma. This is especially true for trauma that takes place (or has done so, in the past) within religious contexts or under religious auspices, for this sort of trauma is among the most personally violating and emotionally harmful. As we have seen, strong connections exist between childhood sexual violence and later incidences of dysfunctional and unjust sexual patterns. It is profoundly disingenuous to condemn the latter while doing little to face, let alone prevent, the former.

Turning to more explicitly theological territory: ecclesiastical conversations, lectures, and courses designed to explore the nature of sin and injustice must be extended to cover the *structural* manifestations of such sin and injustice *in the explicitly sexual spheres of life*. In this manner, churches and religious and educational institutions can build awareness of the assorted and often well-hidden ways in which social injustice deeply impinges upon both freedom and human well-being, sexually speaking. For churches and educational institutions to take these steps would go a long way toward helping young adults to define themselves and others not by hypersexualized—and heavily gendered—social norms or attitudes but rather by each person's fundamental status as dignified and beloved by God. It would thus encourage a positive regard for one's own basic desires, well-being, and decision-making agency while also directing respect for those very same capacities in others. While such a posture will not eliminate the pitfalls of hookup culture, the prevalence of teen sexting, or the dysfunctionality embedded in commercial sex, it will lay a solid groundwork to begin reforming these social practices in the direction of justice.

Beyond educational reform, however, more is needed at the societal level. Our legal systems and policies must be updated to better address the true sexual realities of persons and communities, especially the ways social structures and institutions impact those sexual realities. On campuses, for instance, practices of affirmative consent—including especially the standard of "yes means yes" rather than simply "no means no"—must be actively and enthusiastically promoted at both the administrative and disciplinary levels. In the case of teen sexting, policy reform will entail a recognition that teenagers sext for reasons quite distinct from those that motivate adults to consume child pornography. Young teens like Margarite and Isaiah should, therefore, not be legally penalized as adults would be but rather should be guided—using non-legal tools—toward a more holistic self-understanding and a mutually respectful and caring expression of sexual desire.

As for commercial sex, it is imperative that laws be restructured on an individual level to empower rather than to punish sex workers, and the force of these laws should be directed primarily against the buyers, facilitators, and any others who exploit sex workers, not against the sex workers themselves. Still more broadly, public policy must be aimed at reducing the overall prevalence of commercial sex and fortifying alternative employment options and social supports—so that cisgender women and trans* persons find themselves with genuinely humanizing employment options as well as a strong social safety net. Such changes will expand their possibilities and guard against the dangers and abuse that are currently rife within both sex work and sex trafficking. Moreover, this sort of policy reform, instead of a purely punitive approach, is far likelier to create long-term, sustainable social well-being for both women and children, while also respecting and fortifying their dignity and freedom.

In each of these instances, current US educational and legal approaches have left us with serious shortcomings, including ethical voids that are unhelpfully filled by a myopic focus on consent alone. Further, as I have argued, even consent itself is complicated and compromised by dysfunctional patterns of social sin, both socioeconomic and gender-related. In the face of this pattern, the Christian tradition has continued to put forth an unfortunately truncated understanding of sexual virtue, one that may elevate chastity and marriage but offers little else that is meaningful in a contemporary context. Such a limited approach cannot possibly counter the cultural drift toward the thin version of individual consent that functions as the sole arbiter of ethical legitimacy in the United States today. If Christian ethics as a field is to be of significant use to young adults in navigating these issues, it must pivot away from a narrow-minded focus on chaste, heterosexual marriage as the sole locus for humanizing forms of sexual expression. Instead, it must promote robust, justice-based sensibilities about what it means for humans to thrive in the sexual sphere, including a clear-eyed analysis of the forms of injustice that function to inhibit such thriving.

Otherwise put, it is time for Christian ethics to reenvision and reframe its understanding of sexual virtue such that ethical sex is not limited to "chaste," married sex. Rather, ethical sex is better demarcated as sex that expresses the fullness of human agency, communicates the joy of shared pleasure, and confers a sense of wholeness, indeed *holiness*, upon *all* its participants. And, importantly, Christian ethics must adopt this robust approach proactively and boldly, drawing deeply upon its own internal theological resources as well as broader philosophical insights about what it means for women and other marginalized groups to flourish in contemporary sexual society. In this way, Christian ethics may in fact end up returning persons to themselves, affirming their authentic emotional and relational complexity while nevertheless continuing to insist upon the sublime nature of human freedom.

As we saw toward the start of this work, we find the preliminary seeds of such an understanding in the celebration of human sexuality that characterizes the Song of Solomon. There, desire, pleasure, and agency comingle with relational intimacy to portray the sublime beauty and mutual power of sex. Midway through that love poem, one lover invites the beloved to understand their shared yearning for one another as part of a larger, more abundant and joyous world:

> Arise, my love, my fair one,
> and come away;
> for now the winter is past,
> the rain is over and gone.
> The flowers appear on the earth;
> the time of singing has come,
> and the voice of the turtledove
> is heard in our land. (Song of Solomon 2:10b–12)

In this portion of the poem, individual passion and desire are fused not only with the human yearning to be known, loved, and companioned but with a larger and more comprehensive social vision, one characterized by hope, life, and renewal. In truth, in any society, including our own, individuals' yearnings and desires—sexual and otherwise—are deeply interwoven with the communal ecology within which those individuals find themselves. In a sense, sex summons us out of ourselves and into that broader social world, even as our sexual decision-making both reflects and shapes the communities of which we are a part.

This is the primary reason Christian ethics cannot afford to look past the social and historicized context in which individual sexual decision-making takes place. If our society is characterized by sexual injustice, so too will be our predominant sexual self-understanding. But if our society is animated by a more life-giving vision, one represented by a comprehensive and justice-minded construal of human agency and well-being, individual expression of human sexuality is far more likely to follow suit. It is my fervent hope that the efforts in this volume to renew, refresh, and reenvision Christian sexual ethics in fact help to lead beyond the current sexual impasse, smoothing the road to a genuine "time of singing" yet to come.

Notes

1. National Women's Law Center, "COVID-19 Jobs Day Reports," https://nwlc.org /resources/2020-jobs-day-reports/; and "50 Prominent Women Run Full Page Ad in

The New York Times Calling on President Biden to Implement Marshall Plan for Moms in First 100 Days," *Cision PR Newswire*, January 26, 2021, https://www.prnewswire.com /news-releases/50-prominent-women-run-full-page-ad-in-the-new-york-times-calling -on-president-biden-to-implement-marshall-plan-for-moms-in-first-100-days-30121 4913.html.

2. Scott Horsley, "Job Growth Slows Sharply in Last Employment Report before Election," NPR/KQED, October 2, 2020, https://www.npr.org/sections/coronavirus-live-updates /2020/10/02/919152104/jobs-growth-continues-to-slow-in-last-employment-report -before-election; and Andrea Hsu, "'This Is Too Much': Working Moms Are Reaching the Breaking Point during the Pandemic," NPR/KQED, September 29, 2020, https://www .npr.org/2020/09/29/918127776/this-is-too-much-working-moms-are-reaching-the -breaking-point-during-the-pandemi.

Bibliography

Abraham, Kochurani. "Resistance: A Liberative Key in Feminist Ethics." In *Feminist Catholic Theological Ethics: Conversations in the World Church*, edited by Linda Hogan and A. E. Orobator, 97–107. Maryknoll, NY: Orbis Books, 2014.

Amnesty International. *Amnesty International Policy on State Obligations to Respect, Protect and Fulfil the Human Rights of Sex Workers*. May 26, 2016. https://www.amnesty.org /download/Documents/POL3040622016ENGLISH.PDF.

———. *Explanatory Note on Amnesty International's Policy on State Obligations to Respect, Protect and Fulfill the Human Rights of Sex Workers*. May 26, 2016. https://www.amnesty.org /download/Documents/POL3040632016ENGLISH.PDF.

Anderson, Monica, Emily A. Vogels, and Erica Turner. "The Virtues and Downsides of Online Dating." Pew Research Center, February 6, 2020. https://www.pewresearch.org/internet /2020/02/06/the-virtues-and-downsides-of-online-dating/.

Anderson, Monica, and Jingjing Jiang. "Teens, Social Media and Technology, 2018." Pew Research Center, May 31, 2018. https://www.pewresearch.org/internet/2018/05/31 /teens-social-media-technology-2018/.

Andolsen, Barbara Hilkert. "Agape in Feminist Ethics." *Journal of Religious Ethics* 9 (1981): 69–83.

Antus, Elizabeth L. "Was It Good for You? Recasting Catholic Sexual Ethics in Light of Women's Sexual Pain Disorders." *Journal of Religious Ethics* 46, no. 4 (December 2018): 611–34. https://oi.org/10.1111/jore.12238.

Aquinas, Thomas. *Summa Theologica*. Translated by Fathers of the English Dominican Province. Westminster, MD: Christian Classics, 1981.

Aquino, María Pilar. "Latina Feminist Theology: Central Features." In *A Reader in Latina Feminist Theology: Religion and Justice*, edited by María Pilar Aquino, Daisy L. Machado, and Jeanette Rodríguez, 133–60. Austin: University of Texas Press, 2002.

———. "Latin American Feminist Theology." *Journal of Feminist Studies in Religion* 14, no. 1 (Spring 1998): 89–107.

Armstrong, Elizabeth A., Laura Hamilton, and Brian Sweeney. "Sexual Assault on Campus: A Multilevel, Integrative Approach to Party Rape." *Social Problems* 53, no. 4 (November 2006): 483–99. https://doi.org/10.1525/sp.2006.53.4.483.

Augustine. "The Good of Marriage." In *Treatises on Marriage and Other Subjects*, edited by Roy J. Deferrari. Washington, DC: Catholic University of America Press, 1955.

Bader-Saye, Scott. "The Transgender Body's Grace." *Journal of the Society of Christian Ethics* 39, no. 1 (Spring/Summer 2019): 75–92.

Baker, Carrie N. "Moving beyond 'Slaves, Sinners, and Saviors': An Intersectional Feminist Analysis of US Sex-Trafficking Discourses, Law and Policy." *Journal of Feminist Scholarship* 4 (Spring 2013): 1–23.

Bales, Kevin. *Disposable People: New Slavery in the Global Economy.* Berkeley: University of California Press, 2012.

Barrios, R. J., and Jennifer Hickes Lundquist. "Boys Just Want to Have Fun? Masculinity, Sexual Behaviors, and Romantic Intentions of Gay and Straight Males in College." *Journal of LGBT Youth* 9, no. 4 (2012): 271–96. https://doi.org/10.1080/19361653.2012.716749.

Batstone, David. *Not for Sale: The Return of the Global Slave Trade—and How We Can Fight It.* New York: HarperCollins, 2010.

Bell, Laurie, ed. *Good Girls, Bad Girls: Feminists and Sex Trade Workers Face to Face.* Seattle: Seal Press, 1987.

Bersamin, Melina M., Byron L. Zamboanga, Seth J. Schwartz, M. Brent Donnellan, Monika Hudson, Robert S. Weisskirch, Su Yeong Kim, V. Bede Agocha, Susan Krauss Whitbourne, and S. Jean Caraway. "Risky Business: Is There an Association between Casual Sex and Mental Health among Emerging Adults?" *Journal of Sex Research* 51, no. 1 (2014): 43–51. https://doi.org/10.1080/00224499.2013.772088.

Beste, Jennifer. *College Hookup Culture and Christian Ethics: The Lives and Longings of Emerging Adults.* New York: Oxford University Press, 2017.

Bogle, Kathleen A. *Hooking Up: Sex, Dating, and Relationships on Campus.* New York: New York University Press, 2008.

Bolz-Weber, Nadia. *Shameless: A Sexual Reformation.* New York: Convergent Books, 2019.

Boyle, Joseph, Ronald Lawler, and William E. May. *Catholic Sexual Ethics: A Summary, Explanation, and Defense.* Huntington, IN: Our Sunday Visitor, 2011.

Bradshaw, Carolyn, Arnold S. Kahn, and Bryan K. Saville. "To Hook Up or To Date: Which Gender Benefits?" *Sex Roles* 62, no. 9/10 (2010): 661–69. https://doi.org/10.1007/s11199-010-9765-7.

Braun-Courville, Debra K., and Mary Rojas. "Exposure to Sexually Explicit Web Sites and Adolescent Sexual Attitudes and Behaviors." *Journal of Adolescent Health* 45, no. 2 (2009): 156–62. https://doi.org/10.1016/j.jadohealth.2008.12.004.

Brents, Barbara G., and Kathryn Hausbeck. "Violence and Legalized Brothel Prostitution in Nevada: Examining Safety, Risk, and Prostitution Policy." *Journal of Interpersonal Violence* 20, no. 3 (March 2005): 270–95. https://doi.org/10.1177/0886260504270333.

Brewer, Devon D., Jonathan A. Dudek, John J. Potterat, Stephen Q. Muth, John M. Roberts Jr., and Donald E. Woodhouse. "Extent, Trends, and Perpetrators of Prostitution-Related Homicide in the United States." *Journal of Forensic Science* 51, no. 5 (September 2006): 1101–8. https://doi.org/10.1111/j.1556-4029.2006.00206.x.

Brock, Rita Nakashima, and Susan Brooks Thistlethwaite. *Casting Stones: Prostitution and Liberation in Asia and the United States.* Minneapolis: Fortress Press, 1996.

Brown, Brené. *Daring Greatly.* New York: Penguin Random House, 2012.

Brown, Jennifer L., and Peter A. Vanable. "Alcohol Use, Partner Type, and Risky Sexual Behavior among College Students: Findings from an Event-Level Study." *Addictive Behaviors* 32, no. 12 (December 2007): 2940–52. https://doi.org/10.1016/j.addbeh.2007.06.011.

Burke Ravizza, Bridget. "Feminism a Must: Catholic Sexual Ethics for Today's College Classrooms." In *Women, Wisdom, and Witness*, edited by Rosemary P. Carbine and Kathleen J. Dolphin, 146–65. Collegeville, MN: Liturgical Press, 2012.

Butler, Judith. *Bodies That Matter.* New York: Routledge, 1993.

———. "Contingent Foundations: Feminism and the Question of 'Postmodernism.'" In *Feminist Contentions: A Philosophical Exchange*, edited by Seyla Benhabib, Judith Butler, Drucilla Cornell, and Nancy Fraser. New York: Routledge, 1995.

———. *Gender Trouble: Feminism and the Subversion of Identity*. New York: Routledge, 1990.

———. *Undoing Gender*. New York: Routledge, 2004.

Cahill, Ann J. "Unjust Sex vs. Rape." *Hypatia* 31, no. 4 (Fall 2016): 746–61.

Cahill, Lisa. *Between the Sexes: Foundations for a Christian Ethics of Sexuality*. Philadelphia: Fortress Press, 1985.

Cahill, Lisa Sowle. "Catholic Sexual Ethics and the Dignity of the Person: A Double Message." *Theological Studies* 50, no. 1 (March 1989): 120–50.

———. *Sex, Gender, and Christian Ethics*. New York: Cambridge University Press, 1996.

Calvin, John. *Institutes of the Christian Religion*. Edited by John T. McNeill. Philadelphia: Westminster Press, 1960.

Camosy, Charles C. *Beyond the Abortion Wars: A Way Forward for a New Generation*. Grand Rapids, MI: Eerdmans, 2015.

Campbell, Letitia M., and Yvonne C. Zimmerman. "Christian Ethics and Human Trafficking Activism: Progressive Christianity and Social Critique." *Journal of the Society of Christian Ethics* 34, no. 1 (Spring/Summer 2014): 145–72. https://doi.org/10.1353/sce.2014.0003.

Catechism of the Catholic Church. 2nd ed. Vatican City: Libreria Editrice Vaticana, 1997. http://ccc.usccb.org/flipbooks/catechism/index.html.

Catholic Theological Society of America Committee on the Study of Human Sexuality. *Human Sexuality: New Directions in American Catholic Thought*. New York: Paulist Press, 1977.

Centers for Disease Control and Prevention. "Sexually Transmitted Diseases: Reported Cases and Rates of Reported Cases, United States, 1941–2018." Last modified August 20, 2019. https://www.cdc.gov/std/stats18/tables/1.htm.

———. "Trends in the Prevalence of Sexual Behaviors and HIV Testing National YRBS, 1991–2017." Last modified April 9, 2019. https://www.cdc.gov/healthyyouth/data/yrbs/factsheets/2017_sexual_trend_yrbs.htm.

Children's Defense Fund. "The State of America's Children, 2020." Accessed June 21, 2021. https://www.childrensdefense.org/policy/resources/soac-2020-child-poverty/#:~:text=Children%20remain%20the%20poorest%20age,and%20older%20(10%20percent).

Cloutier, David. *Love, Reason, and God's Story: An Introduction to Catholic Sexual Ethics*. Winona, MN: St. Mary's Press, 2008.

Cloutier, David, and William C. Mattison III. "Bodies Poured Out in Christ: Marriage Beyond the Theology of the Body." In *Leaving and Coming Home: New Wineskins for Catholic Sexual Ethics*, edited by David Cloutier, 206–25. Eugene, OR: Wipf and Stock, 2010.

Copeland, M. Shawn. "White Supremacy and Anti-Black Logics in the Making of U.S. Catholicism." In *Anti-Blackness and Christian Ethics*, edited by Vincent W. Lloyd and Andrew Prevot, 61–74. Maryknoll, NY: Orbis Books, 2017.

Coulter, Robert W. S., and Susan R. Rankin. "College Sexual Assault and Campus Climate for Sexual- and Gender-Minority Undergraduate Students." *Journal of Interpersonal Violence* (2017). https://doi.org/10.1177/0886260517696870.

Crittenden, Ann. *The Price of Motherhood: Why the Most Important Job in the World Is Still the Least Valued*. New York. II. Holt, 2002.

Crooks, Robert L., and Karla Baur. *Our Sexuality*. 13th ed. Boston: Cengage Learning, 2017.

Cunningham, Scott, and Manisha Shah. "Decriminalizing Indoor Prostitution: Implications for Sexual Violence and Public Health." *Review of Economic Studies* 85 (2018): 1683–1715. https://doi.org/10.1093/restud/rdx065.

Davis, Henry. *Moral and Pastoral Theology*. London: Sheed and Ward, 1936.

Day, Keri. "'I Am Dark and Lovely': Let the Shulammite Woman Speak." *Black Theology* 16, no. 3 (2018): 207–17. https://doi.org/10.1080/14769948.2018.1492300.

Delacoste, Frédérique, and Priscilla Alexander, eds. *Sex Work: Writings by Women in the Sex Industry.* 2nd ed. San Francisco: Cleis Press, 1998.

De La Torre, Miguel. *A Lily among the Thorns: Imagining a New Christian Sexuality.* San Francisco: Jossey-Bass, 2007.

Dempsey, Michelle Madden. "Sex Trafficking and Worker Justice: Insights from Catholic Social Teaching." *Journal of Catholic Social Thought* 9, no. 1 (Winter 2012): 71–89.

Doak, Mary. "Trafficked: Sex Slavery and the Reign of God." In *Women, Wisdom, and Witness,* edited by Rosemary P. Carbine and Kathleen J. Dolphin, 45–60. Collegeville, MN: Liturgical Press, 2007.

Douglas, Kelly Brown. "More than Skin Deep: The Violence of Anti-Blackness." In *Anti-Blackness and Christian Ethics,* edited by Vincent W. Lloyd and Andrew Prevot, 3–18. Maryknoll, NY: Orbis Books, 2017.

———. *Sexuality and the Black Church: A Womanist Perspective.* Maryknoll, NY: Orbis Books, 1999.

Dreamworlds 3: Desire, Sex and Power in Music Video. Directed by Sut Jhally. Northampton, MA: Media Education Foundation, 2007. DVD.

Dworkin, Andrea. "Prostitution and Male Supremacy." *Michigan Journal of Gender and Law* 1, no. 1 (1993): 1–12.

Ehrenreich, Barbara, and Deirdre English. *For Her Own Good: 150 Years of the Experts' Advice to Women.* New York: Doubleday, 1978.

Ellison, Marvin M. "Is Pro-Choice What We Mean to Say?" In *Making Love Just: Sexual Ethics for Perplexing Times,* by Marvin M. Ellison, 99–114. Minneapolis: Fortress Press, 2012.

———. *Making Love Just: Sexual Ethics for Perplexing Times.* Minneapolis: Fortress Press, 2012.

———. "Reimagining Good Sex: The Eroticizing of Mutual Respect and Pleasure." In *Sexuality and the Sacred: Sources for Theological Reflection,* 2nd ed., edited by Marvin M. Ellison and Kelly Brown Douglas, 245–61. Louisville, KY: Westminster John Knox Press, 2010.

Evans, Megan L., Margo Lindauer, and Maureen E. Farrell. "A Pandemic within a Pandemic—Intimate Partner Violence during Covid-19." *New England Journal of Medicine* 383, no. 24 (2020): 2302–4. https://www.nejm.org/doi/full/10.1056/NEJMp2024046.

Farley, Margaret A. "Feminism and Universal Morality." In *Changing the Questions: Explorations in Christian Ethics,* edited by Jamie L. Manson, 88–111. Maryknoll, NY: Orbis Books, 2018.

———. "Feminist Ethics." In *The Westminster Dictionary of Christian Ethics,* edited by James F. Childress and John Macquarrie, 229–31. Philadelphia: Westminster Press, 1986.

———. *Just Love: A Framework for Christian Sexual Ethics.* New York: Continuum, 2006.

———. "New Patterns of Relationship: Beginnings of a Moral Revolution." In *Woman: New Dimensions,* edited by Walter Burkhardt, 51–70. New York: Paulist Press, 1975.

———. *Personal Commitments: Beginning, Keeping, Changing.* San Francisco: Harper & Row, 1986.

Farley, Melissa. "Prostitution and the Invisibility of Harm." *Women & Therapy* 26, no. 3/4 (2003): 247–80. https://doi.org/10.1300/J015v26n03_06.

Farley, Melissa, Isin Baral, Merab Kiremire, and Ufuk Sezgin. "Prostitution in Five Countries: Violence and Post-Traumatic Stress Disorder." *Feminism & Psychology* 8, no. 4 (November 1998): 405–26. https://doi.org/10.1177/0959353598084002.

Farley, Melissa, Emily Schuckman, Jacqueline M. Golding, Kristen Houser, Laura Jarrett, Peter Qualliotine, and Michele Decker. "Comparing Sex Buyers with Men Who Don't Buy Sex." Paper presented at the Annual Meeting of Psychologists for Social Responsibility, Boston, July 15, 2011. www.demandabolition.org.

Fielder, R. L., and M. P. Carey. "Prevalence and Characteristics of Sexual Hookups among First-Semester Female College Students." *Journal of Sex and Marital Therapy* 36, no. 4 (July 2010): 346–59. https://doi.org/10.1080/0092623X.2010.488118.

Fielder, Robyn L., Jennifer L. Walsh, Kate B. Carey, and Michael P. Carey. "Sexual Hookups and Adverse Health Outcomes: A Longitudinal Study of First-Year College Women." *Journal of Sex Research* 51, no. 2 (2014): 131–44. https://doi.org/10.1080/00224499.2013 .848255.

Fisher, Bonnie S., Francis T. Cullen, and Michael G. Turner. *The Sexual Victimization of College Women.* Washington, DC: US Department of Justice, National Institute of Justice, December 2000. https://www.ojp.gov/pdffiles1/nij/182369.pdf.

Flack, William F., Jr., Kimberly A. Daubman, Marcia L. Caron, Jenica A. Asadorian, Nicole R. D'Aureli, Shannon N. Gigliotti, Anna T. Hall, Sarah Kiser, and Erin R. Stine. "Risk Factors and Consequences of Unwanted Sex among University Students." *Journal of Interpersonal Violence* 22, no. 2 (February 2007): 139–57. https://doi.org/10.1177/08862605062 95354.

Ford, Craig. "Transgender Bodies, Catholic Schools, and a Queer Natural Law Theology of Exploration." *Journal of Moral Theology* 7, no. 1 (January 2018): 70–98.

Freitas, Donna. *Consent on Campus: A Manifesto.* New York: Oxford University Press, 2018.

———. *The End of Sex: How Hookup Culture Is Leaving a Generation Unhappy, Sexually Unfulfilled, and Confused about Intimacy.* New York: Basic Books, 2013.

———. *Sex and the Soul: Juggling Sexuality, Spirituality, Romance, and Religion on America's College Campuses.* New York: Oxford University Press, 2008.

Friedman, Jaclyn. *Unscrewed: Women, Sex, Power, and How to Stop Letting the System Screw Us All.* Berkeley: Seal Press, 2017.

Fullam, Lisa. "Sex in 3-D: A Telos for a Virtue Ethics of Sexuality." *Journal of the Society of Christian Ethics* 27, no. 2 (Fall/Winter 2007): 151–70.

Gandolfo, Elizabeth O'Donnell. *The Power and Vulnerability of Love.* Minneapolis: Fortress Press, 2015.

Garcia, J. R., and C. Reiber. "Hook-Up Behavior: A Biopsychosocial Perspective." *Journal of Social, Evolutionary, and Cultural Psychology* 2, no. 4 (2008): 192–208. http://dx.doi.org /10.1037/h0099345.

Garcia, Justin R., Chris Reiber, Sean G. Massey, and Ann M. Merriwether. "Sexual Hookup Culture: A Review." *Review of General Psychology* 16, no. 2 (June 2012): 161–76. https:// doi.org/10.1037/a0027911.

Genilo, Eric Marcelo O. *John Cuthbert Ford, S.J.: Moral Theologian at the End of the Manualist Era.* Washington, DC: Georgetown University Press, 2007.

Genovesi, Vincent J. *In Pursuit of Love: Catholic Morality and Human Sexuality.* 2nd ed. Collegeville, MN: Liturgical Press, 1996.

González Faus, José Ignacio. "Sin." In *Mysterium Liberationis: Fundamental Concepts of Liberation Theology,* edited by Ignacio Ellacuria S.J. and Jon Sobrino S.J., 532–42. Maryknoll, NY: Orbis Books, 1993.

Gorry, Jo, Katrina Roen, and James Reilly, "Selling Your Self? The Psychological Impact of Street Sex Work and Factors Affecting Support Seeking." *Health and Social Care in the Community* 18, no. 5 (2010): 492–99. https://doi.org/10.1111/j.1365-2524.2010 .00925.x.

Grigoriadis, Vanessa. *Blurred Lines: Rethinking Sex, Power, and Consent on Campus.* Boston: Eamon Dolan/Houghton Mifflin Harcourt, 2017.

Grimes, Katie. "Butler Interprets Aquinas: How to Speak Thomistically about Sex." *Journal of Religious Ethics* 42, no. 2 (June 2014): 187–215.

Gudorf, Christine E. *Body, Sex, and Pleasure: Reconstructing Christian Sexual Ethics.* Cleveland: Pilgrim Press, 1994.

———. "Parenting, Mutual Love, and Sacrifice." In *Women's Consciousness, Women's Conscience,* edited by Barbara Hilkert Andolsen, Christine E. Gudorf, and Mary D. Pellauer, 181–86. San Francisco: Harper & Row, 1985.

Hamilton, Laura. "Trading on Heterosexuality: College Women's Gender Strategies and Homophobia." *Gender & Society* 21, no. 2 (2007): 145–72. https://doi.org/10.1177 /0891243206297604.

Harrison, Beverly Wildung. *Our Right to Choose: Toward a New Ethic of Abortion.* Boston: Beacon Press, 1984.

Heyer, Kristin. *Kinship across Borders: A Christian Ethic of Immigration.* Washington, DC: Georgetown University Press, 2012.

———. "Social Sin and Immigration: Good Fences Make Bad Neighbors." *Theological Studies* 71, no. 2 (May 2010): 410–36.

Himes, R. Kenneth. "Social Sin and the Role of the Individual." *Annual of the Society of Christian Ethics* 6 (1986): 183–218. https://www.jstor.org/stable/23559619.

Hinze, Christine Firer. "The Drama of Social Sin and the (Im)Possibility of Solidarity: Reinhold Niebuhr and Modern Catholic Social Teaching." *Studies in Christian Ethics* 22, no. 4 (November 2009): 442–60. https://doi.org/10.1177/0953946809340947.

———. "Straining toward Solidarity in a Suffering World: *Gaudium et Spes* after Forty Years." In *Vatican II: Forty Years Later,* edited by William Madges, 165–95. Maryknoll, NY: Orbis Books, 2006.

Hobgood, Mary Elizabeth. "Solidarity and the Accountability of Academic Feminists and Church Activists to Typical (World-Majority) Women." *Journal of Feminist Studies in Religion* 20, no. 2 (Fall 2004): 137–65 and 194–95.

Howes, Hilary. "Mother, Father, Brother, Sister, Husband, and Wife." In *More than a Monologue: Sexual Diversity and the Catholic Church, Volume 1: Voices of our Times,* edited by Christine Firer Hinze and J. Patrick Hornbeck, 43–53. New York: Fordham University Press, 2014.

Human Rights Watch. "Why Sex Work Should Be Decriminalized." Last modified August 7, 2019. https://www.hrw.org/news/2019/08/07/why-sex-work-should-be-decriminalized.

Humbach, John A. "Sexting and the First Amendment." *Hastings Constitutional Law Quarterly* 37, no. 3 (Spring 2010): 433–86.

Ipsen, Avaren. *Sex Working and the Bible.* New York: Routledge, 2014.

Isasi-Díaz, Ada María. *Mujerista Theology: A Theology for the Twenty-First Century.* Maryknoll, NY: Orbis Books, 1996.

Jagannathan, Meera. "'We've Seen an Alarming Spike in Domestic Violence Reports': For Some Women, It's Not Safe to Leave the House OR Stay Home." Market Watch. June 19, 2020. https://www.marketwatch.com/story/its-not-safe-to-leave-the-house-and-its-not -safe-to-stay-in-the-house-how-coronavirus-could-exacerbate-domestic-violence-2020 -03-20.

Jaggar, Alison M. "Prostitution." In *The Philosophy of Sex: Contemporary Readings*, edited by Alan Soble. Savage, MD: Rowman & Littlefield, 1991.

Jeal, Nikki, and Chris Salisbury. "A Health Needs Assessment of Street-Based Prostitutes: Cross-Sectional Survey." *Journal of Public Health* 26, no. 2 (June 2004): 147–51.

John Paul II. *Familiaris Consortio.* Apostolic exhortation. Vatican website. November 22, 1981. http://www.vatican.va/content/john-paul-ii/en/apost_exhortations/documents/hf_jp-ii_exh_19811122_familiaris-consortio.html.

———. *General Audience.* Vatican website. March 12, 1980. http://www.vatican.va/content/john-paul-ii/en/audiences/1980/documents/hf_jp-ii_aud_19800312.html.

———. *Laborem Exercens.* Encyclical letter. Vatican website. September 14, 1981. http://www.vatican.va/content/john-paul-ii/en/encyclicals/documents/hf_jp-ii_enc_14091981_laborem-exercens.html.

———. *Letter of Pope John Paul II to Women.* Vatican website. June 29, 1995. http://www.vatican.va/content/john-paul-ii/en/letters/1995/documents/hf_jp-ii_let_29061995_women.html.

———. *Mulieris Dignitatem.* Apostolic letter. Vatican website. August 15, 1988. http://www.vatican.va/content/john-paul-ii/en/apost_letters/1988/documents/hf_jp-ii_apl_19880815_mulieris-dignitatem.html.

———. *Sollicitudo Rei Socialis.* Encyclical letter. Vatican website. December 30, 1987. http://www.vatican.va/content/john-paul-ii/en/encyclicals/documents/hf_jp-ii_enc_30121987_sollicitudo-rei-socialis.html.

Johnson, Elizabeth A. *Truly Our Sister: A Theology of Mary in the Communion of Saints.* New York: Continuum, 2003.

Johnson, Luke Timothy. *The Revelatory Body: Theology as Inductive Art.* Grand Rapids, MI: Wm. B. Eerdmans, 2015.

Jordan, Mark D. *The Ethics of Sex.* Malden, MA: Blackwell, 2002.

Kalbian, Aline H. "Integrity in Catholic Sexual Ethics." *Journal of the Society of Christian Ethics* 24, no. 2 (2004): 55–69.

Kalish, Rachel, and Michael Kimmel. "Hooking Up: Hot Hetero Sex or the New Numb Normative?" *Australian Feminist Studies* 26, no. 67 (March 2011): 137–51. https://doi.org/10.1080/08164649.2011.546333.

Kara, Siddharth. *Sex Trafficking: Inside the Business of Modern Slavery.* New York: Columbia University Press, 2009.

Kaveny, Cathleen. *Law's Virtues: Fostering Autonomy and Solidarity in American Society.* Washington, DC: Georgetown University Press, 2012.

Keenan, James F. "Contemporary Contributions to Sexual Ethics." *Theological Studies* 71, no. 1 (March 2010): 148–67.

———. "Virtue Ethics and Sexual Ethics." *Louvain Studies* 30, no. 3 (Fall 2005): 180–97.

Keller, Leah H. "Reducing STI Cases: Young People Deserve Better Sexual Health Information and Services." *Guttmacher Policy Review* 23 (2020): 6–12.

Kenney, S. R., Vandana Thadani, Tehniat Ghaidarov, and Joseph W. LaBrie. "First-Year College Women's Motivations for Hooking Up: A Mixed Methods Examination of Normative Peer Perceptions and Personal Hookup Participation." *International Journal of Sexual Health* 25, no. 3 (2013): 212–24. http://doi.org/10.1080/19317611.2013.786010.

Kierkegaard, Soren. *Works of Love.* New York: Harper & Row, 1962.

Kimmel, Michael. *Guyland: The Perilous World Where Boys Become Men.* New York: Harper Perennial, 2009.

King, Jason. *Faith with Benefits: Hookup Culture on Catholic Campuses.* New York: Oxford University Press, 2017.

———. "A Theology of Dating for a Culture of Abuse." In *Leaving and Coming Home: New Wineskins for Catholic Sexual Ethics,* edited by David Cloutier, 29–46. Eugene, OR: Cascade Books, 2010.

Kingston, Sarah, and Terry Thomas. "No Model in Practice: A 'Nordic Model' to Respond to Prostitution?" *Crime, Law and Social Change* 71 (2019): 423–39. https://doi.org/10.1007/s10611-018-9795-6.

Knust, Jennifer Wright. *Unprotected Texts: The Bible's Surprising Contradictions about Sex and Desire.* New York: HarperCollins, 2011.

Kristof, Nicholas D., and Sheryl WuDunn. *Half the Sky: Turning Oppression into Opportunity for Women Worldwide.* New York: Vintage, 2009.

Kuperberg, Arielle, and Joseph E. Padgett. "Dating and Hooking Up in College: Meeting Contexts, Sex, and Variation by Gender, Partner's Gender, and Class Standing." *Journal of Sex Research* 52, no. 5 (2015): 517–31. https://doi.org/10.1080/00224499.2014.901284.

Kwok, Pui-Lan. "Unbinding Our Feet: Saving Brown Women and Feminist Religious Discourse." In *Postcolonialism, Feminism, and Religious Discourse,* edited by Laura E. Donaldson and Kwok Pui-Lan, 62–81. New York: Routledge, 2002.

Lamont, Ellen, Teresa Roach, and Sope Kahn. "Navigating Campus Hookup Culture: LGBTQ Students and College Hookups." *Sociological Forum* 33, no. 4 (2018): 1000–1022. https://doi.org/10.1111/socf.12458.

Laumann, Edward O., Anthony Paik, and Raymond C. Rosen. "Sexual Dysfunction in the United States: Prevalence and Predictors." *Journal of the American Medical Association* 281, no. 6 (February 1999): 537–44. https://doi.org/10.1001/jama.281.6.537.

Lebacqz, Karen. "Appropriate Vulnerability: A Sexual Ethic for Singles." In *Sexuality and the Sacred: Sources for Theological Reflection,* 2nd ed., edited by Marvin M. Ellison and Kelly Brown Douglas, 272–77. Louisville, KY: Westminster John Knox Press, 2010.

———. *Justice in an Unjust World: Foundations for a Christian Approach to Justice.* Minneapolis: Augsburg, 1987.

Lenhart, Amanda. "Teens and Sexting." Pew Research Center, December 15, 2009. https://www.pewresearch.org/internet/2009/12/15/teens-and-sexting/.

Lorde, Audre. "An Open Letter to Mary Daly." In *This Bridge Called My Back: Writings by Radical Women of Color,* 4th ed., edited by Cherrie Moraga and Gloria Anzaldua. Albany: SUNY Press, 2015.

Lunceford, Brett. "The New Pornographers: Legal and Ethical Considerations of Sexting." In *The Ethics of Emerging Media: Information, Social Norms, and New Media Technology,* edited by Bruce E. Drushel and Kathleen German, 99–118. New York: Continuum, 2011.

Lundquist, Jennifer Hickes, and Celeste Vaughan Curington. "Love Me Tinder, Love Me Sweet: Reshaping the College Hookup Culture." *Contexts* 18, no. 4 (2019): 22–27. https://doi.org/10.1177/1536504219883848.

Luther, Martin. "The Large Catechism (1529)." In *The Annotated Luther, Volume 2: Word and Faith,* edited by Kirsi I. Stjerna. Minneapolis: Fortress Press, 2015.

MacKinnon, Catharine A. "Prostitution and Civil Rights." *Michigan Journal of Gender and Law* 1, no. 1 (1993): 13–31.

Madigan, Sheri, Anh Ly, Christina L. Rash, Joris Van Ouytsel, and Jeff R. Temple. "Prevalence of Multiple Forms of Sexting Behavior among Youth: A Systemic Review and

Meta-Analysis." *JAMA Pediatrics* 172, no. 4 (2018): 327–35. https://jamanetwork.com/journals/jamapediatrics/fullarticle/2673719.

Majority Report of the Papal Commission for the Study of Problems of the Family, Population, and Birth Rate. Agathon Associates. http://www.bostonleadershipbuilders.com/0church/birth-control-majority.htm.

Malamuth, Neil M. "Rape Proclivity among Males." *Journal of Social Issues* 37, no. 4 (Fall 1981): 138–57. https://doi.org/10.1111/j.1540-4560.1981.tb01075.x.

Massey, Alana. "Against Chill." *Medium.* April 1, 2015. https://medium.com/matter/against-chill-930dfb60a577.

Massingale, Bryan N. "The Erotic Life of Anti-Blackness: Police Sexual Violation of Black Bodies." In *Anti-Blackness and Christian Ethics,* edited by Vincent W. Lloyd and Andrew Prevot, 173–94. Maryknoll, NY: Orbis Books, 2017.

McCabe, Megan K. "A Feminist Catholic Response to the Social Sin of Rape Culture." *Journal of Religious Ethics* 46, no. 4 (2018): 635–57. https://doi.org/10.1111/jore.12239.

McCool, Megan E., Andrea Zuelke, Melissa A. Theurich, Helge Knuettel, Cristian Ricci, and Christian Apfelbacher. "Prevalence of Female Sexual Dysfunction among Premenopausal Women: A Systematic Review and Meta-Analysis of Observational Studies." *Sexual Medicine Reviews* 4, no. 3 (July 2016): 197–212. http://doi.org/10.1016/j.sxmr.2016.03.002.

McLachlan, Julie Halloran. "Crime and Punishment: Teen Sexting in Context." *Penn State Law Review* 115, no. 1 (Summer 2010): 135–81.

Mescher, Marcus. "The Moral Impact of Digital Devices." *Journal of Moral Theology* 9, no. 2 (2020): 65–93.

Millett, Kate. "Prostitution: A Quartet for Female Voices." In *Woman in Sexist Society: Studies in Power and Powerlessness,* edited by Vivian Gornick and Barbara K. Moran, 60–125. New York: Basic Books, 1971.

Mitchell, Kimberly J., David Finkelhor, Lisa M. Jones, and Janis Wolak. "Prevalence and Characteristics of Youth Sexting: A National Study." *Pediatrics* 129, no. 1 (January 2012): 13–20. https://doi.org/10.1542/peds.2011-1730.

Moloney, Katherine Patricia. "Prostitution Legislation: Toward an Ethical Christian Response." *Crux* 50, no. 3 (2014): 12–21.

Monto, Martin A., and Anna G. Carey. "A New Standard of Sexual Behavior? Are Claims Associated with the 'Hookup Culture' Supported by General Social Survey Data?" *Journal of Sex Research* 51, no. 6 (August 2014): 605–15. http://doi.org/10.1080/00224499.2014.906031.

Nair, Yasmin. "Somaly Mam, Nicholas Kristof, and the Real Sex Trafficking Story." *Yasmin Nair* (blog). June 2, 2014. https://yasminnair.com/somaly-mam-nicholas-kristof-and-the-real-sex-trafficking-story/.

National Center for Children in Poverty. [Table on children in low-income families, by state]. Accessed June 28, 2021. https://www.nccp.org/data-table/?state=US&cat=income&denom=char&data=per&unit=Children&age=18&inc=Low-Income&submit=Create%20table.

National Center for Missing and Exploited Children. "Missing Children Statistics." Accessed June 28, 2021. https://www.missingkids.org/footer/media/keyfacts.

National Coalition Against Domestic Violence. "Domestic Violence and the LGBTQ Community." Last modified June 6, 2018. https://ncadv.org/blog/posts/domestic-violence-and-the-lgbtq-community.

————. "National Statistics." Accessed June 28, 2021. https://ncadv.org/statistics.

National Human Trafficking Hotline. "Sex Trafficking." Accessed June 28, 2021. https://humantraffickinghotline.org/type-trafficking/sex-trafficking.

Nelson, James B. *Embodiment: An Approach to Sexuality and Christian Theology.* Minneapolis: Augsburg, 1978.

Niebuhr, Reinhold. *An Interpretation of Christian Ethics.* New York: Harper & Row, 1935.

————. *The Nature and Destiny of Man, Volume 1: Human Nature.* New York: Charles Scribner's Sons, 1964.

Norma, Caroline, and Melinda Tankard Reist, eds. *Prostitution Narratives: Stories of Survival in the Sex Trade.* North Melbourne, Australia: Spinifex Press, 2016.

Northrup, Christiane. *Women's Bodies, Women's Wisdom: Creating Physical and Emotional Health and Healing.* Rev. ed. New York: Bantam Books, 2020.

Nouwen, Henri J. M. *Life of the Beloved.* New York: Crossroad, 1992.

Nussbaum, Martha. "Human Capabilities, Female Human Beings." In *Women, Culture and Development*, edited by Martha Nussbaum and Jonathan Glover, 61–104. New York: Oxford University Press, 1995.

————. "Objectification." *Philosophy and Public Affairs* 24, no. 4 (Autumn 1995): 249–91.

Nygren, Anders. *Agape and Eros.* Philadelphia: Westminster Press, 1953.

Ortner, Sherry B. "Making Gender: Toward a Feminist, Minority, Postcolonial, Subaltern, etc., Theory of Practice." In *Making Gender: The Politics and Erotics of Culture*, 1–20. Boston: Beacon Press, 1996.

Orwell, George. *Animal Farm.* New York: Penguin, 1946.

Outka, Gene. *Agape: An Ethical Analysis.* New Haven, CT: Yale University Press, 1977.

Overall, Christine. "What's Wrong with Prostitution? Evaluating Sex Work." *Signs* 17, no. 4 (Summer 1992): 705–24.

Parker, Rebecca. "Making Love as a Means of Grace." *Open Hands* 3, no. 3 (Winter 1988): 8–12.

Pateman, Carole. "Defending Prostitution: Charges against Ericsson." *Ethics* 93, no. 3 (April 1983): 561–65.

Paul VI. *Humanae Vitae.* Encyclical letter. Vatican website. July 25, 1968. http://www.vatican.va/content/paul-vi/en/encyclicals/documents/hf_p-vi_enc_25071968_humanae-vitae.html.

————. *The Pastoral Constitution of the Church in the Modern World (Gaudium et Spes).* Constitution. Vatican website. December 7, 1965. http://www.vatican.va/archive/hist_councils/ii_vatican_council/documents/vat-ii_const_19651207_gaudium-et-spes_en.html.

Pazmany, Els, Sophie Bergeron, Lukas Van Oudenhove, Johan Verhaeghe, and Paul Enzlin. "Body Image and Genital Self-Image in Pre-menopausal Women with Dyspareunia." *Archives of Sexual Behavior* 42 (2013): 999–1010. https://doi.org/10.1007/s10508-013-0102-4.

Peskin, Melissa Fleschler, Christine M. Markham, Robert C. Addy, Ross Shegog, Melanie Thiel, and Susan R. Tortolero. "Prevalence and Patterns of Sexting among Ethnic Minority Urban High School Students." *Cyberpsychology, Behavior, and Social Networking* 16, no. 6 (2013). http://doi.org/10.1089/cyber.2012.0452.

Peters, Rebecca Todd. *Solidarity Ethics: Transformation in a Globalized World.* Minneapolis: Fortress Press, 2014.

————. *Trust Women: A Progressive Christian Argument for Reproductive Justice.* Boston: Beacon Press, 2018.

Peterson-Iyer, Karen. "Mobile Porn? Teenage Sexting and Justice for Women." *Journal of the Society of Christian Ethics* 33, no. 2 (Fall/Winter 2013): 93–110.

———. "Prostitution: A Feminist Ethical Analysis." *Journal of Feminist Studies in Religion* 14, no. 2 (Fall 1998): 19–44.

———. "Sex and Sexuality." In *T&T Clark Companion to Christian Ethics*, edited by Tobias Winright, 439–49. London: T&T Clark, 2021.

Pew Research Center. "Mobile Fact Sheet." April 7, 2021. https://www.pewresearch.org /internet/fact-sheet/mobile/.

Phillips, Lynn. *Flirting with Danger: Young Women's Reflections on Sexuality and Domination.* New York: NYU Press, 2000.

Potter, Mark W. "Solidarity as Spiritual Exercise: Accompanying Migrants at the US/Mexican Border." *Political Theology* 12, no. 6 (2011): 830–42. https://doi.org/10.1558/poth .v12i6.830.

Potterat, John J., Devon D. Brewer, Stephen Q. Muth, Richard B. Rothenberg, Donald E. Woodhouse, John B. Muth, Heather K. Stites, and Stuart Brody. "Mortality in a Long-Term Open Cohort of Prostitute Women." *American Journal of Epidemiology* 159, no. 8 (April 2004): 778–85. https://doi.org/10.1093/aje/kwh110.

Power to Decide (formerly National Campaign to Prevent Teen and Unplanned Pregnancy). "Sex and Tech: Results from a Survey of Teens and Young Adults." December 2008. https://powertodecide.org/what-we-do/information/resource-library/sex-and-tech -results-survey-teens-and-young-adults.

Rahner, Karl. "The Experiment with Man: Theological Observations on Man's Self-Manipulation." In *Theological Investigations*, Vol. 9, 205–24. London: Darton, Longman and Todd, 1972.

RAINN: Rape, Abuse and Incest National Network. "Victims of Sexual Violence: Statistics." Accessed June 28, 2021. https://www.rainn.org/statistics/victims-sexual-violence.

Reimer-Barry, Emily. "Another Pro-Life Movement Is Possible." *Proceedings of the Catholic Theological Society of America* 74 (June 2019): 21–41.

Rickaby, Joseph. *Of God and His Creatures: An Annotated Translation of the Summa Contra Gentiles of St. Thomas Aquinas.* The Catholic Primer, 2005. https://d2y1pz2y630308 .cloudfront.net/15471/documents/2016/10/St.%20Thomas%20Aquinas-The %20Summa%20Contra%20Gentiles.pdf.

Roberts, Dorothy E. *Killing the Black Body: Race, Reproduction, and the Meaning of Liberty.* New York: Vintage, 1998.

Rosin, Hanna. *The End of Men: And the Rise of Women.* New York: Riverhead Books, 2012.

Rudy, Kathy. *Beyond Pro-Life and Pro-Choice: Moral Diversity in the Abortion Debate.* Boston: Beacon Press, 1996.

Rupp, Leila J., Verta Taylor, Shiri Regev-Messalem, Alison C. K. Fogarty, and Paula England. "Queer Women in the Hookup Scene: Beyond the Closet?" *Gender & Society* 28, no. 2 (2014): 212–35. https://doi.org/10.1177/0891243213510782.

Ryan, Elizabeth M. "Sexting: How the States Can Prevent a Moment of Indiscretion from Leading to a Lifetime of Unintended Consequences for Minors and Young Adults." *Iowa Law Review* 96, no. 357 (2010): 357–83.

Salzman, Todd A., and Michael G. Lawler. *Sexual Ethics: A Theological Introduction.* Washington, DC: Georgetown University Press, 2012.

———. *The Sexual Person: Toward a Renewed Catholic Anthropology.* Washington, DC: Georgetown University Press, 2008.

Schweizer, Eduard. "Σαρξ, Σαρκικος, Σαρκινος." In *Theological Dictionary of the New Testament*, Vol. 7, edited by Gerhard Kittel and Gerhard Friedrich, 98–151. Grand Rapids, MI: Wm. B. Eerdmans, 1971.

"Sexual Abuse Statistics." TeenHelp.com. Accessed June 28, 2021. https://www.teenhelp.com /sexual-abuse-trauma/sexual-abuse-statistics/.

Shah, Krupa. "Sexting: Risky or [F]risky? An Examination of the Current and Future Legal Treatment of Sexting in the United States." *Faulkner Law Review* 2, no. 1 (2010): 193–216.

Shelley, Louise. *Human Trafficking: A Global Perspective*. New York: Cambridge University Press, 2010.

Shively, Michael, Kristina Kliorys, Kristin Wheeler, and Dana Hunt. *A National Overview of Prostitution and Sex Trafficking Demand Reduction Efforts, Final Report*. Washington, DC: National Institute of Justice, 2012. https://nij.ojp.gov/library/publications/national -overview-prostitution-and-sex-trafficking-demand-reduction-efforts.

Shrage, Laurie. "Should Feminists Oppose Prostitution?" *Ethics* 99, no. 2 (January 1989): 347–61.

Snapp, Shannon, Ehri Ryu, and Jade Kerr. "The Upside to Hooking Up: College Students' Positive Hookup Experiences." *International Journal of Sexual Health* 27, no. 1 (2015): 43–56. https://doi.org/10.1080/19317611.2014.939247.

Soderlund, Gretchen. "Running from the Rescuers: New US Crusades against Sex Trafficking and the Rhetoric of Abolition." *NWSA Journal* 17, no. 3 (Autumn 2005): 64–87.

Soelle, Dorothee. *To Work and To Love: A Theology of Creation*. Philadelphia: Fortress Press, 1984.

Spell, Sarah A. "Not Just Black and White: How Race/Ethnicity and Gender Intersect in Hookup Culture." *Sociology of Race and Ethnicity* 3, no. 2 (April 2017): 172–87.

Spohn, William. "Jesus and Christian Ethics." *Theological Studies* 56, no. 1 (1995): 92–107.

Steck, Christopher. "Solidarity, Citizenship, and Globalization: Developing a New Framework for Theological Reflection on U.S.-Mexico Immigration." *Journal for Peace and Justice Studies* 14, no. 2 (2004): 153–78. https://doi.org/10.5840/peacejustice20041426.

Traina, Cristina L. H. "Feminism and Natural Law: Recapitulation and Reconsideration." Unpublished manuscript, presented at the Society of Christian Ethics Annual Meeting. Washington, DC, January 2020.

———. "Maternal Experience and the Boundaries of Christian Sexual Ethics." *Signs* 25, no. 2 (Winter 2000): 369–405.

UNICEF. "Nearly 385 Million Children Living in Extreme Poverty, Says Joint World Bank Group/UNICEF Study." October 3, 2016. https://www.unicef.org/media/media_92856 .html.

United Nations Department of Economic and Social Affairs, Statistics Division. *The World's Women, 2015: Trends and Statistics*. New York: United Nations, 2015. https://unstats.un .org/unsd/gender/downloads/worldswomen2015_report.pdf.

United Nations Office on Drugs and Crime. *Estimating Illicit Financial Flows Resulting from Drug Trafficking and Other Transnational Organized Crimes*. Vienna: United Nations Office on Drugs and Crime, 2011. http://www.unodc.org/documents/data-and-analysis /Studies/Illicit_financial_flows_2011_web.pdf.

———. *Global Report on Trafficking in Persons, 2020*. Vienna: United Nations Office on Drugs and Crime, 2020. https://www.unodc.org/documents/data-and-analysis/tip/2021/GLOTiP _2020_15jan_web.pdf.

UN Women. "Facts and Figures." Accessed June 21, 2021. http://www.unwomen.org/en/news/in-focus/commission-on-the-status-of-women-2012/facts-and-figures.

US Census Bureau. "Income, Poverty and Health Insurance Coverage in the United States: 2016." September 12, 2017. https://www.census.gov/newsroom/press-releases/2017/income-poverty.html.

US National Human Trafficking Hotline/Polaris. "2019 Data Report." Accessed June 22, 2021. https://polarisproject.org/wp-content/uploads/2019/09/Polaris-2019-US-National-Human-Trafficking-Hotline-Data-Report.pdf.

Valenti, Jessica. *The Purity Myth: How America's Obsession with Virginity Is Hurting Young Women*. Berkeley: Seal Press, 2010.

Wade, Lisa. *American Hookup: The New Culture of Sex on Campus*. New York: W. W. Norton, 2017.

Wade, Lisa, and Caroline Heldman. "Hooking Up and Opting Out: Negotiating Sex in the First Year of College." In *Sex for Life*, edited by Laura Carpenter and John DeLamater, 128–45. New York: NYU Press, 2012.

Walk Free Foundation. *Global Slavery Index 2018*. https://www.globalslaveryindex.org/resources/downloads/.

Watson, Ryan J., Shannon Snapp, and Skyler Wang. "What We Know and Where We Go from Here: A Review of Lesbian, Gay, and Bisexual Youth Hookup Literature." *Sex Roles* 77, no. 11/12 (2017): 801–11. https://doi.org/10.1007/s11199-017-0831-2.

West, Christopher. *Fill These Hearts: God, Sex, and the Universal Longing*. New York: Doubleday, 2018.

———. *Theology of the Body for Beginners*. West Chester, PA: Ascension Press, 2004.

Whitehead, Evelyn Eaton, and James D. Whitehead. *Fruitful Embraces: Sexuality, Love, and Justice*. Bloomington, IN: iUniverse, 2014.

Williams, Delores S. "Sin, Nature, and Black Women's Bodies." In *Ecofeminism and the Sacred*, edited by Carol J. Adams, 24–29. New York: Continuum, 1993.

———. *Sisters in the Wilderness: The Challenge of Womanist God-Talk*. Maryknoll, NY: Orbis Books, 1993.

Winner, Lauren F. *Real Sex: The Naked Truth about Chastity*. Grand Rapids, MI: Brazos Press, 2005.

World Health Organization. *HIV Prevention, Diagnosis, Treatment and Care for Key Populations: Consolidated Guidelines*. July 2014. https://apps.who.int/iris/bitstream/handle/10665/128049/WHO_HIV_2014.8_eng.pdf.

———. "Sexual and Reproductive Health." Accessed June 28, 2021. https://www.who.int/reproductivehealth/topics/gender_rights/sexual_health/en/.

Young, Iris Marion. *Responsibility for Justice*. New York: Oxford University Press, 2011.

Zimmerman, Kari-Shane Davis. "In Control? The Hookup Culture and the Practice of Relationships." In *Leaving and Coming Home: New Wineskins for Catholic Sexual Ethics*, edited by David Cloutier, 47–61. Eugene, OR: Cascade Books, 2010.

Zimmerman, Yvonne C. *Other Dreams of Freedom: Religion, Sex, and Human Trafficking*. New York: Oxford University Press, 2013.

Index

abortion, 1, 34, 50–51n20

Abraham, Kochurani, 35

abuse. *See* sexual assault and abuse

acquaintance rape, 62

adolescents. *See* children and adolescents

affirmative consent, 81n43, 166

African Americans. *See* BIPOC communities

agency. *See* sexual agency

AIDS/HIV, 104, 111, 140

alcohol use. *See* substance use

Amnesty International, 104, 109, 110, 113, 128, 133n34

anthropological framework: characteristics of, 3–4, 33; for hookup culture, 56; for sexting, 91–93; for sex trafficking, 139, 143–46; theological, 12, 102, 143

Antus, Elizabeth, 77–78

Aquinas, Thomas. *See* Thomas Aquinas

Armstrong, Elizabeth, 78

Asian and Asian-American communities, 14, 108

Augustine of Hippo, 8, 28

autonomy: in deconstructionist feminism, 16; defined, 51n24; as moral guidepost, 33; personhood and, 32, 33, 91; sexting and, 91, 92; of sex-trafficked persons, 144; of sex workers, 111–13, 117; social power and, 48. *See also* freedom of choice

Baker, Carrie, 143, 146, 148

Bales, Kevin, 153, 158n7

Batstone, David, 142

Bazelon, Emily, 109

Bennetts, Leslie, 126

Beste, Jennifer, 57, 61, 64

Bible: on commercial sex, 119–21; on dignity, 25; liberation in, 25–27, 48; relational reciprocity in, 28–29; soul-body unity in, 22–24. *See also* Christianity

BIPOC communities: abuses on bodies of, 14, 39; in COVID-19 pandemic, 165; gender-based power disparities in, 49; sex trafficking in, 147; sex workers in, 103–4, 107, 109, 121, 122; use of term, 51–52n39. *See also* racism

birth control. *See* contraception

Black communities. *See* BIPOC communities

body-soul unity, 22–24, 29, 36, 95

Bolz-Weber, Nadia, 25, 40

Boyd, Danah, 86

Brock, Rita Nakashima, 119, 126, 127

Brown, Brené, 40

bullying, 84, 88, 97

Burke Ravizza, Bridget, 13

Butler, Judith, 16, 35–36, 66

Cahill, Lisa Sowle, 2–3, 16

Calvin, John, 9, 33

Campbell, Letitia, 146

campus sexual culture. *See* hookup culture

Canadian Organization for the Rights of Prostitutes. *See* Sex Professionals of Canada

Catholic Church: anti-trafficking efforts in, 138; *Catechism of the Catholic Church,* 10, 119; on commercial sex, 119; on contraception, 34; dignity in teachings of, 24–25; exclusion of women from leadership positions, 148; on freedom of choice, 33; integrity as viewed by, 40; labor as viewed by, 124; procreative

About the Author

KAREN PETERSON-IYER is an assistant professor of theological and social ethics in the Department of Religious Studies at Santa Clara University. She is the author of *Designer Children: Reconciling Genetic Technology, Feminism, and Christian Faith*, as well as book chapters and journal articles examining topics within sexual ethics, bioethics, and labor ethics. She holds a PhD in religious ethics from Yale University.